The Observing Self

Contents

The
Observing Self

Rediscovering the essay

GRAHAM GOOD

Routledge
London and New York

First published in 1988 by
Routledge
a division of Routledge, Chapman and Hall
11 New Fetter Lane, London EC4P 4EE

Published in the USA by
Routledge
a division of Routledge, Chapman and Hall, Inc.
29 West 35th Street, New York NY 10001

© 1988 Graham Good

Printed in Great Britain by
Biddles Ltd, Guildford

British Library Cataloguing in Publication Data
Good, Graham,
    The observing self: rediscovering the essay.
    1. Essays in English, to 1950. Critical studies
    I. Title
    824'.009

    ISBN 0 415 00729 1
         0 415 00730 5 Pbk

Library of Congress Cataloging in Publication Data
Good, Graham
    The observing self: rediscovering the essay/Graham Good.
    p. cm.
    Bibliography: p.
    Includes index.
    ISBN 0 415 00729 1 (US). ISBN 0 415 00730 5 (US: pbk.)
    1. English essays – History and criticism. 2. American essays – History and
    criticism. 3. Essays. 4. Self in literature.
    I. Title.
    PR921.G66 1988
    824'.009–dc19 87-33694

Preface

When I told people that I was writing a book on "the essay," I had to overcome two kinds of negative association with the genre. One was with the basic teachers' job of setting and marking "essays," as if this genre was confined to the lower reaches of the educational system, and should be gratefully put aside when time permitted for reading and writing "scholarly articles." The other was with *belles lettres*, an archaism whose use is now entirely dismissive, like the neologism based on it: "belletristic." This conjures up the image of a middle-aged man in a worn tweed jacket in an armchair smoking a pipe by a fire in his private library in a country house somewhere in southern England, in about 1910, maundering on about the delights of idleness, country walks, tobacco, old wine, and old books, blissfully unaware that he and his entire culture are about to be swept away by the Great War and Modern Art. The "image" of the essay, when not stuck in the classroom, seems to be stuck in the Edwardian period, neglecting its immense importance as precisely an expression and vehicle of Modernism: Yeats, Eliot, Woolf, Lawrence, Forster, Pound – in fact nearly all the key poets and novelists of that movement were also outstanding essayists in different ways. Naturally, these essays are widely read, but usually with some other purpose in mind. Both for students and for other readers, essays are seen somehow as adjuncts to "major" genres or ideas, not as works in themselves.

This book aims to provide a study of the essay as a literary form, first through an "historico-philosophical" introduction and, second, through a set of eight chapters devoted to individual essayists. The hyphenated term, borrowed from the subtitle of Georg Lukács's *The Theory of the Novel*, is cumbersome but precise; my approach is not historical in the sense of offering an extrinsic survey of all of the literature that might be classed as essays, but in the sense of identifying a certain conjuncture in intellectual history which made possible that form of writing first practiced by Montaigne in the late sixteenth century. In some ways, as I discuss in Chapter 1, the rise of the essay is comparable to the rise of the novel, to borrow Ian Watt's phrase. But after this my approach is not primarily historical; I do not follow the essay's development in terms of general intellectual or literary history (though it is a prime and somewhat underused source for both of these), and only note external factors (growth of the periodical press, etc.) in so far as they are necessary to understand the essayists I discuss. My main focus is on the way they realize the different potentials of the form of writing first tried, or "essayed," by Montaigne. The concept of "prose style," which has traditionally governed literary study of the essay, is only one element in my analysis, which basically tries to show how the essay "constructs" its object in terms of ideas and general rhetorical strategies, as well as the features traditionally grouped by the category of "style." My approach is largely derived from the texts of Lukács and Adorno discussed in the third part of Chapter 1.

The selection of essayists – Montaigne, Bacon, Johnson, Hazlitt, James, Eliot, Woolf, Orwell – also requires some comment. There are various reasons for limiting this study to a single national context (though two American expatriates are included). The essay has been practiced most continuously in England, despite the fact that its founder was French (Montaigne could certainly be considered the co-founder of the *English* essay, given the great popularity of Florio's translation, but is in any case indispensable in considering the genre at all). The empirical and individualistic quality of English culture and the early dominance of bourgeois values were obviously hospitable to the essay, though we should remember before connecting the genre too closely to capitalism and protestantism à la Max Weber that its inventor was a French Catholic and a minor nobleman. Although this study is not historical in the external sense, it recognizes that the potential offered by the essay form is realized differently in different periods. The English essay has the advantage of showing a consecutive tradition, enabling us to represent at least the major literary periods: Renaissance (Bacon), Eighteenth Century (Johnson), Romantic period (Hazlitt), Victorian (James), and Modern

(Woolf, Eliot, Orwell). But why these, rather than Addison, Steele, Lamb, Stevenson, Forster, Lawrence, and Aldous Huxley – all outstanding essayists? My selection does not imply any superiority in those selected, or attempt to create a "great tradition" of essayists in the Leavisite mode. My choices result partly from interest in those particular figures, partly from a sense that they represent a range of uses as well as historical phases of the form, and partly from a limitation of space – no work on the essay should aim to be "exhaustive." The list of possible inclusions could go on and on: in France, Sainte-Beuve, Baudelaire, Valéry, Sartre, and Camus; in Germany, Schiller, Mann, Benjamin, Adorno; in Spain, Unamuno and Ortega . . . . There is abundant material for a comparative study of the European essay, as well as for the essay in the Americas, where the question of national and cultural identity in the New World dominates the form in Latin America, as well as figuring largely in English and French Canada and the USA. The development of the genre in Japan also accounts for the otherwise odd fact that one of the best-loved and most studied English authors there is Charles Lamb! In face of all of this my own study looks very restricted in scope; but it is an attempt to renew interest in the essay *as a form*. The wealth of essayistic material is of course read and studied, but generally in relation to some outside focus: to illustrate the author's views and shed light on his work in "major" genres; or to illustrate the course of intellectual history. The essay, for reasons I will discuss in the last chapter, has remained the "invisible" genre in literature, commonly used but rarely analyzed in itself.

My focus is on the inner workings of the essay, and on the center rather than the periphery of the genre's area. That is, my main aim is not to "define" the essay in the sense of drawing up lines of demarcation enabling one to say whether this or that piece of writing counts as an essay. Nevertheless, we do need some approximate working definition to begin with. What defines the essay in this extrinsic sense? First, it is normally in *prose*. The term "essay" has been used for works such as Pope's *Essay on Man*, which are in verse, but this is fairly exceptional. The spontaneous, improvised quality of essayistic thinking is incompatible with formal verse, especially rhymed couplets, and Pope's *Essay* is in any case highly schematic in its thought. The language of the essay, with its stress on accuracy of representation rather than elaboration of style, demands prose, though of course not all prose has these qualities. A second feature of the essay, related to this, is that it is in the vernacular. In writers like Montaigne and Bacon, the choice of the vernacular over Latin indicates the relative informality of the writing, though Bacon eventually had his essays published in Latin; as he wrote in the Preface to the 1625 edition of his *Essays*, "I do conceive, that the Latin volume of them (being in the universal language) may last as long as books last" (57). (Ironically, of course, English has supplanted Latin as the universal language, and may well outlast the age of the book.) Montaigne knew Latin well, having been taught it by his father in an early application of the "immersion" method, yet although Latin was more his mother tongue than French, he chose to write in the latter.

Length, however, is probably the key external feature distinguishing the essay among the prose forms. It belongs somewhere in the middle of the continuum of prose forms. The shortest are part-words or derivatives of words like acronyms or logos. Then come single words or short phrases like the commands of propaganda ("Brits Out!") or the slogans of advertising ("Coke – it's the real thing!"). Next is the sentence, in both senses: a complete syntactic unit, and an utterance expressing a memorable thought (other versions of this form are the adage, the commonplace, the aphorism, and the proverb). Beyond this is the paragraph, a group of sentences developing a thought at greater length; these are usually published in collections like Pascal's *Pensées*, Gissing's *The Private Papers of Henry Ryecroft*, most of Nietzsche's works, Adorno's *Minima Moralia*, Benjamin's *Einbahnstrasse* (One-way Street) and Handke's *Der Gewicht der Welt* (The Weight of the World). These collections have some affinities with Renaissance prose miscellanies, which sometimes have thematic titles connected with woodland, like Ronsard's *Bocages*, Bacon's *Sylva Sylvanum*, or Jonson's *Timber* and *Underwoods*, a nomenclature perhaps echoed much later in Heidegger's *Holzwege* (Woodland Paths). The essay, as a group of paragraphs occupying anything from one to a hundred pages, fills the middle of the prose spectrum. After it come forms of the book: the monograph (short), the treatise (longer), and then the megavolume or multivolume forms: the anthology (like the Bible or a college literary anthology), the encyclopedia, and the compendium or anatomy (to use Northrop Frye's term). The term "essay" has sometimes been used for book-length works, perhaps most notably in John Locke's *Essay concerning Human Understanding*. Rosalie Colie (89) describes it as a "radical expansion" of the form used by Montaigne and Bacon; although the early parts of Locke's work are systematically argued, the later ones are more like *collections* of essays where "we can recognize from the chapter titles the kind from which the whole enterprise sprang" in that those pieces can be read as single essays. She also points out that Locke's empirical approach allies his work with the essay form. But generally his text bears out the idea that the single overall design necessary to hold together a book-length prose work precludes the informal spontaneity of the essay. The demands made on the reader's concentration would also exceed the easy-going rhythm of most essays, as would even a much shorter piece of rigorous philosophical reasoning.

Within these limits, *kinds* of essay can be distinguished by form, approach, or content. The letter and the sketch are cognate forms which overlap to some extent with the essay. Essays can be couched as letters, like Montaigne's "Of the Education of Children" or Lukács's "On the Nature and Form of the Essay," and there are a number of fictional letters in *The Spectator*, for example. The essay could be defined as a letter addressed to any reader, in fact. The "sketch" implies a descriptive piece that could be presented fictionally or non-fictionally, either as a short story or as an essay. The "article" I would see as the prose form equivalent to the essay within the discourse of the official academic disciplines, and as such essentially different from the essay – a point to be taken up later. However, many lectures, often with an academic setting, have later been published as essays – here the quality of oral delivery seems to counter the customary formality of the setting to produce a result akin to the written essay. Certainly this form differs from the classical oration, where the emphasis is on persuasion rather than "disinterested" consideration, although the essay-form whose title announces that it is "in defense of" some usually unpopular cause (idleness, cheap comics, etc.) represents a survival, in parodic terms, of oratorical advocacy.

Different types of essay can also be distinguished by tone or content. But forming sub-genres in terms of tone or style seems to offer little, in that all essays are more or less "familiar," while "lyrical" essays (a term used in connection with Camus, for example) turn out either to be simply "descriptive," or to verge on being prose poems. The most useful classification is based on content, or rather on the basic activities which give essays a recognizable and persistent forward movement. I distinguish four principal types: the travel essay, the moral essay, the critical essay, and the autobiographical essay. Of course these are not mutually exclusive categories: many essays contain a mixture of elements from two or more, especially the last. Nor are they exhaustive: other categories could be and are used. But the four seem to me to cover the main essayistic activities: traveling, pondering, reading, and remembering. Their four objects are also interconnected: books and places, mores, and memories. These provide the occasions for essayistic reflections, but of course they could also provide book-length treatments, which would differ in more than length. The travel book typically covers a journey, perhaps over an entire country or region or continent, while the essay tends to concentrate on a particular place. Or it may concern simply a walk: in some ways the essay is *essentially* a peripatetic or ambulatory form. The mixture of self-preoccupation and observation, the role of chance in providing sights and encounters, the ease of changing pace, direction, and goal, make walking the perfect analog of "essaying." The autobiographical essay, similarly, focuses on a single crucial episode rather than the whole life, like Hazlitt's account of his first meetings with Wordsworth and Coleridge in "On My First Acquaintance With Poets," or Orwell's account of his schooldays in "Such, Such Were the Joys." The moral essay, although it takes on major as well as minor issues of human life and society, is quite sharply distinguished from the systematic coherence and consistency one would expect from a study in ethics. In fact the topic of the moral essay is often human inconsistency, as if to acknowledge those parts of human behavior which escape from systems of values. Book- and essay-length autobiography and travel writing have the personal and amateur viewpoint in common, but the moral essay, defined as a reflection on an aspect of human nature, effectively loses its content to the disciplines of philosophy, or to the new "human sciences," psychology, anthropology, and sociology, once it attains the dimensions of a book.

Although organizing the study around the different types of essay would have produced some interesting juxtapositions, I finally opted for the category of individual author, simply because the distinctive features show more clearly that way than through divisions by form or by content: Henry James's travel essays have more in common with his critical essays than with other travel essays, for example. I also came to feel that an approach to the essay as form should tend to the essayistic rather than the systematic or methodical, and for this reason I have kept the citations of other criticism to a minimum in my individual chapters, and listed the secondary material in Bibliographical Notes for each chapter. It is noteworthy that the main "theoretical" texts I discuss in Chapter 1 are themselves in essay form. I am not maintaining that criticism should always try to imitate the form of its object, but in this case it should not go totally against it. If a "theory" were outlined and then "applied" to various texts, this would aim for a kind of control of the texts which would essentially reverse the process of essayistic writing. As Adorno puts it in "The Essay as Form," "it is scarcely possible to speak of the aesthetic unaesthetically, stripped of any similarity with its object, without becoming narrow-minded and *a priori* losing touch with the aesthetic object" (153). But the relation of essay form to criticism and theory will be discussed more thoroughly in the last chapter.

Note on references

Sources of quotations from the principal essayists discussed in this book are given at the beginning of the Bibliographical Notes for the appropriate chapter, i.e. Montaigne (Chapter 2), Bacon (Chapter 3), Johnson (Chapter 4), Hazlitt (Chapter 5), Henry James (Chapter 6), Virginia Woolf (Chapter 7), T. S. Eliot (Chapter 8), and George Orwell (Chapter 9). Other sources cited are given in the Reference List preceding the Bibliographical Notes at the end of the book. The Bibliographical Notes for Chapter 1 list general works on the essay form.

Acknowledgments

I would like to thank Janice Price, Managing Director of Methuen and now Publisher, Humanities Division, Routledge, for her generous help and encouragement over the five years from this book's inception to its publication. Thanks are also due to the University of British Columbia for granting me study leave in 1985–6, when most of the research and writing was done. I am grateful to the editor of *College Literature* for permission to use part of my article "Ideology and Personality in Orwell's Criticism," which appeared in Vol. 11, No. 1 (Winter 1984), pp. 55–69; and to the editor of *Prose Studies* for permission to use part of my article "Language, Truth, and Power in Orwell" from Vol. 7, No. 1 (May 1984), pp. 78–93. Finally, I owe a special debt of gratitude to my wife, Robyn Groves, for her unfailing sympathy and support over the years of this project.

1

The essay as genre

The essay as knowledge

Like the novel, the essay has no real precedent in the generic system of classical antiquity. The essay was not one of those Renaissance genres based on a desire to revive the literary models of antiquity. Its initial impulse was away from genre altogether, in the direction of formlessness. Bakhtin defines as a novel "whatever form of expression within a given literary system reveals the limits of that system as inadequate, imposed or arbitrary" (Holquist and Clark, 276), and the essay could easily be included here. The specific genre in relation and reaction to which Montaigne developed the *essai* was the compendium of sayings, like Erasmus's *Adagia*. Rosalie Colie states,

> Montaigne began his essays . . . as remarks in the service of carefully selected adages. His powerful personality, however, soon swamped such objective aims . . . . The essay is, really, in part a fulfillment of the implications of adage-making; by working from adages into a new context, it developed into a form of its own. (35–6)

Montaigne's earliest essays seem designed to establish the truth about a given topic by collecting relevant quotations from classical and later writers. But the handling of these citations gradually changes, until in the later essays quotation becomes a way of bringing a new voice into a conversation, rather than of providing authoritative support. We can see a similar change from Bacon's early essays, which read like linked aphorisms, to his later versions, where his personal voice comes through more strongly, and there is more discussion and qualification of the quotations.

Beyond this kind of derivation of the essay from specific

1

earlier *forms*, we can also see essayistic discourse as a special instance of the widespread departure from the *procedures* of medieval discourse that took place in the late sixteenth century. Foucault has expressed this change succinctly: "*Commentary* has yielded to *criticism*" (80). The task of commentary is first to assemble, and only then to add to, all of the existing writing on the topic. This compilation represents the discursive dimension of the object's existence, which is not radically separate from its non-discursive existence. Foucault's example is from natural *history*, itself an odd locution for us now. This history is its *written* history, the complete file to date, as it were.

> When one is faced with the task of writing an animal's *history*, it is useless and impossible to choose between the profession of naturalist and that of compiler: one has to collect together into one and the same form of knowledge all that has been *seen* and *heard*, all that has been *recounted*, either by nature or by men, by the language of the world, by tradition, or by the poets. (40)

On the same page Foucault quotes Montaigne's expression of impatience with this infinite growth of secondary discourse (which is also reminiscent of the limitless "textuality" of post-structuralism): "Il y a plus affaire à interpreter les interpretations qu'à interpreter les choses, et plus de livres sur les livres que sur autre subject: nous ne faisons que nous entregloser" (G ii:520); "It is more of a job to interpret the interpretations than to interpret the things, and there are more books about books than about any other subject; we do nothing but write glosses on one another" (F 818). The *critical* attitude to this accumulated lore is to review and select only parts of it, those which correspond to observable fact. This implies a clear separation of the order of words from the order of things, and a comparison of the first to the second to check its accuracy of representation. "Criticism questions language as if language were a pure function, a totality of mechanisms, a great autonomous play of signs; but, at the same time, it cannot fail to question it as to its truth or falsity, its transparency or opacity" (40).

In his *Essais*, Montaigne confronts the accumulation of classical learning in a *critical* manner; this decisively separates him from the medieval approach. In the Middle Ages, according to Curtius, "all authors are authorities" (49); later, he adds: "Medieval reverence for *auctores* went so far that every source was held to be good" (52). Montaigne's critical or skeptical attitude to sources allies his writing with empirical science, with its stress on observation and proof; Bacon, of course, was one of its founders, while Sir Thomas Browne's *Pseudodoxia Epidemica* aims to sift the true from the false in the accumulation of pseudo-scientific lore. But the essay did not become part of this new mode of learning, despite certain affinities. It emerges between the old and the new learning, rejecting the old method of uncritically accumulated commentary, but also refusing the systematic ambitions of the new science, despite sharing its conception of language. Empirical science aims to be cumulative and progressive, though in a critical and selective way, preserving and building only on proven observations and laws. The essay does not aim at system at all; its empirical data are used in a much more limited way.

In so far as its utterances are not presented as fictional, the essay does imply a claim to count as knowledge. But this knowledge is not part of an organized whole; in fact, as knowledge, it is specifically *un*organized. The form emerges during the reorganization of knowledge in the late sixteenth and early seventeenth centuries, but it is not actually incorporated into the "new philosophy" of the seventeenth century (essentially what we now call "science"). We can see the essay as a commentary which has broken free from its "text," and implicitly from "textuality" conceived as the unity and interdependence of all writing, to become self-contained and *sui generis*. At the same time, the essay remained independent of the new enterprise of empirical science, as sketched for example in Bacon's *The Advancement of Learning*. In this work, Bacon attacks academic Scholastics on the same grounds as Montaigne does. Joseph Mazzeo in *Renaissance and Revolution* paraphrases Bacon's view thus: "Their thought remained entirely within the compass of their books, and, far from discovering new knowledge, they spent their time in disputation and commentary. Neither fresh ideas nor fresh observation could possibly arise from such an approach to learning" (196). But although reorganized and founded on empirical principles and methods, Bacon's project for modern science was specifically "cooperative, public, and cumulative" (190). The essay, even as practiced by Bacon himself, did not fulfill these aims, though it was not opposed to them either, as R. S. Crane's article on "The relation of Bacon's *Essays* to his Program for the advancement of learning" makes clear. The essay refused both the classical-medieval and the modern-scientific syntheses of knowledge, though it drew freely on the first and shared the empirical impulse of the second. In Montaigne we see that impulse playing over the inherited stock of ideas and selectively comparing them with his own direct observation and experience.

What sort of knowledge does the essay, then, offer? The essay presupposes an independent observer, a specific object, and a sympathetic reader. It also presupposes a language capable of rendering and communicating observations, whether physical or mental. Its starting-point is like that of Cartesian philosophy: an isolated self confronting a world of which nothing is known for certain. But the two forms of writing immediately diverge: Descartes is seeking certain knowledge, and a method for finding it. The skepticism of the essay takes a different form. It is spontaneous and unsystematic, and accepts its *occasional*, even accidental, nature. Like Cartesian philosophy and Baconian science, its observations are free, and do not seek authority from tradition and doctrine. But unlike them, the essay does not try to organize a new discipline on this new basis.

The essay exists outside *any* organization of knowledge, whether medieval or modern. In it, an open mind confronts an open reality. An uncertain, unorganized world enters an unprejudiced awareness, and the essay results as a record and provisional ordering of the encounter. In a sense, self and object organize each other, but only in a temporary way. Nothing can be built on this configuration, no rules or methods deduced from it. Self and object define each other, but momentarily. The self will go on to other definitions through other objects; the objects (whether places, works of art, or issues) will find other definitions in other selves. The essay makes a claim to truth, but not permanent truth. Its truths are particular, of the here and now. Other times and places are not its affair. Descartes wanted a fresh start for knowledge, but the essay starts afresh every time. Nothing is carried over.

The essay opposes doctrines and disciplines, the organizing structures of academic knowledge – hence the essay's neglect in the higher levels of the academic literary system. Hence, also, its wide cultivation at the lower levels as a preliminary form still reliant on personal knowledge, of use only until the student has acquired enough impersonal knowledge to write research papers and perhaps eventually scholarly articles, where the personal element is minimized. Doctrine and discipline were originally paired concepts, the first referring to teaching (as performed by *doctores*), and the second to learning (as performed by students or *discipuli*). But gradually the first term fell into disuse because of its association with authority, especially religious, and the accent fell on knowledge as "learning" and "discipline"; Bacon did not entitle his *magnum opus* "the Advancement of Teaching." Doctrine and discipline, in their medieval or modern forms alike, are inimical to the spirit of the essay, and Chaucer's Clerk of Oxenford ("gladly wolde he lerne and gladly teche") so often cited with relish by academics, would be an antitype to the essayist. Montaigne states explicitly, "je parle enquerant et ignorant . . . Je n'enseigne poinct, je raconte" (G ii:224); "I speak as one who questions and does not know . . . I do not teach, I relate" (C 237).

The essay offers personal experience, not disciplinary expertise. Modern "disciplines" tightly govern the content and form of individual contributions. First, the area of proper investigation is distinguished from other areas, and the borderlines carefully watched. Then, the proper *method* of investigation is defined in theory and practice. Finally, access to the discourse is limited: the general reader is discouraged from participating because the tone and style indicate a "specialist" audience of initiates, while access to publication is normally limited to those who have the appropriate certification (such as a "doctorate") and position (a university appointment). Rules also govern the relations between contributions *within* the discipline. Each acceptable contribution has to take account of previous contributions on the topic, especially *recent* ones. The disciplinary enterprise is defined as collaborative, cumulative, and progressive (though in practice it is often competitive and repetitive). Supposedly, disciplines advance from year to year through new work by individuals. These new items are not self-sufficient, but are judged by the effectiveness of their relations (addition, correction, reaffirmation) to the existing discourse. (All of this neglects the ample evidence that controversies in many disciplines rage for a few years and are then simply abandoned unresolved as interest shifts elsewhere.) Contributions are impersonal in the sense that two trained specialists could conceivably produce substantially the same article unknown to each other (the fear of this is actually quite common in academia). In contrast, the discourse of the essay is uniquely personal and thus *non*-disciplinary (though not necessarily *un*disciplined). Its claim to significance does not rest on its finding a place in an organized, interpersonal body of knowledge.

The essay cultivates diversity where the disciplines seek unity. Disciplines aim to "cover the field" they have defined, and this spatial image corresponds to the temporal idea of progress. Gradually the "gaps" in the discourse are filled in, until theoretically the discipline could be declared finished. But long before this happens, it is discovered that the whole field has to be covered again, this time on correct principles; or a new and more "successful" discipline invades its territory. In any case, the drive to unity always dominates the disciplines. They seek to derive general rules from specific instances, subordinating them through classification and hierarchical arrangement. Paradoxically, this stress on generality produces a discourse of little interest to the common reader, who is more likely to appreciate the particularity of the essay. The particularities of the essay are of general interest because they are still the "raw data" of experience, unclassified and unassigned to any discipline. When generalities do arise in the essay they come as spontaneous responses to phenomena. The particular has priority over the general and often overturns it: the essay is more hospitable to exceptions than to rules. The essay presents "special" instances to the "general" reader, where the disciplines present "general" conclusions to the "specialist."

Although the essay is not itself a "learned" work in the sense of contributing to a common system of knowledge, the essayist often uses his own personal learning. There are often quotations in the essay, but rarely footnotes. The modern "article" is required to have an apparatus of citations and references which bind it into the "textuality" of its discipline. In contrast the essayist often quotes from memory (Montaigne began the essayistic tradition of doing so *fallibly*), and in any case the reader is not expected to want to find or verify the quotation as if he were a *discipulus*. Quoting in the essay introduces an element of dialogue; disciplinary prose quotes to provide authority for its statements through an accepted *doctor* of its discipline. Montaigne writes: "Je ne dis les autres, sinon pour d'autant plus me dire" (G i:157); "I quote others only to make myself more explicit" (C 52); and again, "je fay dire aux autres ce que je ne puis si bien dire" (G i:448); "I make others say what I cannot say so well myself" (C 159). The essay does not, like the professional contribution, aim to be "definitive," that is, to define for others in terms of the discipline what the correct explanation of a given phenomenon is. This "definitive" quality is in any case liable to be superseded by a later contribution which can adduce new evidence or deploy a new approach. The essay cannot be superseded in this way since it makes no claim to be definitive in the first place.

Ultimately, the essayist's authority is not his learning, but his experience. The essay's claim to truth is not through its consistency in method and result with an established body of writing. Its method is not collaborative and its findings do not need corroboration. Its claim is to yield flexibly to individual experience. Instead of imposing a discursive order on experience, the essay lets its discourse take the shape of experience. Judgments may result, but there are no prejudgments, no prejudices. Conclusions may arise, but they are not foregone conclusions, nor can they be used as a foundation by another writer, though they may be cited for interest. They are provisional, and cannot be detached from their occasion. Reflections in the essay rise from and return to particular experiences. The literature and philosophy of the past are not a realm *apart* from experience and used to judge it; rather, reading and thinking are themselves felt as experiences mixed in with other experiences.

Thought in the essay stays close to its objects and shares their space and atmosphere. The connections between thoughts in the essay are often made through things, rather than being linked directly in a continuous argument. The term "reflection" is perhaps better than "thought," since it suggests the intellectual mirroring of an object. The truth of the essay is a *limited* truth, limited by the concrete experience, itself limited, which gave rise to it. The essay is a provisional reflection of an ephemeral experience of an event or object. If one event followed another, we would have a narrative; if one object followed another, we would have a descriptive catalogue; if one thought followed another, we would have a logical argument. But in the essay, event and reflection, object and idea, are interwoven and limit each other's development. The ideas are valid for here and now, while the sense-impressions of the object-experience are still fresh in the mind. Thought in the essay tends to be presented *as experienced*, not as afterthought; as it responds to objects and events on the spot, not as it is later arranged and systematized. This is the essential uniqueness of essayistic discourse: neither the order of thoughts nor the order of things predominates. Each constantly interrupts and interpenetrates with the other. As Montaigne puts it, "La raison a tant de formes, que nous ne sçavons à laquelle nous prendre; l'experience n'en a pas moins" (G ii:516); "Reason has so many shapes that we do not know which to take hold of; experience has no fewer" (C 344). The essay's fabric is woven from these alternations.

The essay offers knowledge of the moment, not more. The moment is one of insight, where self and object reciprocally clarify and define each other. Orwell believed a writer's prose became most distinctly personal exactly where he was most forgetful of self and most intent on the object. The essay is built around this moment of reciprocal identification. A loss of self is followed by a sharpened sense of self. But this illumination is temporary; it can be recorded and shared by other individuals, but not incorporated into any collective enterprise. Its wisdom is not abstractable from the moment. The essayist's truths are "for me" and "for now," personal and provisional. The essay stays closer to the individual's self-experience than any other form except the diary.

The mixture of elements in the essay – the unsorted "wholeness" of experience it represents – can only be held together by the concept of self. The selection and order of the ideas and objects can have no other basis. The order is "as it occurred *to me*," not "as it usually occurs." But the generality that is lost at one level is regained at another: *everyone's* experience of being an individual is mixed in this way. The essayist's personality is offered as a "universal particular," an example not of a particular virtue or vice, but of an "actually existing" individual and the unorganized "wholeness" of his experience. This creates a new kind of writing, as Montaigne was well aware: "Les autheurs se communiquent au peuple par quelque marque particuliere et estrangere; moy, le premier, par mon estre universel, comme Michel de Montaigne, non comme grammarien, ou poëte, ou jurisconsulte" (G ii:223); "Authors communicate with the world in some special and peculiar capacity: I am the first to do so with my whole being, as Michel de Montaigne, not as a grammarian, or a poet, or a lawyer"

(C 236). A particular individual presents himself in a general (i.e. unspecialized, non-disciplinary) way, and thus attains a knowledge unavailable to those who study human nature *en masse*. Montaigne justifies his self-study thus: "chaque homme porte la forme entiere de l'humaine condition" (G ii:222); "Every man carries in himself the complete pattern of human nature" (C 236). Although "man" is differently realized in every individual, the study of one man is nevertheless one way to study "man." The essayist is representatively unrepresentative, typical of how we experience ourselves as untypical.

The essay as art

Despite its non-fictional status, the essay has a strong affinity with the novel. Much of Ian Watt's theory in *The Rise of the Novel* can be applied, *mutatis mutandis*, to the rise of the essay. Both emerge from the same intellectual climate:

> The general temper of philosophical realism has been critical, anti-traditional and innovating; its method has been the study of the particulars of experience by the individual investigator, who, ideally at least, is free from the body of past assumptions and traditional beliefs; and it has given a peculiar importance to semantics, to the problem of the nature of the correspondence between words and reality. (12)

We can attribute to the essayist the same aim Watt ascribes to his philosopher and novelist: "the production of what purports to be an authentic account of the actual experience of individuals" (27). The world view of the essay is essentially the one Watt finds in the novel: in place of the medieval unity, "a developing but unplanned aggregate of individuals having particular experiences at particular times and at particular places" (31). This, Watt states, is the basic perspective of the middle class, who provided most of the audience for both genres. In terms of eighteenth-century England, in fact, Watt sees the *Tatler* and *Spectator* as preparing the way for the novel, both in general taste and through specific features, especially the de Coverley Papers, which show many techniques later used in the novel (51). Conversely, many novelists from Cervantes and Fielding to Mann and Musil have included essays or essayistic material in their novels.

We can see the same essay–novel conjuncture at work also in

the late sixteenth and early seventeenth century in continental Europe. Watt's title should have been qualified as the "Rise of the *English* Novel," since as Claudio Guillén has shown in *Literature as System* the new genre was recognizable in Spain by 1605. As he points out, it takes two works to constitute a genre; in this case, the anonymous *Lazarillo de Tormes* (1556) and Alemán's *Guzmán de Alfarache* (1604) together formed the genre of the picaresque, as a kind of inversion of the quest romance, preserving its loose, episodic structure, but negating its values and world view. Cervantes then combines both in *Don Quixote* (1605, 1615) by sending out his quest-romance knight into the picaresque world. The knight of medieval and Renaissance romance approaches his world armed with knowledge of the codes, conventions, and traditions of his calling, as well as with his sword, shield, and lance. Don Quixote is the ultimate "textualist" in this regard, refusing to acknowledge any reality that does not fit his mental and literary constructs, and thus incapable of learning anything new. The picaro is just the opposite: beginning as a naïf, he soon discards his credulity and acquires the skills needed to survive and prosper at the expense of others. His amoral attitude and observant empiricism eventually make him into an accomplished rogue.

The figure of the essayist, emerging in the same period in Montaigne's *Essais* (1580) and Bacon's *Essays* (1597), belongs somewhere between the two. He is more rooted in society than either, but still has a detached, skeptical view of his environment. His "essays" are equivalent to the "episodes" of knightly adventure or picaresque trickery: none of these forms is tightly integrated into a plot or systematic structure. Like the two others in the trio, the essayist goes out on each foray, physical or intellectual, into an open world where almost anything can be encountered. But generally his adventures do not involve the physical violence that constantly befalls (or is inflicted by) the knight or rogue. We imagine the essayist as more sedate: either actually sitting reading or watching, or walking (the praise of which is a *topos* of the genre). The essayist goes out not to vanquish villains and succour maidens, nor to cheat and swindle, but out of disinterested curiosity. His implied rank is middle class, or, especially in the early essay, lower gentry, like Montaigne. (Don Quixote, or rather Alonzo Quijano, as he was known before his knighthood, came from this class, and it is tempting and easy to imagine him as an essayist if he had spent his time reading Montaigne's *Essais* instead of *Amadís de Gaul*.)

Certainly the essayist does not live in fear of hunger, homelessness, robbery, and violence, like the picaro. Nor are we usually conscious of him as having work to do: this would give him too specific a place in society and too *interested* a viewpoint. Like the *honnête homme* of French seventeenth-century literature, the ideal essayist should be *disinterested*, his outlook uncolored by any particular trade or profession. This does not conflict with the essayist's own fascination with particularities, as it is precisely his *general* interest that leads him to observe them. This disinterest negates the stress on self-interest in bourgeois economics, at least from Adam Smith onwards, which actually the picaro reflects more strongly, though in an anarchic, antisocial way. The essayist's disinterest is then a kind of bourgeois self-critique, which also found expression in Arnold's attacks on the "narrowness" of the middle-class outlook. In the same way, the essayistic theme of "the praise of idleness" is a critique of the bourgeois stress on the virtue of "industry." However, the leisure implied in the essayist's attitude does not imply great wealth, or, usually, a moral or ascetic revulsion against the ways of the world. Since "experience" of one kind or another is his theme, he presents himself as an "experienced" individual, which tends to further connote "maturity," being middle-aged as well as middle-class. The essayist is contemplative, but not as a monk or scholar who has never known the world; rather as someone who has been active in public affairs, like Montaigne, who wrote his essays in temporary retirement from office, as Seneca did his letters. This situation often gives the essay a pastoral mood: its perspective is removed form the centers of power and influence, though the tone remains urbane. Rural innocence and city experience combine, just as the essayist himself, though well read and well traveled already, is not too set in his ways and opinions to reject new experiences and attitudes. André Gide's concept of *disponibilité* perfectly describes the essayist's state of mind: spontaneous, available, eager, and curious.

Freedom is the essay's essential mood and quality, in that the essayist is free temporally (he has leisure), spatially (he can walk and travel), economically (he has at least a "sufficiency"), but most of all mentally (he is unprejudiced, curious, observant about himself and the world, quick to respond to new experience and new ideas). Of course, to use Sartre's term, every freedom is *situated;* but each new "essay" or venture is a *re*-situation of the self in relation to the object or event described. In this respect it is a highly "existentialist" form: neither the self nor the world is fixed, but reciprocally shape or reshape each other within the experimental or experiential field of each essay. Montaigne writes of his endeavor of self-portraiture, "Je ne puis asseurer mon object. . . . Si mon ame pouvoit prendre pied, je ne m'essaierois pas, je me resoudrois; elle est tousjours en apprentissage et en espreuve" (G ii:222); "I cannot fix my subject. . . . Could my mind find a firm footing, I should not be making essays but coming to conclusions; it is, however, always in its apprenticeship and on trial" (C 235). The essayist is as "errant" in the physical sense as the knight or the picaro, but his identity and values are much more fluid than theirs. They are either proud or repentant of their deeds in relation to a fixed code of morality, but neither attitude characterizes the essayist. Where the picaro routinely repents of his ways at the end of his confession, Montaigne says simply, "je me repens rarement" (G ii:224); "I rarely repent" (C 237). Nor is he given to boasting or seeking high renown in the world's eyes. He accepts the fluidity of the self and the relativity of the conscience, and uses the essay as the record of their provisional accords with the world.

I have been presenting the essay as a sort of fiction, in the context of the novel, and seeing the essayist as a sort of hero, whose function is well captured by some eighteenth-century periodical titles, like *The Tatler, The Spectator,* or *The Observer.* And in fact the "Character," the sketch of a human type like "The Happy Milkmaid," invented by Theophrastus and popularized in early seventeenth-century England by Sir Thomas Overbury, was an important influence on the development of the essay, especially the de Coverley papers of Addison and Steele. But despite its affinities with fiction, the essay is rightly classed in libraries as *non-*fiction. This distinction has blurred in the recent "non-fiction novel" as well as in recent critical theory, which tends to treat all writing, including history and philosophy, as "fictional." And certainly, as Hayden White (1975) has shown, historiography makes use of narrative techniques and mythic plots which are common to fiction. Since no event can be exhaustively represented, it is argued, the selected aspects must be arranged according to a pre-existing schema. But it does not follow that, because every representation is a construct, it is thereby a fiction. Nor does it follow, incidentally, that a fiction cannot represent reality; it does so under certain rhetorical conditions, i.e. an understanding with the reader implicit in the choice of genre that what is represented is figuratively rather than literally true. The essayist implies that his representations *are* literally true *within the terms of his relationship to his reader.*

This relationship is defined throughout the essay tradition from Montaigne onwards as one of friendship; Montaigne gave the death of his friend Etienne de La Boétie as his main reason for beginning essay-writing as a substitute for their conversations. Thus the kind of truth offered in the essay is not that of the witness stand or the scientific laboratory, both of which require fixed and consistent *evidence*, but a mixture of anecdote (perhaps heightened and "pointed" for effect), description (again selective), and opinion (perhaps changing). You do not show that Orwell was writing "fiction" by pointing out discrepancies between his notebooks and the published text of *The Road to Wigan Pier*, because individual details are not decisive. If, however, you can prove that Orwell never saw a hanging or shot an elephant, then you have a case for reclassifying "A Hanging" or "Shooting an Elephant" as short stories (curiously, Orwell never wrote any) rather than essays. They would be equally effective as either, but the reader would respond within a different framework for actual or imagined events. To describe an event in fiction carries an implication that it is in some way typical, whereas in the essay this is not implied, and would have to be made explicitly if at all.

We have considered the essay as a non-fictional cognate of certain kinds of fiction. But what of the broader category of art? Like the novel, the essay existed a long time before people began to speak of it as an art. Montaigne sees his activity as artless rather than artistic: he begins his essay "Of Friendship" with an account of a mural painter who uses "grotesques" to fill up the gaps and margins. Montaigne continues: "Que sont-ce icy aussi, à la verité, que crotesques et corps monstrueux, rappiecez de divers membres, sans certaine figure, n'ayants ordre, suite ny proportion que fortuite?" (G i:198); "And what are these things of mine, in truth, but grotesques and monstrous bodies, pieced together of divers members, without definite shape, having no order, sequence, or proportion other than accidental?" (F 135). Perhaps with the diffidence of someone working in what was not yet an acknowledged genre, Montaigne sees his work as artless, an *ad hoc* response to chance circumstances and thoughts as they occurred to him. His "grotesques" are on the fringes of the established art forms, and have the disunity of the experiences they reflect. They are like rough sketches made on the spot as compared to finished "studio" works. They fill in the edges of the recognized and prestigious arts. Their content is miscellaneous and often humble or homely, and in this respect their visual analog is seventeenth-century Dutch or Spanish painting of "low life" or "still life," perfected by Rembrandt and Velásquez. Here, the close study of particular objects and individual characters shows the same impulse that is at work in the essay and the realistic novel. In *Adam Bede*, George Eliot expresses her preference for Dutch over Italian paintings in these terms:

> I turn, without shrinking, from cloud-borne angels, from prophets, sibyls, and heroic warriors, to an old woman bending over her flower-pot, or eating her solitary dinner, while the noonday light, softened perhaps by a screen of leaves, falls on her mob-cap, and just touches the rim of her spinning-wheel, and her stone jug, and all those cheap common things which are the precious necessaries of life to her. (Ch. 17)

The sensibility described here, with its ability to find significance and beauty in the detail of a small world and little-regarded people and things, is often found in the essay, which also turns aside from the grand design and the imposing statement for minor truths.

The essay as aesthetic knowledge

Up to this point, we have been seeing the essay as a form of knowledge which is unorganized either by the medieval structures of learning or by the modern disciplines of empirical science and post-Cartesian philosophy, and seeing it as a form of art historically, philosophically, and to some extent formally akin to realistic fiction and painting. Now we are in a position to see that it offers aesthetic knowledge, that is to say knowledge which is organized artistically rather than scientifically or logically. The essay's open-minded approach to experience is balanced by aesthetic pattern and closure. It is not a work of art in the full sense, but a kind of hybrid of art and science, an aesthetic treatment of material that could otherwise be studied scientifically or systematically. The subject matter of the essay is constantly being taken up by disciplines like psychology, sociology, and the recent attempts at systematic poetics. Yet the essay has survived repeated appropriations of its content by the developing "human sciences." The scientific treatment does not exclude the artistic, and the two *can* happily coexist, though a new discipline often seeks to establish itself with attacks on "amateur" or essayistic treatments of a subject that it claims now for the first time to study in properly organized fashion; this we have seen in successive attempts to "professionalize" literary study. Unfortunately, the essay usually goes unrecognized either as knowledge (because it is seen as too "artistic") or as art (because it is "knowledgeable" rather than "creative").

There is, however, one intellectual tradition which stresses the value of the essay as providing a unique combination of empirical knowledge and aesthetic form. This is a branch of the tradition of systematic aesthetics in Germany, which runs from Baumgarten in the mid-eighteenth century, through Kant and Hegel, down to Emil Staiger's *Grundbegriffe der Poetik* in the mid-twentieth. Although the essay is not much discussed before Lukács, this tradition always took seriously the cognitive aspect of art, and thus prepared the ground for a serious philosophical account of the essay. Lukács's contributions to genre theory – of the novel in *The Theory of the Novel* (1916), of the novella in his essay "Solzhenitsyn: *One Day in the Life of Ivan Denisovich*" (1964), and of the essay in "On the Nature and Form of the Essay" (1909) – could be read as filling in the gaps in Hegel's *Aesthetics*, which did not treat any of the three in any detail. Adorno, too, whose "The Essay as Form" (1958) we will be discussing, belongs to the tradition; like Lukács, he wrote a systematic aesthetics, though (perhaps appropriately) both reserved their accounts of the essay for separate, self-contained pieces. Since Kant's placing of aesthetic judgment as a mediator between *Verstand*, the theoretical philosophy of Nature, and *Vernunft*, the practical philosophy of morality, art as knowledge and knowledge of art have been central issues in German philosophy. In the twentieth century this produced a theory of the essay as a combination of both, and provided an account of the genre much more profound than anything in England or France, though paradoxically those two cultures have had longer and fuller traditions of actual essay-writing than Germany, as Adorno notes. The relatively late development of the genre in Germany meant that it lacked the associations with science and philosophy it had in France and England. Instead, it tended to be associated with art; thus Germanic theory usually equates the *critical* essay with the essay as such, defining it as that form of art which has art as its subject matter.

The *locus classicus* of this approach is Lukács's "On the Nature and Form of the Essay," which is cast as a letter to Leo Popper, dated from "Florence, October 1910," and printed as a preface to the collection of essays *Soul and Form*. In it, Lukács tries to define the genre he is using in the rest of the book. Exactly the same occasion, the collection of his own essays, provoked Adorno's reflections on the form as a preface for *Noten zur Literatur* (1958). For Lukács, who in 1910 is showing a strong influence from Pater and Wilde, especially Wilde's "The Critic as Artist," the modern essay's content is "usually" art, though he acknowledges that many essays deal with life-problems directly (3), and in fact includes the Platonic dialogue and the medieval mystical vision as earlier periods' equivalent forms of "essayistic" or non-systematic thought. Essays are "intellectual poems," he maintains, quoting the elder Schlegel (19). They are *secondary* creations, or recreations, but creations none the less. "The essay has to create from within itself all the preconditions for the effectiveness and validity of its vision. Therefore two essays can never contradict one another: each creates a different world" (11). This principle of non-contradiction of course differentiates the essay from the scholarly article, which is, at least in theory, open to correction, qualification, or rebuttal within the discourse of its discipline. For Lukács, critical essays have creative autonomy in common with the works of art they discuss. We could formulate the implicit claim of the Lukácsian essay as something like: my view of this work recreates the work within my world, and represents the work as I see it; as such it cannot enter into conflict with your view. But Lukács does not maintain this view consistently in the rest of his book; for instance "Richness, Chaos and Form: A Dialogue Concerning Lawrence Sterne," which is incidentally a revealing picture of the intellectual and social milieu of his youth, contains a quite vehement argument about the literary value of *Tristram Shandy*.

But Lukács does not take a purely aestheticist view of the

essay; for him, it is mimetic as well as creative; it aims at a kind of truth, as well as imaginative response. The analogy he takes is portrait painting. The essay's re-creation of its object is part creation and part mimesis, analogous to the painter's striving for a "likeness" of his sitter (10–11). Lukács claims that we do not need independent knowledge of the subject in order to sense the likeness. Here he seems to verge on a Leavisite "vitalism of the text" in asking the essayist to rival the portraitist's struggle to bring his subject "to life":

> Here too [in the essay as well as in the portrait] there is a struggle for truth, for the incarnation of a life which someone has seen in a man, an epoch or a form; but it depends only on the intensity of the work and its vision whether the written text conveys to us this suggestion of that particular life. (11)

This intuitive intensity in the critic-essayist is directed towards "the mystical moment of union between the outer and the inner, between soul and form" (8); by re-experiencing the form he can re-create the moment of formation, and this is something quite different from merely explaining the work, though that might superficially appear to be the goal. Lukács's approach and terminology is full of early twentieth-century vitalism or *Lebensphilosophie*, where form is simply seen as a temporary accommodation for the restless, renewing energy of the life-force; the essay form is more sympathetic to his vitalism than the fully elaborated intellectual system because it emphasizes dynamic process rather than finished product: "the essay is a judgment, but the essential, the value-determining thing about it is not the verdict (as is the case with the system) but the process of judging" (18). In this view, the essay is seen as a renewal of the "life" of art works in the lives of the critic and of his readers.

The second important contribution to Germanic essay-theory is Max Bense's "Uber den Essay und seine Prosa" (1947). Like Lukács he offers an account of the essay as an aesthetic form of knowledge, with both a creative and a cognitive dimension. His key term is "configuration": "The essayist is a combiner, an indefatigable producer of configurations around a particular object....Configuration is an epistemological category which cannot be reached by axiomatic deduction, but only through a literary *ars combinatoria*, in which imagination replaces strict knowledge" (422; my translation). The essay, according to Bense, only declares its "tendency" or ethical message after a "combinatorial play of idea and image"; its presentation combines "the experimental demonstration of a natural effect and the repatterning of a kaleidoscope" (423–4; my translation).

Bense's idea of configuration as the essay's way of relating objects and ideas is an interesting one, and we might see in it a secular or humanist adaptation of the medieval idea of "Figura." Auerbach's classic article of that title shows how the pervasive analogism of medieval thought virtually constituted a "figural method," used to unify the whole of Christian history, and still surviving in modern literary criticism in terms like "adumbrate" or "prefigure." The essay would then, after the break-up of this unity, represent a temporary individual patterning of an experience from a single viewpoint, a miniaturized attempt to create a provisional "world" through a now purely private and momentary "configuration" without access to a higher synthesis but still recapturing a brief sense of "wholeness." This would connect with Bense's finding an "epic" or world-creating drive in the essay; but instead of the epic hero enacting and embodying the life-world of his people, as in Hegel's theory of the epic, the isolated essayist has to give meaning and pattern to his own experience, through repeated reconfigurations of it.

Another analogous concept to Bense's "configuration" is Walter Benjamin's "constellation," which represents the basic structure of his essays, and is discussed in his "Epistemo-critical Prologue" to *The Origin of German Tragic Drama*, written in the mid-1920s as his *Habilitationsschrift* but, perhaps predictably, rejected by the University authorities and not published until long after his death. Although he is not speaking specifically of the essay, his succinct simile "Ideas are to objects as constellations are to stars" (34) could form the basis of an approach to the essay in general as well as a key to Benjamin's own practice of it. The moment of intellectual insight works in the same way as the "image" provided by the constellation unites and characterizes a previously unpatterned aggregate of stars. Analysis and recreation converge to produce simultaneously "the salvation of phenomena and the representation of ideas" (35); the ideas are embodied or illustrated concretely at the same time as the object is intellectually illuminated.

This idea, as well as those of Bense and Lukács, is certainly influential on Adorno's "The Essay as Form," which can be seen as a kind of summation, as well as development, of the earlier contributions. Adorno sees the essay in musical terms as involving thematic rather than conceptual unity: this is reflected in the title of the essay-collection to which "The Essay as Form" serves as preface: *Noten zur Literatur,* where the word "notes" has the sense of musical accompaniment as well as written comment. Adorno was himself a musicologist and composer, and as Susan Buck-Morss puts it, he "didn't write essays, he *composed* them, and he was a virtuoso in the dialectical medium. His verbal compositions express an 'idea' through a sequence of dialectical reversals and inversions" (101). The essay in general he sees as a musical composition of ideas, which, if organized in other ways, could become parts of systems of knowledge. He writes: "Its transitions disavow rigid deduction in the interest of establishing internal cross-connections, something for which discursive logic has no use. . . . the essay verges on the logic of music, the stringent and yet aconceptual art of transition" (169). In other words, the ideas in an essay are arranged aesthetically, forming a pattern of relationships rather than a straight line of necessary consequences; its ideas need not *follow* in the logical sense. "In the essay, concepts do not build a continuum of operations, thought does not advance in a single direction, rather the aspects of the argument interweave as in a carpet. The fruitfulness of the thoughts depends on the density of this texture" (160). That is, there are multiple points of contact among the thoughts, rather than a hierarchy in which, say, ideas of a higher order of generality *govern* the more particular ones.

Since the insights are of equal value, they are best united by a spontaneous *aesthetic* design, comparable to the symbolic patterns that are meant to be grasped simultaneously in modernist works like Eliot's *Four Quartets,* which also uses musical structures. As Adorno says of the essay, "It coordinates elements rather than subordinating them" (170). This latter observation clearly reflects his own stylistic practice, which like Benjamin's is heavily paratactical. The difficulties many readers experience with their essays are partly due to expecting hierarchical distinctions between the general message, the subordinate points, and the illustrations of the points; but Benjamin and Adorno on principle omit these structures, so that each paragraph, each sentence and even each clause stands on its own. The reader has to pattern the work for himself, and this can take as much effort as reading a complex modernist poem. Of course their practice is by no means typical of essays in general, which are usually much easier on the reader. But this is really due to their being less densely textured, not to their having tight logical structures. As we will see, Bacon's essays have clear rhetorical outlines, but Montaigne's essays, particularly the longer ones, are often densely textured through layers of additions as well as being hard to "follow" in a linear way. Thus Adorno's comment about the essay co-ordinating rather than subordinating its elements does not merely apply to his own writing, which simply carries that form to an extreme. In fact his essays might be much more widely appreciated through greater awareness of their musical structures, such as the repetition of themes in different keys, in different connections, and in harmony or dissonance with other themes.

Adorno's account of the essayist's "composition" of his thought bears an intriguing similarity to Eliot's account of poetic creation (to be discussed in Chapter 8). In each case the mind takes an almost passive attitude to its ideas or images, allowing them to form "wholes" almost of their own arranging. Adorno writes, "the essay urges the reciprocal interaction of its concepts in the process of intellectual experience....Actually, the thinker does not think, but rather transforms himself into an arena of intellectual experience, without simplifying it" (160–1). The essay aims, in other words, to preserve something of the *process* of thinking, whereas systematic thought presents a fully finished and structured *product*. Adorno's image for this kind of spontaneous, unstructured conceptualizing is a man forced to speak the language in a foreign country without access to grammars and dictionaries, learning through trial and error, through personal experience of different situations. We might say that through repeated "essays" in and of the language, he eventually acquires a "feel" for it, and that the essay learns its objects in the same way. The essayist, like the immersion-method language learner, has to improvise, and may make mistakes, but this insecurity and uncertainty are vital to the energy of his work.

Adorno provides two similes for the results of the essayist's thinking process, which correspond to the two sides of the dialectic of "form" and "life" in Lukács's essay. The first is of the essay's formation or taking shape: "Through their own movement the elements crystallize into a configuration" (161).

The second is a dynamic simile of *trans*formation or dissolving shape: "It [the essay] is a force field [*Kraftfeld*], just as under the essay's glance every intellectual artifact must transform itself into a force field" (161). As force field, the essay breaks up and energizes its object as a second force field with which it interacts; as configuration, as "a constructed juxtaposition of elements" (170), the essay shows an "affinity with the visual image" (170), since it is "composed of tensions, which, as it were, have been brought to a standstill" (170). Through this crystallization "it constructs the interwovenness of concepts in such a way that they can be imagined as themselves interwoven in the object" (170). In other words, the essay presents us with interpenetrating ideas and images, with objectified concepts or conceptualized objects. For Adorno, the essay produces a unique combination of subject and object, like a constellation's combination of human design and celestial phenomenon. But the essay's insights cannot be transferred into organized discourse; they remain within the bounds of the text, which in this respect is as autonomous as a work of art.

Adorno's treatment of the subjective component of the essay remains curiously impersonal, like Eliot's treatment of the poet's "crucible" of experience. For Adorno, ideas and objects seem to combine and form patterns like molecules in a scientific experiment, and the same is true to a lesser extent of Bense, Lukács, and Benjamin. They seek to construct a subjectivized object in which the object is central and the subject simply refracts aspects of it. My approach has given the subjective aspect of the essay equal prominence. The similes these writers use for the essay can be adapted to this emphasis quite easily. Lukács, for example, speaks of the essay as creating a "likeness" of its object in the same way as a portraitist seeks a "likeness" of his sitter. But the portraitist, we might add, also represents his *own* likeness in his painting, in the sense that we can recognize a family resemblance in the different portraits by the same artist. In fact we tend to identify portraits by the artist's rather than the sitter's name: a Rembrandt, rather than the particular dignitary depicted. If we compare two portraits of the same figure by different artists, the differences between the artists' visions will be as apparent as the resemblances which establish the identity of the sitter. That is why I prefer to see the concept of "likeness" as Janus-faced, including the artist as well as his model. The literary term "characterization" can encompass both

dimensions, and is a good one for the essay: it is a characterization of its object (a place, a work, a person), but also of its
maker; a *reciprocal* characterization, in fact. Bob Hullott-Kentor,
in his introduction to Adorno's "The Essay as Form," writes,
"The idea is to phenomena as is an expression to a face" (143).
This is an excellent simile; but the facial expression, as well as
being *of* that person's emotion, is often *to* an onlooker; further,
when that expression is artistically represented by the onlooker,
his personality is expressed in the representation as well. The
result is a kind of fusion of expressions: an aspect of the object
has elicited an aspect of the observing subject, and in the essay
(as in the portrait) the two aspects are represented together.

The heart of the essay as a form is this moment of
characterization, of recognition, of figuration, where the self
finds a pattern in the world and the world finds a pattern in the
self. This moment is not the result of applying a preconceived
method, but is a spontaneous, unpredictable discovery, though
often prepared by careful attention and observation. This
discovery can be about the self or about the world, but is mostly
about a combination of both. Self and object are configured in a
mutually illuminating way. But the insight is confined to that
moment; the generalization cannot be separated from its
particular circumstances of time and space, and made into a law
– it remains an isolated occurrence. The essay's ideas are
essentially *inapplicable* elsewhere, because essayistic experience
is not governed by known laws. Instead, chance plays a
dominant role in the essay's world. What happens happens *to
me*, and has no design other than what I can give it. The essay is
the record of these provisional designs. Events are not pro-
vidential. The world is chaotic and disenchanted, but also free
for me to order it "for now." The essay is always a "first
account" of its object, since it does not borrow its first
principles from outside its particular situation. Nor can its
reflections be used as a basis for further accumulation of
knowledge, though they may provide illumination. The
essayist is like a traveler; he can choose the places he visits, and
compare his impressions with others', but he cannot determine
what happens while he is there, or whether his experience is in
any way typical. The place is always the place at one time, for
one person.

In the essay, the identity of neither self nor object is
predetermined. Both are changeable, and take a particular

shape in conjunction, in configuration, with each other. The essay is a reflection of and on the changing self in the changing world, not the pure, abstract, Cartesian construction of the self or Newtonian construction of the world, but a construction of, and a response to, this time and place in the world, by this self. The indeterminacy of both self and world attains a temporary determination in the essay. The essay aims to inspire confidence not by its authority, not by the mastery of general laws and principles applied to the particular, but by its capacity to record the particulars of experiences and responses accurately *as particulars*. The essay is an act of personal witness. The essay is at once the *in*scription of a self and the *de*scription of an object. Self and object are freed from their places in social and scientific systems respectively, but at the price of remaining within the limits of a specific situation.

This view of the essay is suggestive of existentialism; indeed, the essay was a key form for Camus and Sartre, and Heidegger too turned away from systematic philosophy to the essay. Sartre's title for his volumes of essays is *Situations* – many good insights into the potentials of the essay form can be gained from the titles of collections. Existentialism, like the essay, prefers open intellectual experience, accepting the limitations on the knowledge that results: knowledge that is for here, for now, and for me – situated knowledge, in fact. This idea has to be distinguished from the Nietzschean relativism or "fictionalism" which proclaims that there are no "truths," only "constructs" or "myths" which are imposed as history by the victorious. As Adorno puts it: "the essay is not intimidated by the depraved profundity which claims that truth and history are incompatible" (158). Moral and logical absolutes have to be discarded in favour of a spontaneous response to personal encounters with others, with the past, or with works of art. The essays of Sartre and Camus are their best non-fictional prose, as their attempts at full-scale system (which in some ways is at odds with existentialism anyway) clearly demonstrate. Sartre's *Les Mots* is a classic of the extended autobiographical essay because it is not dominated by a method, unlike the vast and overblown *Critique of Dialectical Reason* or the monstrous 2,750-page *L'Idiot de la famille*, his study of Flaubert. Likewise, Camus's early essays, collected in *L'Envers et l'endroit* and *Noces* are much preferable to the treatise *L'Homme revolté*. Adorno says much the same of Lukács in "The Essay as Form," that he was better as an essayistic critic than a systematic one, and the same could even be said of Adorno himself; his beautifully titled collection *Prisms* is more satisfying, for example, than the abstractions of *Negative Dialectics*.

However, it is not necessary to denigrate the treatise in general in order to praise the essay. It is simply that the prestige of the full-scale treatise within academic disciplines has occluded the essay and turned it into a minor form, perhaps because its insights are non-transferable. They are thus felt as less useful; they do not offer a theory or a method which can then be *applied* to other objects. The essay starts without these pre-conceptions, and it is fitting that none of the writers we have discussed offers a "theory" of the essay, that is, a set of propositions capable of controlling or marshalling this vast field. Instead, each put forward an "essay on the essay." At first sight this might seem weaker than a theory; but it is stronger in the sense that each is demonstrating or enacting the form while commenting on it. It is not an accident that systematic poetics has had so little to say about the essay. Instead of a theory, then, Adorno and Lukács give us meta-essays, essays raised to a higher power of self-consciousness.

With Benjamin and Adorno, and indeed with Sartre and Lukács, we have to confront the paradoxical relationship between Marxism and the essay. Lukács calls the essayist "the pure type of the precursor" (16), maintaining that the essay is to the fully articulated intellectual system as John the Baptist is to Christ. Unlike Eliot, whose essays will be discussed later in connection with this idea, Lukács went on to deliver systematic treatises. But Adorno rejects this "precursor" idea and sees "theory" as Lukács's downfall as an essayist: "It [the essay] neither deduces itself rigidly from theory – the cardinal fault of all Lukács's later essayistic work – nor is it a down-payment on future syntheses. Disaster threatens intellectual experience the more strenuously it ossifies into theory" (165) – a disaster, one is tempted to add, which Adorno himself did not entirely avoid. Certainly Sartre did not. Of the four, Benjamin is the most consistently essayistic, and even his attempts at longer works remain more or less essay-collections or amassed fragments. The tension in his writing between Marxism and Messianic religion can perhaps best be understood by seeing both as "totalizing" systems of signification, one modern and one ancient, one worldly and one other-worldly, which he only approaches through particular objects. His religion and his Marxism are both inhibited by his essayism, his intent focus on the particular, and his Proustian faith that past worlds could be resurrected whole from the material relics. Conversely his essayism is incessantly checked and complicated by his desire to transcend the here and now. Despite his stretching of the form to its limits, Benjamin is best understood as an essayist, including the travel and autobiographical pieces in *One-Way Street* as well as the critical essays in *Illuminations*. The essay must obviously be at odds to some extent with Marxism and religion in that both the latter approach phenomena in the light of accepted principles or articles of faith, where the essay works from particular phenomena outwards (and not very far outwards). The intensity of Benjamin's essays is this hint of "total" vision amidst the detail of highly particularized objects. Adorno's brilliantly chosen epigraph from Goethe for his "The Essay as Form" is apposite here: "Bestimmt, Erleuchtetes zu sehen, nicht das Licht." "Destined to see the illuminated, not the light" (151). The source of visionary power and meaning, the first principles from which the world can be totalized, remain hidden from the essay, yet its indirect effects are everywhere. Benjamin differed from other essayists only through the power of his visionary urge to glimpse the source of his illuminations. Adorno's musicalization of ideas to form a "setting" or "accompaniment" to the object is less mystical, and provides a more general approach to the essay as counterpoint of image and idea, aesthetics and thought, as well as a continuing refusal of ideological system in favor of the unique "constellation" of subject and object, self and world.

2
Montaigne: the growth of experience

Like *Don Quixote*, its near contemporary, Montaigne's *Essais* is a highly self-conscious and frequently self-referential text. Cervantes' Book II (1615) is set in a world in which Book I (1605) has been published and widely read and discussed. With Montaigne, also, the later essays comment freely on the earlier ones, and Book III (1588), in particular, several times mentions how its author's life has been changed by the fame following the publication of Books I and II (1580). The volumes were not presented as separate entities, however, but as parts of a single, growing whole: each new edition in Montaigne's lifetime (as well as the first posthumous one, in 1595) incorporated additions to the essays already published, as well as completely new essays. In the middle of the long essay "On Vanity" (III,9), Montaigne states: "Mon livre est tousjours un. Sauf qu'à mesure qu'on se met à le renouveller afin que l'acheteur ne s'en aille les mains du tout vuides, je me donne loy d'y attacher (comme ce n'est qu'une marqueterie mal jointe), quelque embleme supernuméraire" (G ii:402); "My book is always one. Except that at each new edition, so that the buyer may not come off completely empty-handed, I allow myself to add, since it is only an ill-fitted patchwork, some extra ornaments" (F 736).

The changes are almost entirely additions, with very few excisions, but Montaigne was not bothered by the occasional inconsistency or awkwardness which resulted. He gives two reasons: that one should not tamper with statements once they have been published, and that the later opinions may be worse than the original ones. "Mes premieres publications furent l'an mille cinq cens quatre vingts. Depuis un long traict de temps je suis envieilli, mais assagi je ne le suis certes pas d'un pouce" (G ii:403); "My first edition was in the year 1580. Since then I have

26

grown older by a long stretch of time; but certainly I have not grown an inch wiser" (F 736). Thus during the author's lifetime the essays develop with his personality, yet still contain the earlier states, changed, of course, by the new context created by the additions. This is what Montaigne meant by saying that his book was "consubstantial" with himself: the book and the self continue to influence each other and reflect each other, with the book finally becoming the "portrait" (Montaigne's own repeatedly used and seriously intended description of his work) of its author. However, the earlier and later selves are superimposed and blended in a way which could hardly have an equivalent in painting.

As a "book of the self" Montaigne's *Essais* has several important differences from the diary or confession. The relation with time is different: in the diary, each entry is limited to one day and represents the state of mind of that day, or specifically of the time of writing, just as the content is limited to the events or thoughts of that day. With autobiography or confession the diary's multiple series of viewpoints (produced by the series of "entries" into the text) is replaced by a single one, often considerably later than the events described. In Montaigne's book, the text accretes around a set of *topics*, not a series of dates or events. Montaigne cheerfully accepts the occasional "transposition de chronologie" (G ii:403) which results from this building up of temporal layers into a kind of palimpsest. In some editions, including Donald Frame's standard modern translation of the complete *Essais*, three time-strata are actually indicated in the text as A (pre-1588), B (1588), and C (post-1588). There are arguments for and against this practice: it is sometimes useful and interesting to have additions distinguished, but it tends to expose the incremental process too obtrusively. Montaigne's editions of course did not have these indications; but then again, even the longest essays were printed without paragraph divisions, so his editing practices are hardly obligatory for modern versions.

In some ways the concept of the "book" has priority for Montaigne over the individual "essay" as the essential organizing unit. The essays were never seen as even potentially publishable in any other form; the periodicals which could have provided an alternative venue did not yet exist. Montaigne's headings describe the individual essays as "Chapters," a long-established term for a prose work's sections, and the term "essais" is often used apologetically, though part of this is due to Montaigne's ironic self-deprecation. The book-title *Essais* can be seen as an anticipation of similar "collective" titles for volumes of relatively "scattered" writings, like *Explorations, Illuminations,* or *Prisms,* and it was only with Bacon's use of the term "essays" that it came to denote a new genre. With Montaigne the *"essai"* is still a sketchy concept, a kind of linking medium between the established forms of the "sentence" or quotation on one side, and the "book" on the other. Several crucial instances of the term *"essai,"* in which it hovers between the then established usage as "attempt" or "trial" and an anticipation of the generic usage, *also* describe a movement away from book learning and authority towards the verdict of the independent mind, or, to use Foucault's terms, between traditional commentary and independent criticism. The essay "On Books" (II, 10) begins: "Je ne fay point de doute qu'il ne m'advienne souvent de parler de choses qui sont mieus traictées ches les mestres du mestier, et plus veritablement. C'est icy purement l'essay de mes facultez naturelles, et nullement des acquises" (G i:447); "I have no doubt that I often speak of things which are better treated by the masters of the craft, and with more truth. This is simply a trial of my natural faculties, and not of my acquired ones" (C 159). This "essay" is an "essay" of the unaided self (like *ownself* in Orwell's Newspeak) without the authority of (though sometimes with reference to) traditional learning. The piece entitled "On Democritus and Heraclitus" (I, 50) begins with a similar justification for taking on a subject on which he has little formal expertise: "Le jugement est un util à tous subjects, et se mesle partout. A cette cause, aux essais que j'en fay ici, j'y employe toute sorte d'occasion. Si c'est un subject que je n'entende point, à cela mesme je l'essaye" (G i:334); "Judgment is a tool to use on all subjects, and comes in everywhere. Therefore in the tests that I make of it here, I use every sort of occasion. If it is a subject I do not understand at all, even on that I essay my judgment" (F 219). There is a pronounced air of bravado here, of defying established practice, and the choice of *"essais"* as the book title can also be seen as an effort to pre-empt criticism of the author's lack of expertise or credentials. In the two examples quoted, "essays" were essays *of* something (natural faculties, or the faculty of judgment) *on* something else (a topic or occasion). There is also a sense in the use of *"essayer"* of risk, uncertainty, and inconclusiveness, a feeling of venturing outside the paths of conventional methods.

Montaigne was highly conscious that his way of writing departed from the prescribed forms of classical rhetoric as laid out in Cicero and Quintilian and, as Curtius describes in *European Literature and the Latin Middle Ages*, passed down to the Renaissance. In the essay "On Presumption" (II, 17), with his usual disarming modesty (though we should remember that the device of self-deprecation is itself found in the rhetoric handbooks), Montaigne says his work lacks both formal elegance and formal structure, and that the term "style" may be inappropriate for what he calls "un parler informe et sans regle, un jargon populaire et un proceder sans definition, sans partition, sans conclusion, trouble, à la guise de celuy d'Amafa-nius et de Rabirius" (G ii:38); "a formless and irregular utterance, a popular jargon that runs on without definitions, without divisions, without conclusions, and is as vague as that of Amafanius and Rabirius" (C 197). These two characters are from Cicero's *Academica*, where they are described as speaking "artlessly on low subjects, in vulgar language, without defini-tions or divisions" (G i:635–6, n. 74). Of course, a positive claim is advanced behind the self-denigration. This is essentially that Montaigne's form and style (or formlessness and unstylishness) are better adapted both to his personality and to his subject matter. His way of writing may be against his better judgment, he says, but it is to his taste; quite simply, it suits him: "mon langage n'a rien de facile et poly: il est aspre et desdaigneux, ayant ses dispositions libres et desreglées; et me plaist ainsi, si non par mon jugement, par mon inclination" (G ii:38); "my language has no ease or grace; it is rough and contemptuous, free and irregular in its arrangement; and my inclination, if not my judgment, likes it so" (C 197). This forsaking of the forms of "art" (i.e. rhetoric) may appear to result in formlessness, but actually it yields to a "natural" form (i.e. natural to the particular self): "Comme à faire, à dire aussi je suy tout simplement ma forme naturelle" (G ii:39); "As in deeds, so in words, I simply follow my natural way" (C 198).

It is worth emphasizing that as well as seeing his formal "essays" as a natural form of *self*-expression, Montaigne sees their informality as their way of adapting to the *object* of the essay. He claims that, for him, matter takes priority over manner. The natural structure of the particular content is preferred to the imposed or inherited structures of rhetorical art, of which definition and division are the most basic. In the essay "On Vanity" (III, 9), Montaigne writes,

> J'entends que la matiere se distingue soy-mesmes. Elle montre assez où elle se change, où elle conclud, où elle commence, où elle se reprend, sans l'entrelasser de parolles de liaison et de cousture introduictes pour le service des oreilles foibles ou nonchallantes, et sans me gloser moy-mesme. (G ii:439)

> I want the matter to make its own divisions. It shows well enough where it changes, where it concludes, where it begins, where it resumes, without any interlacing it with words, with links and seams introduced for the benefit of weak or heedless ears, and without writing glosses on myself. (F 761)

In a sentence whose looseness epitomizes that of the whole essay, Montaigne describes unapologetically his dispensing with the reader-aids common to ancient and modern rhetoric: introductions, summaries, subheadings, etc. One begins to see some justice in his calling his style "contemptuous," although he shows his awareness of the demands he makes on the reader, particularly in the longer essays of the third book, which he says are going to need at least an hour to absorb (in an earlier essay on his own reading habits, he gives one hour as his maximum attention span). This length he now sees as necessary to fully arouse the reader's attention, and to get to grips with the subject thoroughly. He is not interested in readers who are unwilling to give him an hour of their undivided attention, and to make the effort to follow the natural path of his thought without the convenience of subheadings, markers, and retrospects.

The two claims that Montaigne makes in defending himself against the charge of neglecting the rhetorical arts – that his writing follows the natural form of his "self" *and* that of his "matter" – should be examined together, even though Montaigne makes them separately and even in a contradictory-sounding way. At one point, for example, he says to the reader: "Qu'on ne s'attende pas aux matieres, mais à la façon que j'y donne" (G i:448); "No attention should be paid to the matter, only to the shape that I give it" (C 159). Here, of course, he is speaking of his personal "manner" (façon), not the conventional forms of rhetoric that he was earlier contrasting with his "matter." At different times, then, Montaigne saw his experimental form of writing as adapted to the natural expression of the self or of the object, though he did not seem to see both operating at the same time, as I have claimed the essay does. This "naturalness" which the two have in common is essentially that they are non-selective, at least in any systematic or preconceived way. The spirit is one of writing things down as they occur or emerge without worrying about overall cohesion, consistency, or any other set "frame" or filter for discourse. Anything can be included, at any point, at least in theory. Montaigne's aim is an unrepressed thinking-writing, a spontaneous flow of subjective responses around an object, rather than the application of a preconceived method or structure.

Montaigne also claims to be non-selective, even random, about the topics of his essays. In his experiment in writing the self, any occasion can serve as a theme and illustrate the self's distinctiveness. In the essay "On Democritus and Heraclitus" (I, 50), Montaigne announces, "Je prends de la fortune le premier argument" (G i:334); "I take the first subject that chance offers me" (C 130). This is justified by the fact that "Tout mouvement nous descouvre" (G i:335); "Every action reveals us" (C 131). But the kind of knowledge obtainable in this way is subject to the limitations of the perceiving self, which shape the perceived object. In a striking anticipation of Kant's unknowable *Ding an sich*, Montaigne writes "Les choses, à part elles, ont peut estre leurs poids et mesures et conditions; mais au dedans, en nous, elle [l'ame] les leur taille comme elle l'entend" (G i:335); "Things in themselves perhaps have their own weights, measures and states; but inwardly, when they enter into us, the mind cuts them to its own conceptions" (C 131). Montaigne never fully reconciled his accounts of subjective and objective knowledge on the theoretical level; but of course he was not aiming at a systematic epistemology.

The variety of individuals' subjective reactions is contrasted not only with the ultimately unknowable truth, but with traditional doctrines. In the case of death, for example, Montaigne focuses on death-for-me, as a unique individual, not on death as described by the Church or any other orthodoxy. These views may be considered (in practice Montaigne refers almost entirely to classical authors, and very rarely to Christian ones); but what really counts is the presence of death to the individual consciousness. Montaigne's neglect of doctrine harmonizes with his neglect of rhetoric; both are forms imposed on individual consciousness from outside. Not that he rejects doctrine: his essay "That it is Folly to Measure Truth and Error by our own Capacity" (I, 27) shows him in a Catholic and submissive mood, maintaining that we are too quick to dismiss as impossible things like miracles which are beyond our experience. It is simply that his approach to his subject matter is non-doctrinal, whether for or against; it starts from a quite different point, from individual experience. Doctrine and rhetoric naturally go together as traditional matter and manner; Montaigne's writing escapes both, and substitutes the *"essai"* for both. In Montaigne's use, as in this example from "On Experience" (III, 13), the word hovers between writing and living: "toute cette fricassée que je barbouille icy n'est qu'un registre des essais de ma vie" (G ii:532); "all this medley that I am scribbling here is but a record of my life's experiences" (C 361). The *literary* formlessness of his writing, which Montaigne deprecates here, but also implicitly defends, results from the surrender of rhetoric to experience, of form to content. Thus the "essais de ma vie" are both written and lived. Montaigne writes essays about his own life, and since one of his main activities is writing essays, the form and content tend to converge into a single activity of "essaying": testing and tasting one's own life while experiencing it, thinking about it and recording the thoughts, reading and revising and adding to those thoughts, and comparing them to the recorded thoughts of others. The essay is a sample of the self as it is involved in this complex of activities, and the essayist is a taster for his reader: "J'ay assez vescu, pour mettre en compte l'usage qui m'a conduict si loing. Pour qui en voudra gouster, j'en ay faict l'essay, son eschançon" (G ii:533); "I have lived long enough to give an account of the way of life that has carried me so far. For anyone who has a mind to try it, I have, in the capacity of his wine-taster, made the test" (C 362).

Perhaps the best way to "essay" (or taste, or test) Montaigne's essays and their development is to take for examples a short early essay, a middle-length middle-period essay, and a long, late essay, as this increasing length does represent an underlying trend, despite a number of exceptions. "Of Idleness" (I, 8) is one of the early pieces (1572–4) which are about one page long; it is of special interest partly because the topic became a staple of the later essay tradition, and because it shows the still uneasy relationship between general and personal levels of experience. In fact the essay is exactly split between the two; half a page is devoted to each. Montaigne begins with a long, formal sentence containing two formal similes for the unoccupied mind: fallow land and female body, both in need of seed from another source in order to become usefully productive. Human minds are the same: "Si on ne les occupe à certain sujet, qui les bride et contreigne, ils se jettent desreiglez, par-cy par là, dans le vague champ des imaginations" (G i:29); "If we do not occupy them with some definite subject which curbs and restrains them, they rush wildly to and fro in the ill-defined field of the imagination" (C 27). After elaborating this idea and illustrating it with quotations from Virgil, Horace, and Martial, Montaigne plunges abruptly into the personal and anecdotal. His recent retirement to his house, he tells us, was intended to give his mind (*"esprit"*) a complete rest: "de le laisser en pleine oysiveté, s'entretenir soy mesmes, et s'arrester et rasseoir en soy" (G i:29); "to leave it in complete idleness to commune with itself, to come to rest, and to grow settled" (C 27). Experience has shown him, however, that the actual result is the opposite; the mind acts like a runaway horse, the image implied in the earlier quotation about the "field" of imagination. Thus far his particular experience of mental idleness bears out the general rule and invalidates his original project.

But there is an odd twist at the end of the essay: instead of curbing his runaway horse or sowing his weed-infested field by some orderly system of study, Montaigne says he has decided to *write down* his wild thoughts in order to study their oddity at his leisure, and perhaps eventually cure his mind through shame of these disordered jottings. There is a concealed shift from "the mind's need to fix on an object" to "the interest of recording the mind's unfixed movement": the "record" turns out to be precisely the "object" needed. At this point Montaigne still sees the *informality* of the essay as *deformity*; in terms of the recurrent reproductive simile in the essay, it is monstrous, abortive. Later, he will be able to see the essay as a paradoxical "informal form," a discourse in which subject and object can attain a reciprocal (though only provisional) conformation or configuration. At this moment, he is still somewhat ashamed (though fascinated) by his spontaneous mental productions, seeing them as aberrations from moral and literary order, and not yet as sources of their own kind of truth. The essay seems to intend to defer to classical wisdom about the uselessness of the idle mind, but subverts that conclusion by recording his "idle" thoughts as possible evidence in a psychological or philosophical experiment.

Gradually Montaigne overcomes this fear of formlessness, and acquires confidence in a new kind of ordering, a new kind of accommodation between the mind and its objects. Smoother transitions tend to replace the abrupt shift in the essay "Of Idleness" between the opening's formal rhetoric, conventional similes, and classical quotations, and the ending's familiar tone, anecdotal content, and lack of logical consistency. "On Books" (II, 10) is a good example of Montaigne's middle-length essays from the period 1578–80. It has a fairly coherent overall structure, consisting of an introduction discussing Montaigne's reading habits and poor memory, a main "body" concerned with his favourite poets, moral philosophers, and historians, and a conclusion (perhaps better described as a postscript or appendix) which consists simply of reading notes transcribed from the backs of some of his books. In his opening self-presentation, Montaigne shows himself more at ease with his experiment in leisure (another possible translation of "oysiveté" as well as the somewhat pejorative "idleness"). But he continues to be defensive about his form of writing, as if concerned to answer an imagined question, "Why am I reading Montaigne and not an acknowledged master of the topic he is discussing?" Montaigne disclaims any intent to provide objective, authoritative knowledge in his book of essays: "Ce sont icy mes fantasies, par lesquelles je ne tasche point à donner à connoistre les choses, mais moy" (G i:447); "These are my fancies, in which I make no attempt to convey information about things, only about myself" (C 159). In other words, what he is offering in this essay is not an authoritative "Great Tradition," but an openly subjective self-portrait in books. He chooses not to defend the value of his comments as adding to knowledge about the texts, or as offering insights or aids to appreciation, but this does not mean that he actually thought of them as valueless. Strategically, he simply wants to distinguish his "impressions" from learned "judgments," and to justify the former as refractions of himself rather than contributions to learning. In modern terms, Montaigne's "approach" is descriptive and reader-oriented in contrast to the prescriptive and evaluative tradition in poetics. But Montaigne does not defy traditional rankings of authors; he in fact defers to them, attributing any failure of appreciation to his own shortcomings as a reader: "mon jugement...n'est pas si sot de s'opposer à l'authorité de tant d'autres fameux jugemens anciens" (G i:450); "My judgment...is not so foolish as to oppose the authority of so many other famous minds of antiquity" (C 162).

This distinction between authoritative literary judgment and personal literary experience could be seen as a parting of the ways between official academic criticism and informal essayistic criticism, a separation which still exists. Montaigne did not aim, like F. R. Leavis, to create a revolution of established taste, but rather to inaugurate a new way of writing about literature – or, rather, *books*: the distinction is important, since "Literature" implies some kind of overarching unifying concept. The other significant aspect of Montaigne's title "On Books" is that he can deal with reading and writing as parts of a single continuing activity: his books and his Book, as it were. The prose paragraphs which end the essay were originally written in the back papers of his own books before he had really started writing essays. These notes, meant to record his impressions after finishing reading, and motivated by his sense of having a poor memory, could be seen not only as the germ of the literary essay, but of the essay as such. In them Montaigne attempts quick character sketches of various historians, trying to intuit their moral natures from their writings. In some ways he treats their books as "consubstantial" with their selves, as he claimed for his own Book. He appropriates them, as it were, through their books, speaking of them in the possessive: "Voicy ce que je mis, il y a environ dix ans, en mon Guicciardin....En mon Philippe de Commines il y a cecy" (G i:460–1); "This is what I put down about ten years ago in my Guicciardini....In my Philippe de Commines there is this" (C 172). Montaigne's writing is thus generated out of his reading as a kind of friendly dialogue in textual form.

In the literary discussions in the main body of this essay, Montaigne is quite explicit about his goal of finding and characterizing the private self of the author he is reading. He prefers intimate forms like the familiar epistle to public orations and official records. He is curious about the "humeurs privées" and "naïfs jugemens" (G i:456) – "personal humours" and "natural opinions" (C 167) – of "his" authors. Montaigne expresses great impatience at the slow pace and rhetorical elaboration of public discourse. His page-long diatribe against this style as practiced by Cicero is like a compendium of everything the essay form will strive to avoid. These long-winded discourses, Montaigne says, are appropriate for institutions: "Ils sont bons pour l'escole, pour le barreau et pour le sermon, où nous avons loisir de sommeiller" (G i:455); "They are good for the school, the bar, and the pulpit, where we have leisure to doze" (C 166). Montaigne prefers writing which is frank, personal, and goes straight to the point; structuring devices of any kind are irrelevant: "Pour moy, qui ne demande qu'à devenir plus sage, non plus sçavant ou eloquent, ces ordonnances logiciennes et Aristoteliques ne sont pas à propos" (G i:455); "For me, who only want to become wiser, not more learned or more eloquent, these logical and Aristotelian orderings of the material are of no use" (C 166). What Montaigne seeks is the directness and immediacy appropriate between friends, rather than the formality of public occasions where individual personality is lost or muted.

In this essay, Montaigne presents his personal experience with literature; at its most pleasurable and productive, the experience of a book is the experience of another personality. He is most conscious of the audacity of what he is doing when he has to record a negative experience of an acknowledged "great" author. He asks with apparent trepidation: "La licence du temps m'excusera elle de cette sacrilege audace, d'estimer aussi trainans les dialogismes de Platon mesmes et estouffans par trop sa matiere?" (G i:455); "Will the licence of the age excuse my sacrilegious boldness in thinking that even Plato's dialogues drag, and stifle their meaning on a plethora of argument?" (C 167). Excessive elaboration both dissipates the force of the points and conceals the self of the author; hence Montaigne's preference for brevity and simplicity of style. This simplicity makes language fitter to deal with real complexity and change in the self and its experiences. Montaigne acknowledges the variousness of literary experience by showing that the same author can express himself differently at different times: even the magniloquent Cicero can also produce the intimate *Letters to Atticus*. The reader's experience is also changeable, and Montaigne again expresses a sense of audacity in confessing that he is no longer entertained by Ariosto and Ovid as he was in his youth (G i:450; C 161). The idea of writing about reading as a personal experience was clearly a new and perhaps questionable one.

Experience is the unifying idea towards which his essays all seem to be working in one way or another, while already embodying it. His last and perhaps his greatest essay is "On Experience" (III, 13), and it is fittingly placed at the end of his "book of the self." Here the experience of essaying and the essaying of experience are given their fullest treatment in the course of Montaigne's full-length portrait (it is important that the picture includes the whole body, not just the face). At the outset, Montaigne contrasts experience to reason as a way of satisfying our natural desire for knowledge. Reason seeks to group phenomena according to their resemblances, and to deduce general laws from them. Experience, however, is of the variety and diversity of phenomena. Although Montaigne defers to reason as the higher faculty, he feels that "La ressemblance ne faict pas tant un comme la difference faict autre" (G ii:516); "Resemblance does not make things as much alike as difference makes them dissimilar" (C 344). In other words the centrifugal force of reason is outweighed by the centripetal force of experience; variety is greater than unity; uncertainties outnumber certainties. It is as if Montaigne here differentiates his enterprise from that of Descartes. Both seek a starting-point in the individual self, and the sections of Descartes's *Discourse on the Method of Properly Conducting One's Reason and of Seeking the Truth in the Sciences* (1637), to give it its full title, have some essayistic qualities. They include personal reminiscences and concrete details, such as the setting of his reflections in Germany in winter: "I spent the whole day shut up in a room heated by an enclosed stove, where I had complete leisure to meditate on my own thoughts" (35). Curiously, Montaigne's "On Experience" also mentions German stoves, which he says often cause discomfort to those who, like the French, are used to an open fireplace: "cette chaleur croupie, et puis la senteur de cette matiere reschauffée dequoy ils sont composez, enteste la plus part de ceux qui n'y sont pas experimentez; à moy non" (G ii:534); "that airless heat, and the smell of the red-hot material of which they are made, give most people who are not used to them a headache; but not me" (C 363). Evidently Descartes was not afflicted either, since it was in this atmosphere that he discovered the *cogito*. But the personal and concrete elements in his text have a different function than in Montaigne: the particularities are only a prelude to the moment of enlightenment, in the same way that a religious confession is centered on the moment of conversion. After the point of certainty has been found, the text moves onto a much more general plane, where phenomena can be ordered according to the principles that have been discovered. We might say that Descartes's *Discourse* is essayistic up to that point, but philosophical after it; and that the essay provides a jumping-off point for modern philosophy which it tends to fall back to in the work of philosophers like Nietzsche and Heidegger. There is no Cartesian point of certainty in Montaigne, either philosophical or religious; his view of experience and way of recording it do not allow for such a moment. His equivalent to Descartes's "cogito ergo sum" is a question: "Que sçay-je?" ("What do I know?" – this was the inscription on the medal he had struck in 1576).

Despite his initial deference towards reason as a higher faculty, Montaigne goes on to show great distrust of its results, at least as displayed in the tradition of philosophy up to his time (what his reaction would have been to Descartes's method we can only guess). The build-up of commentaries on texts and commentaries on those commentaries seems to him a process of obscuring meaning, not of clarifying it. Confined to itself, to its world of books and interpretations of books, the human mind simply gets entrapped in its own products: "Les hommes mescognoissent la maladie naturelle de leur esprit: il ne faict que fureter et quester, et va sans cesse tournoiant, bastissant et s'empestrant en sa besongne, comme nos vers de soye, et s'y estouffe. '*Mus in pice*'" (G ii:519); "Men do not recognize the natural infirmity of the mind; it does nothing but ferret and search, and is all the time turning, contriving, and entangling itself in its own work, like a silk-worm; and there it suffocates, 'a mouse in pitch'" (C 347). To the medieval pairing of the Book of God and the Book of Nature, Montaigne implicitly adds a Book of the Self, through the study of which one can attain wisdom and virtue. We will learn more about anger, for example, by remembering our own rages than by reading up about anger in Aristotle. "J'aimerois mieux m'entendre bien en moy qu'en Ciceron. De l'experience que j'ay de moy, je trouve assez dequoy me faire sage, si j'estoy bon escholier" (G ii:526); "I would rather understand myself well by self-study than by reading Cicero. In the experience that I have of myself I find enough to make myself wise, if I were a good scholar" (C 354). The main lesson of self-study is the fallibility of the mind, the way one's mental models of reality often fail to match it. The first achievement is awareness of one's own ignorance: "Car encore faut-il quelque degré d'intelligence à pouvoir remarquer qu'on ignore" (G ii:528); "For it needs some degree of knowledge to observe that one does not know" (C 356). Attention to one's own experience teaches the mind to be humble and to accept correction of its errors. Too strong an attachment to schemas, dogmas, and principles can rob the mind of its precious flexibility of response, of its self-correcting capacity. "La grandeur de l'ame n'est pas tant tirer à mont et tirer avant, comme sçavoir se ranger et circonscrire" (G ii:571); "The soul's greatness consists not so much in climbing high and pressing forward as in knowing how to adapt and limit itself" (C 399). Learning gained from experience is a better guide than theory, morally and practically. Nature has provided us with the mental qualities we need:

> Comme elle [la Nature] nous a fourni de pieds à marcher, aussi a elle de prudence à nous guider en la vie; prudence non tant ingenieuse, robuste et pompeuse comme celle de leur [les philosophes] inven- tion, mais à l'advenant facile et salutaire, et qui faict tresbien ce que l'autre dict. (G ii:526)

> As nature has provided us with feet for walking, so she has given us wisdom to guide us through life; a wisdom less subtle, robust, and spectacular than that of the philosophers' invention, but correspon- dingly easy and salutary, which actually performs very well what the other only promises. (C 354)

Montaigne claims that the study of personal experience gets better results than reason and theory, partly because it takes the body into account. Most of Montaigne's essays refer to physical experience at some point, and the essay "On Experience" considers it at great length. The Cartesian *cogito* ruled out bodily experience as an unreliable source of knowledge, and until Sartrean existentialism reinstated it, it tended to be peripheral in philosophy. Montaigne's view ("philosophy" is hardly the appropriate word, since he never tired of attacking that discipline) is quite opposed to this reduction of human existence to cogitation. He reminds us of our bodies and of his own, often through the themes of sickness and aging. Here, if anywhere, experience is the best guide, Montaigne tells us. "L'experience est proprement sur son fumier au subject de la medecine, où la raison luy quite toute la place" (G ii:532); "In the realm of medicine, experience is at home on its own dunghill, where reason gives place to it entirely" (C 361). Doctors, schooled in theory and generality, and looking only for the resemblance of our condition to a known type, cannot rival the individual's experience of his own body and how different circumstances affect it. Life is lived physically and individually: this is the justification for Montaigne's long description of his own bodily constitution and habits. He also records in detail the effects of his body's passage from youth to age: the body's existence in time is the very basis of experience for him. The mind should accept this fact. Montaigne has no time for those philosophies or religions which teach the inferiority of bodily existence and the desirability of transcending it as far as possible. True wisdom consists in the acceptance of Nature as God has ordered it: "Pour moy donc, j'ayme la vie et la cultive telle a pleu à Dieu nous l'octroier . . . . J'accepte de bon cœur, et recognoissant, ce que nature a fait pour moy, et m'en agrée et m'en loue" (G ii:574); "For my part then, I love life and cultivate it in the form which it has pleased God to bestow it on us . . . . I heartily and gratefully accept what nature has done for me, and I am pleased and proud of myself that I do" (C 402–3). Montaigne rejects asceticism, or any other view which emphasizes the split in man between divine and earthly, rational and irrational, virtuous and sinful. To him, human experience is whole: its physical and mental dimensions should be in balance and harmony. "Que l'esprit esveille et vivifie la pesanteur du corps, le corps arreste la legereté de l'esprit et la fixe" (G ii:575); "Let the mind rouse and enliven the heaviness of the body, and the body check and steady the frivolity of the mind" (C 404).

Nature is the final harmonizing concept in Montaigne, and he ends his last essay and his entire book with the clearest declaration of this belief: "Nature est un doux guide, mais non pas plus doux que prudent et juste" (G ii:574); "Nature is a gentle guide, but no more wise and just than she is gentle" (C 404). Nature works inside and outside the individual, in his body and mind and those of his fellow humans and in the physical world around him. But the harmony of mind and Nature is always being disturbed by the tendency of the mind to set up its own designs against and above those of Nature, and to try to live within the human constructs of reason and traditional learning – in other words within the world of "art" in the wide sense, including medicine, rhetoric, and philosophy, for example. It is easier to live "selon l'art que selon nature, mais bien moins noblement aussi, et moins recommandablement" (G ii:570–1); "It is easier to follow art than nature but it is also much less noble and commendable" (C 399). Man becomes the prisoner of his own culture, and suffers from its distortions of nature.

Montaigne is not preaching an unthinking or anti-intellectual submission to Nature. The essays constantly show him leading an active intellectual life. The mind too has its rights and needs, and its restlessness needs to be satisfied with regular exercise. It should have the humility to accept its own untrustworthiness, without abdicating in favour of an unreflective stupor. In fact it takes a considerable and persistent intellectual effort to live in harmony with Nature, a state which Montaigne sees as philosophical acceptance, not reversion to the instinctual level. The starting-point of the essay was the mind's *natural* desire for knowledge. The task is to bring that desire back to Nature in a wiser and more accepting condition. To do this thought has to stay close to life, rather than constructing a separate world. It has to be reapplied to the experience in which it originates and of which it is a part. Thought should enhance the process of living rather than evade or ignore it. Reflection should increase enjoyment: "Il y a du mesnage à la [la vie] jouyr; je la jouys au double des autres, car la mesure en la jouyssance depend du plus ou moins d'application que nous y prestons" (G ii:572); "It needs good management to enjoy life. I enjoy it twice as much as others, for the measure of enjoyment depends on the greater or less attention that we give to it" (C 401). In so far as thought leads to acceptance and appreciation of Nature, it is good. Life has to be *cultivated* as well as simply lived, so long as cultivation does not become an end in itself as it does with so many of the learned and dogmatic. Thought itself should, in a sense, be natural. "Des opinions de la philosophie, j'embrasse plus volontiers celles qui sont les plus solides, c'est à dire les plus humaines et nostres: mes discours sont, conforméement à mes meurs, bas et humbles" (G ii:574); "Of philosophical opinions I embrace for preference those that are most substantial, that is to say the most human, and the most natural to us. My reflections, in keeping with my actions, are humble and unassuming" (C 403). Life, thought, and discourse should all be *in keeping* with each other.

The Montaignean essay, we can say, is the way of writing

which approximates most closely to the natural form of thought, which in turn is trying to approximate to inner and outer Nature. It is "artless" in the sense that it does not impose a rhetorical design on thought; it reflects the process of thinking rather than reporting and ordering its results. It is "formless" in the sense that it follows the forms of thinking rather than supplying its own ready-made ones. Just as the mind should adapt and yield to the flow of experience, the essay should yield and adapt to the flow of thought. In Montaigne the essay fully submits neither to the order of art nor the order of knowledge, though it participates in both. It prizes those particularities which overturn any kind of schematism, and has room for oddities, anomalies and exceptions. The untidiness of Montaigne's essays is a mark of their openness and receptivity, their welcoming of chance occurrences in thought or event. The unevenness makes demands on the reader, but enables him to re-experience the original process of reflection. It requires the same kind of "yielding" to the text, the giving up of conventional expectations of unity and relevance and consistency, that created the essays in the first place. "On Experience" represents the furthest expansion of this essayistic principle of all-inclusiveness, so that Montaigne gives us the smallest details of his existence, his habits of eating, sleeping, defecating, exercising, love-making, talking, and reading; and its furthest point of departure from the original intention to collect together "sentences" containing compact general truths. Yet those sayings are still there; they are not shut out, simply redeployed in the course of Montaigne's own thinking. He sees no reason not to use them if he's found them to be true. But the priorities have been reversed; now they are illustrations rather than authoritative starting-points. The later stages of Montaigne's project do not cancel the earlier ones, but resituate them, and the whole book, like many of the individual essays, has the cumulative all-inclusive form of experience itself.

3

Bacon: ramifications of counsel

The textual development of Bacon's *Essays* followed a similar path to Montaigne's. The work went through three editions in Bacon's lifetime (1597, 1612, and 1625), and in each edition the individual essays were increased in number and (in most cases) in length. The first edition contained ten essays, along with other texts, and was reissued in 1598, 1604, and 1606 – a testament to its popularity. Partly in response to pirated editions, Bacon prepared a second edition with thirty-eight essays (though forty are listed on the title page), published in 1612. The third edition, entitled *The Essayes Or Counsels, Civill and Morall*, was published in 1625 and contained fifty-eight essays, including twenty new ones and revised and enlarged versions of most of the others. John Florio's translation of Montaigne's *Essais* appeared in 1603; but before this Bacon had already borrowed at least the title for his own first edition. Scholars are divided about how well and at what point Bacon knew Montaigne's work, and also how great an influence the Frenchman was on him (see Adolph, 58–60). Bacon himself appears to minimize the debt in his original dedication of the second edition to Prince Henry (suppressed because of Henry's death), where he states of the term "essay": "The word is late, but the thing is ancient; for Seneca's epistles to Lucilius, if you mark them well, are but essays, that is, dispersed meditations, though conveyed in the form of epistles" (quoted in Adolph, 60). The first words almost certainly refer to Montaigne, but Bacon prefers to emphasize the classical antecedent of Seneca, who of course was also a key source for Montaigne, despite the admittedly epistolary form.

Despite differences of style and philosophy, Bacon and Montaigne are working in what is recognizably the same genre, which is distinct from the genre used by Seneca. Seneca's influence on the two later authors is moral, not formal; he is writing in an established classical genre, the familiar epistle, and using it as a means to instruct his young correspondent Lucilius in an established philosophy, that of Stoicism. There are many personal details, but the main thrust of each piece is didactic, and in that respect is like an informal sermon which the preacher illustrates from his own life. The form invented by Bacon and Montaigne reverses these priorities: the general statements are derived from observation and experience, rather than experience being used to illustrate a pre-established doctrine. Both developed the essay form out of the brief collection of apothegms on a given topic, by a process of expansion in which the linking commentary on those sayings gradually took precedence over them. Bacon's essays, however, even the late ones, remain less exploratory and less personal than Montaigne's. Even in England, Montaigne's influence, strengthened by Florio's translation, was at least equal to Bacon's.

Bacon's essays do not include the frequent self-reference that Montaigne's do, so it is interesting to turn to the prefaces he wrote for the successive editions to gain some idea of how he saw the enterprise. Although the writing in the later editions grows more intimate in tone, the three dedications are to men of increasingly high rank and less intimate connection to Bacon: in 1597 "To Mr. Anthony Bacon, his dear Brother"; in 1612 "To my loving Brother Sir John Constable, Kt." (Constable was his brother-in-law); and in 1625 "To the right honourable my very good lord the duke of Buckingham, his grace, and lord high admiral of England" (W 446). The first dedication defends what Bacon fears might seem premature publication of "these fragments of my conceits." His excuse is the danger of pirated editions; like Cervantes and many other authors of the time he has a clear sense of personal literary property and literary theft. He begins: "I do now, like some that have an orchard ill neighboured, that gather their fruit before it is ripe, to prevent stealing." Having found nothing in the essays "contrary or infectious to the state of religion, or manners, but rather, as I suppose, medicinable," he decides on publishing them. "Only I disliked now to put them out, because they will be like the late new halfpence, which though the silver were good, yet the pieces were small." Already showing his gift for the quick and apposite concrete simile, Bacon presents his work as fruit, as medicine, and as coin. The fruit metaphor recurs in the third dedication, but now with a sense of maturity and harvest: the essays are "of the best fruits, that by the good increase which God gives to my pen and labours I could yield." He places the *Essays* in the context of his life's output, noting that "of all my other works [they] have been most current; for that as it seems they come home to men's business and bosoms" (58).

In several respects, these emphases differ from Montaigne's. Montaigne's *Essais* were the major work of his life, where Bacon's *Essays* were a relatively minor project compared to his scientific works like *The Advancement of Learning*. Montaigne's stated aim, reflected in his practice, was to create a self-portrait in ideas and descriptions, where Bacon's was to provide reliable counsels for others, to find a place in their "business and bosoms." But the most important distinction from our point of view can perhaps be put through Pater's line from the "Conclusion" to *The Renaissance*: "Not the fruit of experience, but experience itself, is the end" (222). This would apply to Montaigne's form of the essay: Bacon himself offers his essays as "fruits" rather than "experiences," the results of inquiry, not the process of inquiry. The "currency" of his ideas in the world he sees as a proof of their validity, which is expressed in the "new coins" simile for the essays. They coexist with the old coinage of apothegm and proverb, if we extend Bacon's metaphor, but are newly minted, formed by fresh observation of the contemporary world. Bacon is more conservative than Montaigne in that he is still aiming at aphoristic form, but based on observation and experience, not the authority of book learning. Rhetorically, too, he is more conservative, using such traditional classical devices as "definition" and "division" of the topic, and providing convenient summaries for the reader, all of which Montaigne neglected deliberately.

All of this makes it easy to underestimate Bacon and see Montaigne as the "true" essayist and the real innovator, as well as being a more vivid, open, and sympathetic personality. Montaigne's loose, exploratory, and digressive style contrasts strongly with Bacon's neat, compact, and orderly manner, but both styles are influential in the development of the essay, and in some ways Bacon is a better model. The short, aphoristic sentence is used effectively by writers like Adorno and Benjamin, while Orwell's essay openings rival some of Bacon's attention-getting first sentences. Bacon uses classical rhetoric (especially definition, division, and simile) not because it is classical, but because it is effective. Usefulness is the keynote of his essay-writing, and this aim is just as modern as the self-revelation which is Montaigne's central aim. Auerbach in *Mimesis* called the *Essais* "the first work of lay introspection" (270); the *Essays* might be seen as the first volume of lay extraversion, the ancestor, in fact, of "self-help" books and magazine articles. The rules of conduct which Bacon articulates are based on impartial study, not religious authority, and although moral considerations do enter into account, they are not the organizing center of Bacon's inquiry, and tend more to act as a counter-movement and source of tension. (In this morally neutral approach Macchiavelli's *The Prince* is of course an important predecessor, but is a systematic political treatise, unlike Bacon's gathering of a diversity of topics.)

Montaigne's basic philosophy is of acceptance, including self-acceptance: this is why he is able to set his own unrepentant, unreformed self before us. The Baconian self, however, is not Bacon himself, but more like the "you" of modern magazine literature: the secular novice, the recipient of guidance. The keynote is not, as in Montaigne, self-acceptance or acceptance of things as they are, but self-improvement and the reforming and reorganizing of human affairs in general. The *Essays* represent the "civil and moral" dimension of Bacon's overall project: to find out how things actually work in society and nature, and then take advantage of this knowledge in practical terms for individual and collective betterment. He is looking for different kinds of truth than Montaigne for different kinds of reasons. Both adopt a critical attitude to the accumulated lore of the past, but where Montaigne refocuses on the present, Bacon does so largely on the future. In current parlance he might be described as "goal-oriented." Bacon was both more of a pragmatist and more of a Utopian than Montaigne. Both sought to accommodate the mind, cleared of the prejudices of inherited orthodoxy, to Nature, but for Bacon this new knowledge was a prelude to power over it. In his treatise *Valerius Terminus: Of the Interpretation of Nature*, Bacon declares that knowledge of Nature is ultimately "a restitution and reinvesting, in great part, of man to the sovereignty and power, for whensoever he shall be able to call the creatures by their true names, he shall again command them, as he had in his first state of creation"

(W 375). He adds that the possibilities range from "the meanest mechanical practice" to human immortality. In an apparent paradox, these Utopian goals depend for their realization on the study of the least important-seeming evidence; only humility can realize the highest ambition. Bacon attacks in *Filum Labyrinthi*, a summary of the principles of his own thinking, the prejudice against natural philosophy (i.e. science) and in favour of abstract, non-empirical thinking:

> He [i.e. Bacon] thought also, there was found in the mind of man an affection naturally bred and fortified, and furthered by discourse and doctrine, which did pervert the true proceeding towards active and operative knowledge. This was a false estimation, that it should be as a diminution to the mind of man to be much conversant in experiences and particulars. (*W* 400)

Bacon attributes this mentality to Aristotle and his successors, the schoolmen (or scholastics) whose work rested merely on "agitation of wit," not empirical investigation. The *Essays* represent one version of Bacon's "active and operative knowledge," founded on observation of the "experiences and particulars" of human behavior, but not organized as a systematic treatise like, say, Hobbes's *Leviathan*, but as local or topical groupings of ideas.

The practicality of Bacon's philosophy is perhaps most clearly shown at the basic level of individual health. Here more than anywhere the practice of self-observation is vital. He writes in "Of Regiment of Health": "There is a wisdom in this beyond the rules of physic: a man's own observation, what he finds good of, and what he finds hurt of, is the best physic to preserve health" (156). Medical theory, professed by doctors and reflected in their prescriptions, is not entirely rejected by Bacon, however: he recommends taking both physicians and "physic" with caution. Some doctors are patient-oriented and humor the patient too much, while others are too disease-oriented and neglect the patient. Bacon advises taking one of "middle temper" (157), or, failing that, consult one doctor of each type! This strategy of avoiding extremes is characteristic of Bacon, and provides a typically neat rhetorical pattern as well, a triad consisting of opposite errors with the truth in the middle. Although Bacon basically shares Montaigne's naturopathic view of human health, he does not refer to his own physical experience as Montaigne does, but addresses himself to the

47

reader as "you": his approach is essentially prescriptive rather than descriptive. This accounts for his occasional resemblance to Polonius lecturing Laertes on how to conduct himself in Paris.

Bacon's conception of the self is more social than Montaigne's; he shows much more concern about how the individual fits into social structures. In that sense his view is both more and less "selfish" than Montaigne's: more, in that the "self" of Bacon's essays is seeking advancement or advantage of some kind; less, in that for this very reason the "self" is more adaptive and eager to learn and change. Montaigne's essays focus on self-reflection, Bacon's on self-improvement. Both see the self as changeable, but for Montaigne the changes are a process of self-unfolding, for Bacon of self-adaptation. Montaigne assumes the autonomy of the self, Bacon its relativity. To employ Sartre's terms, the "self" of Bacon's essays has a *situation* within which it has formed a specific *project*. Where Montaigne is "self-centered" (though not in the pejorative sense of "egocentric"), Bacon is "other-centered." The essay "Of Wisdom for a Man's Self" illustrates this concept of the self being checked and balanced by its society. "Divide with reason between self-love and society, and be so true to thyself as thou be not false to others, specially to thy king and country" (130). Polonius's view is somewhat more straightforward:

> This above all, to thine own self be true,
> And it must follow, as the night the day,
> Thou canst not then be false to any man.
> (*Hamlet*, I.iii.79–81)

For Bacon, being true to yourself has to be *checked* in order to be true to others, whereas for Polonius the second follows naturally from the first. For Bacon there is a certain incompatibility between the goals of self and society which requires careful adjustment. He goes on to explore this through the imagery of centrality: "It is a poor centre of a man's actions, *himself*. It is right earth, for that only stands fast upon his own centre, whereas all things that have affinity with the heavens move upon the centre of another, which they benefit" (130). Society, Bacon argues, is centered on the sovereign, who thus has more excuse for self-centeredness. The selfish ends of his subordinate, however, will inevitably be "eccentric to those of his master"; corrupt officials "set a bias upon their bowl," and are "crooked" in the original sense of that metaphor. Thus a man should keep his place relative to the center, Bacon tells us. But the moral character of the argument is undermined at the end, where we are told that self-wisdom, besides being depraved "in many branches thereof" (a typically Baconian parenthesis undercutting the main proposition), doesn't work, because it produces the illusion of being immune to the vagaries of Fortune, "whose wings they thought by their self-wisdom to have pinioned" (130). In other words, selfish wisdom turns out to be a form of stupidity, based on a misreading of one's proper place and legitimate ends. Self-interest cannot achieve its own ends without harmonizing them to a great extent with the public interest.

Most of the essays that deal with social conduct observe this uneasy balance between seeking the maximum self-advantage and fearing some form of retribution from others. The concept of Fortune, bringing down those who have risen too high, is implicit in many essays where it is not specifically mentioned. Advice about how to succeed is always closely accompanied by advice on how to handle others' reactions to one's success. The prominence of these themes is evident in a number of the essay titles: "Of Praise," "Of Vainglory," "Of Honor and Reputation," "Of Fame," "Of Fortune," "Of Ambition," and others of a similar kind. Bacon views society in much the same way as Freud views the psyche, as a system of compensations and adaptations, where every effect sets off a compensatory counter-effect. Success and failure, possession and dispossession, good fortune and adversity, are not phenomena that can be considered separately because they interact reciprocally all the time. Lack produces desire, desire ambition, ambition perhaps succeeds and provokes resentment, and so on. Bacon sees society as a closed system with a finite quantity of desired rewards (power, prestige, wealth, etc.) that is constantly being redistributed. But the redistribution is circular; society is not evolving consistently in any direction, but tending to return to its norm.

This Baconian economy of desire and possession is seen clearly in the essay "Of Envy." The division of the topic in the second paragraph announces that the author will deal with those who feel envy, those who attract it, and the difference between public and private envy. This is a good example of how Bacon's essay structure reflects his "compensatory" dialectical vision: even his sentences are often built around a similar positive/negative contrast. Envy has a kind of equilibrium function: the envious seek to bring down the envied to their own level, either imaginatively or actually.

> A man that hath no virtue in himself ever envieth virtue in others. For men's minds, will either feed upon their own good or upon others' evil; and who wanteth the one will prey upon the other; and whoso is out of hope to attain another's virtue will seek to come at even hand by depressing another's fortune. (83)

The balance of Bacon's sentences perfectly enacts the balance he is describing. For Bacon, envy is produced by a perceived imbalance, by an inequality seen in relation to a previous or normative equality. When someone "rises," his former equals are liable to envy him, as are the new associates, who when "others come on they think themselves go back" (84). Envy is based on comparability: "envy is ever joined with the comparing of a man's self; and where there is no comparison, no envy; and therefore kings are not envied but by kings" (85). As for moral evaluation, Bacon sees some public benefit from the effects of this private vice: "it is a bridle also to great ones, to keep them within bounds" (85). Envy only endangers the state when it is directed beyond individuals to an entire governing class: then it leads to sedition. Bacon's tripartite "divisio" of his topic has produced a powerful dialectic: the envious and the envied are seen as a symbiotic pairing from each viewpoint, and the opposition resolved from a "social" viewpoint, which in turn "compensates" the negative nature of private envy with its (sometimes) positive public effects.

Bacon's fullest account of class society is given in the essay "Of Nobility," but again it is balanced by a consideration of private nobility, i.e. what it means to an individual and his human relationships to be of noble rank. Once again we have a dialectic of public and private experience, but this time the public viewpoint is examined first. As in many other essays, "but" is the key word, the hinge which unites contrary movements. The nobility is a beneficial class in a monarchy because it "attempers sovereignty" (99), *but* a nuisance in a democracy like Switzerland or the Netherlands because "utility is their bond, and not respects" (99). Bacon then returns to the first proposition, and proceeds to develop and qualify it, viewing the supposedly positive role of the nobility within monarchy from the standpoint of the other constituents of the state, the monarch and the populace: "A great and potent nobility, addeth majesty to a monarch, but diminisheth power; and putteth life and spirit into the people, but presseth their fortune" (99). The analysis has proceeded by shifting the positive/negative opposition from the first contrast (nobility in monarchy vs. nobility in democracy) to the first *half* of that contrast (positive vs. negative effects of nobility in monarchies). The pattern of oppositions works down to the sentence level, where, besides the ubiquitous "but" construction, the texture often consists of balanced equations ("is" and "is not") and imperatives ("let" and "let not").

Bacon includes a multiplicity of effects and viewpoints within a short space, and the compactness and apparent simplicity of his style often lead casual readers to underestimate the complexity of his thought. Bacon imposes different demands on his readers than Montaigne. With Montaigne the difficulty is disunity and digressiveness from the stated topic. Bacon sometimes creates the opposite problem: an obtrusive and almost oppressive sense of structure. But his orderliness is not simplicity. As he divides and subdivides his topic, usually informing you as he is doing it, he makes room for multiple viewpoints and contradictory effects which it is easy to gloss over in a first reading. Stanley Fish, in a long chapter on Bacon's *Essays*, reads them as self-consuming artifacts (in keeping with the title of his book) in the sense that the general propositions are less and less able to contain and subsume their detailed developments. I would use a different analogy for the process of the essays: a kind of "ramification" of the topic, like one of the "trees" from Bacon's other works, showing the different "branches" of knowledge spreading out from the original trunk. Another way to put it would be as a process of "qualification," in the sense both of "more precise specification" and of "partial contradiction." Although Fish's textual model works no worse here than in his other seventeenth-century examples, it is not at all necessary to regard the later complications as "consuming" the earlier generalities. And although Bacon's procedure is often dialectical, i.e. it establishes positives by including negatives, his aim in this is not, as Fish claims, to provide the reader with an experience of uncertainty, but to tabulate the results (positive and negative, certain and less certain) of his own experience, observation, and analysis.

Bacon's own repeatedly stated purpose in writing the essays is to provide texts of "use," especially in the sphere of "men's business," (57) to quote his phrase from the third preface. The essays are intended as guides to how individuals really act and react, and what the consequences are for society at large. To that end the essays have clear and easily remembered analytic structures: Bacon's advice in "Of Dispatch" about conducting brief and effective meetings applies to his essay writing as well:

> Above all things, order and distribution, and singling out of parts is the life of dispatch, so as the distribution be not too subtle: for he that doth not divide, will never enter well into business, and he that divideth too much, will never come out of it clearly. (135)

This glimpse of Bacon's style as a committee chairman helps us to place his brisk and "business-like" tone, and the resemblances between one of his essays and an "agenda" in the original sense of the word as "matters to be acted on." We might recall also Bacon's general conception of knowledge as "active and operative." "Of Negotiating" is another strikingly practical set of precepts about maximizing your own advantages in bargaining with others. Bacon begins by announcing three ways of negotiating: by letter, by speech, and by proxy. Each alternative is dealt with at greater length than the preceding one, and is divided into more options. Letters are best when there might later be need to produce evidence; speech is better where maximum flexibility is desired, or where social superiority might give one an advantage by intimidating the other. Proxies should be chosen according to the nature of the task: "bold men for expostulation, fairspoken men for persuasion, crafty men for inquiry and observation, forward and absurd men for business that doth not well bear out itself" (202). Bacon does not show any of the breadth and detachment of Montaigne in considering human affairs of this kind; he focuses exclusively on getting results and "optimizing" (Bacon's thinking translates easily into the language of modern counseling) one's interests.

Bacon's happiest and most expansive essays are those where he elaborates his designs without having to take into account the reactions of the "other" which elsewhere provide a check to his projects. Plans can be laid out in a purely positive way, without the incessant negative limitation caused by the realities of life in society. The essays "Of Gardens" and "Of Building" sketch out ideal designs for a country house and estate, and they can easily be imagined in modern magazines like *Homes and Gardens*. Inevitably, Bacon's ideal garden is divided into three parts, but the essay has one of his finest "arresting" openings: "God Almighty first planted a garden. And indeed it is the purest of human pleasures" (197). Bacon the natural scientist next comes to the fore, with listings of plants and flowers according to their seasons (year-round, all-weather use is his governing principle in the design). He includes in the 30 acres (this is on a "prince-like" scale, Bacon tells us) an area of heath to be left in a state of "natural wildness," but even this turns out to be carefully planned and planted. Usefulness is again the key to the palace design in "Of Building," which opens: "Houses are built to live in, and not to look on; therefore let use be preferred before uniformity, except where both may be had" (193). The detailed plans, besides stressing the importance of choosing a good "seat" (i.e. site), include considerations of heating, access, seasonal change, and even the placing of the servants' kitchen away from the main stairwell so that the smell of their dinner won't drift up to the master's quarters.

Bacon's unique mixture of Utilitarianism and Utopianism comes out even more strongly in his piece "Of Plantations" (i.e. colonies). After warning against founding settlements in already inhabited country, against expecting a quick profit, and against using criminals as settlers, Bacon recommends a group of "gardeners, ploughmen, laborers, smiths, carpenters, joiners, fishermen, fowlers, with some few apothecaries, surgeons, cooks, and bakers" (162). He stresses the need to adapt and use local resources, and to show patience with the slow establishment of the community, not overwhelming it with new immigrants, and waiting some years before "planting" with women. This model settlement is a step towards Bacon's *New Atlantis* Utopia, with its groups of busy scientists. His essay "Of Usury" again displays his propensity for rational planning, here in the economic sphere. He sets himself the problem of keeping the advantages of usury while avoiding its disadvantages, and comes up with a scheme for a two-tier rate of interest: 5 per cent as the base rate, with higher rates for special projects.

Bacon is one of those rare writers who are equally at home sketching perfect theoretical schemes and noting down the concrete particularities of actual experience. His "planning" essays and his "business" essays correspond to these two aspects, but the two are not exclusive, in that both types are more or less well planned and businesslike, whatever their topic. His orderly dividing and subdividing of his material can be seen as abstract and schematic, or organic. He himself, as we saw earlier, felt that his essays had grown to maturity between 1597 and 1625, and that they could be finally called with truth the "fruits" of his experience. But orderly fruition of human endeavor is not a purely "natural" matter; it requires the guidance of "art" as well. The essay "Of Nature in Men" asserts that an individual's nature is something that can be shaped and modified, but not fundamentally changed, at least not without risk of reversion. Where Montaigne's persistent theme is the acceptance of nature inside and outside the self, Bacon's is self-cultivation, growth directed towards an end. The essay concludes: "A man's nature, runs either to herbs or weeds; therefore let him seasonably water the one, and destroy the other." The essays are meant as helps and guides in the planning of this kind of positive and negative work on the self. The dialectical form of the Baconian essay imposes a more logical structure on thought and experience, something that Montaigne warns against. But Bacon never becomes a formalist in the scholastic sense; he is too intent on the realities of experience, and his orderliness is geared to a kind of usefulness that Montaigne was not very interested in.

4

Johnson: the correction of error

Dr Johnson's greatest fame, aside from his status as a "character," is through his work in the basic "disciplines" of modern literary study: philology (the *Dictionary*), editing (the Shakespeare edition), biography, and criticism (both in *The Lives of the Poets*). His essays, perhaps because the genre was never really incorporated into institutional or disciplinary practice, have never received as much attention. The opinions expressed in the literary essays have been discussed in the general context of Johnson's criticism, but the moral essays, which form the great majority of his work in the genre, are less known. In our time, the very phrase "moral essay" is liable to provoke a fear of "preaching." Also, much of the content of this sub-genre has been taken over by psychology; and the other sub-genres (the travel essay, critical essay, and autobiographical essay) have survived better into the post-Freudian era. The moral essay's mixture of psychological observation and moral precept did not remain viable much after Robert Louis Stevenson's series entitled *Virginibus Puerisque* (1881). Johnson's moral essays are probably the purest examples of the form in the English tradition. His task as an essayist, as he saw it, was to observe social and individual behavior accurately and to judge it carefully and dispassionately. This emphasis on impartial moral judgment distinguishes his work from both Montaigne's cheerful inconsistency and Bacon's emphasis on getting practical results from the study of human nature. It also separates him from Addison and Steele, whose moralizing was more intermittent and lighter in tone. But before considering Johnson's use of the essay we need to discuss the developments of the form which he inherited from them.

The principal changes in the essay in the early eighteenth

century are associated with the move from book to periodical publication. Frequent periodical publication (daily in the case of *The Spectator*) itself creates a sense of spontaneity, an immediate social responsiveness that gives the individual contributions the feeling of participating in a general conversation. Montaigne's spontaneity is more like a dialogue of the self with itself, and when he does envisage or address a reader it is another private individual like himself. Both relationships (author with self, author with reader) are enclosed within the spaces of the Library and the Book. The periodical essay, however, is out in the open on the tables of the coffee-houses and reception rooms. Through periodical publication, Addison tells us, "Knowledge, instead of being bound up in Books, and kept in Libraries and Retirements, is thus obtruded upon the Publick;...canvassed in every Assembly and exposed upon every Table" (*Spectator* 124). The periodical essay *circulates* in the world, provoking discussion and response, reflecting as well as expressing opinion. The association of knowledge with books and with retirement is still strong in Montaigne; in contrast, *The Spectator* essays socialize and urbanize knowledge, distributing it as simply a printed part of a continuing conversation. Their role is comparable to television as well as newspapers in our own time.

When Steele started *The Tatler* in 1709, he distinguished it from the competing journals of news and opinion by giving it a fictional author-editor: Isaac Bickerstaff, borrowed from Swift's pamphlets of 1708. This device was taken over in *The Spectator*, but this time the persona was more sedate and aloof, without the Tatler's active involvement in the metropolitan scene and its gossip and fashions. As the Spectator puts it, "I have acted in all the Parts of my Life as a Looker-on, which is the Character I intend to preserve in this Paper" (*Spectator* 1). His justification for writing essays is that his friends have urged him to use this way of sharing with others the accumulated thoughts and observations which he is too taciturn to express in conversation. This emphasis on the self-effacing presentation of social life contrasts with Montaigne's avowed aim of making a self-portrait; nevertheless the Spectator's shyness and anxiety to preserve his distance itself becomes a means of comic characterization. Ironically, his visit to the country is precisely what puts this aloofness at risk by making him socially conspicuous as Sir Roger de Coverley's guest, and he hastens back to the anonymity of the city: "I can there raise what Speculations I please without being observed my self, and at the same time all the Advantages of Company with all the Privileges of Solitude" (*Spectator* 131).

Besides the fictitious "author-editor," Addison and Steele also introduced other characters, and in *The Spectator* made them into a Club which represented what they saw as the main sectors of English society: Sir Roger represents the country squires, Sir Andrew Freeport typifies the wealthy trading class, Captain Sentry gives the military viewpoint, Will Honeycomb contributes the perspective of the man-about-town, and the Clergyman that of the Church. The circle of their discussions, intended as a microcosm of the nation, is further extended by the "letters to the editor," some of which may be fictitious, others not. The distinction is itself the subject of an essay (*Spectator* 542) which, by deliberately blurring the fiction/reality division, gives the fictitious characters a greater sense of possible "reality," a device common to the early novel from Cervantes onwards. Where Montaigne's multiplicity is that of a single self over time, that of *The Spectator* is produced by the variety of participating characters and textual forms.

Johnson was highly conscious of the precedents set by Addison and Steele. He adopted all of their main innovations: the fictional author-editor and other characters, and also the allegories, dream-visions, literary-critical papers, letters, and tales. For almost exactly two years (20 March 1750 to 14 March 1752) he wrote two essays a week for *The Rambler*, following this with occasional contributions to *The Adventurer* in 1753–4, and a series of weekly essays for *The Idler* from 15 April 1758 to 5 April 1760. Johnson only wrote essays in series and under the pressure of regular periodical publication. Boswell relates that many of the *Ramblers* were composed at the very last minute and sent off to the printer unrevised, a fact the biographer found hard to reconcile with the air of deliberation the writing seems to possess:

> many of these discourses, which we should suppose had been laboured with all the slow attention of literary leisure, were written in haste as the moment pressed, without even being read over by him before they were printed. It can be accounted for only in this way; that by reading and meditation, and a very close inspection of life, he had accumulated a great fund of miscellaneous knowledge, which, by a peculiar promptitude of mind, was ever ready at his call,

and which he had constantly accustomed himself to clothe in the most apt and energetick expression. (*Life of Johnson*, Everyman edn, London: Dent, 1960, vol. 1, 118–19)

Johnson himself was unwilling to allow the shortness and informality of the genre to act as excuses for disorganized writing, and was scathing about those who did: "he therefore who wants skill to form a plan, or diligence to pursue it, needs only entitle his performance an essay, to acquire the right of heaping together the collections of half his life, without order, coherence, or propriety" (5:77; *R* 158).

Boswell's point is that, however spontaneous the actual composition may have been, Johnson's essays do not *sound* spontaneous; rather, they sound like the expressions of a mind already made up, and a conscience certain of its values. The Rambler does not ramble much, either on foot or in writing. At the outset he seems to take a somewhat condescending view of the form of publication he is using. He sees the periodical writer as having a much easier task psychologically than other writers, since he gets what we would now call instant feedback: "it heightens his alacrity to think in how many places he shall hear what he is now writing, read with ecstasies to morrow" (2:7–8; *R* 1). The writer of a book, in contrast, has to persevere in isolation over a long period, during which the public may lose interest in his topic. The essayist, Johnson says, can adapt quickly to these changes of taste, and the shortness of his pieces means that his investment and his risk are much less. Johnson makes the same distinction as Addison in *Spectator* 124 between the delayed reaction to a book and the much quicker response to an essay, but he appears in *Rambler* 1 to find book writing and reading morally preferable because they involve more time and effort. However, in the last *Rambler* (208), after two years of writing two essays a week, Johnson has changed his opinion about the genre's ease:

He that condemns himself to compose on a stated day, will often bring to his task an attention dissipated, a memory embarrassed, an imagination overwhelmed, a mind distracted with anxieties, a body languishing with disease: He will labour on a barren topick, till it is too late to change it; or in the ardour of invention, diffuse his thoughts into wild exuberance, which the pressing hour of publication cannot suffer judgment to examine or reduce. (5:318; *R* 208)

It is hard, however, to find many instances of this kind of loss of control over the text in *The Rambler;* the same deliberate tone prevails throughout.

Johnson's denigration of literary popularity may be another indication of his awareness of *The Spectator;* as he foresaw in *Rambler* 1 and confirmed at the end of the series in *Rambler* 208, his periodical never rivaled Addison and Steele's in popular success. Already in *Rambler* 23, Johnson takes on those of his readers who criticize him for not closely following the model of *The Spectator.* Here are two of the objections he lists:

> Some were angry that the Rambler did not, like the Spectator, introduce himself to the acquaintance of the publick, by an account of his own birth and studies, and enumeration of his adventures, and a description of his physiognomy. Others soon began to remark that he was a solemn, serious, dictatorial writer, without sprightliness or gaiety, and called out with vehemence for mirth and humour. (3:128–9; R 23)

In dealing with these lively critical reactions, Johnson compares the status of the essay series in progress to that of the unpublished manuscript: in both cases readers feel they can influence the writer because changes are still possible. The same person reacts quite differently, Johnson holds, to a published work, where he tends to accept the author's design, than to a manuscript, where he feels the need to justify having been consulted by offering all kinds of suggestions for changes. Johnson's impatience with this attitude on the part of his readers is manifest again at the end of the *Rambler.* In his rather defensive retrospective on the series, Johnson maintains that if "I have never been a favourite of the publick" it is because "I have seldom descended to the arts by which favour is obtained" (5:316; R 208). Among these he includes dealing with ephemeral topics and gossiping about living people; instead of courting popularity in these ways, he has maintained the highest standards of language and morality:

> I have laboured to refine our language to grammatical purity, and to clear it from colloquial barbarisms, licentious idioms, and irregular combinations . . . . The essays professedly serious . . . will be found exactly conformable to the precepts of Christianity, without any accommodation to the licentiousness and levity of the present age. (5:319–20; R 208)

Implicitly, Johnson claims he has deliberately been addressing only a select group of readers whose standards are as high as his own, and who do not need to be attracted by the kinds of stylistic and moral laxity which make for a mass circulation.

Of Johnson's later essay series, the twenty-nine papers he contributed to *The Adventurer* in 1753 continue in much the same vein as *The Rambler,* but in the 104 *Idlers* of 1758–60 Johnson did in fact go some way towards the model of *The Spectator.* The papers are shorter, lighter in tone, and more topical. The fictional characters who appear, such as Jack Whirler, Betty Broom, and Tom Restless, are more likable and lively than the usually negative examples of human conduct in *The Rambler.* Although it is a tribute to Johnson's versatility that he was able to practice successfully the style he had earlier denigrated, his contribution to the development of the essay is the form of moral disquisition he used in *The Rambler* and *The Adventurer,* and it is on these that our discussion will focus, with some comments on his literary essays.

At first sight it might seem that the Johnsonian moral essay, explicitly devoted to inculcating, or at least not controverting, the established precepts of Christianity, may actually come uncomfortably close to preaching. Its pursuit of normative ethical judgments may, in other words, seem to lack what we earlier spoke of as the essence of the essay genre, the unique, unpredictable configuration of self and observation, subject and object. Hazlitt follows this line of attack in his review of Johnson's essays in "On the Periodical Essayists" (Lecture 5 of *English Comic Writers*) and concludes that "he was not a man of original thought or genius, in the sense in which Montaigne or Lord Bacon was . . . . The Rambler is a splendid and imposing commonplace book of general topics, and rhetorical declamation on the conduct and business of human life" (Everyman edn, London: Dent, 1930, 100). Hazlitt's argument seems to imply a return to the kind of moral-scientific compendium the essay originally broke away from; but he underestimates the skeptical, empirical, aspect of Johnson's essays. He also attacks Johnson's style as being inappropriate to essayistic subject matter: "His subjects are familiar, but the author is always upon stilts" (101). However, Hazlitt's parting comments imply a greater consonance of thought and language, though both are denigrated: he calls Johnson a "complete balance-master" both in his rhetoric, "where one clause answers to another in measure and quantity," and in his morality: "he never encourages hope, but he counteracts it by fear; he never elicits a truth, but he suggests some objection to answer it" (102). Hazlitt, as usual, has formulated an essential insight here, but has unfairly made Johnson's thought and style sound mechanical and repetitive. There *is* a deep-seated corrective tendency in Johnson's thought, a desire to redress imbalances, adjust competing claims, and arrive at impartial assessments. But they are still moral investigations, not expositions. They show Johnson's unique adaptation of what was still a relatively new and experimental genre.

The basic strategy of the Johnsonian essay is to bring into right proportions attitudes and actions whose importance has been under- or overestimated. For Johnson, the particular class, profession, group, or individual is always liable to lose perspective on its own relative merit or importance or scope. This is as true of writers as of those they write about, and Johnson frequently reduces the claims of intellectuals by showing that they too often have a partisan, self-interested approach to public affairs, and overestimate their own significance. First of all, the writer must observe due proportion between his topic and the literary form he is using. In keeping with this, Johnson is careful to limit the scope of his own essays. In writing of anger, for example, he mentions but does not develop the terrible effects of the rage of tyrants, stating: "this gigantick and enormous species of anger falls not properly under the animadversion of a writer, whose chief end is the regulation of common life, and whose chief precepts are to recommend themselves by their general use" (3:57; *R* 11). In other words, the essay should not attempt epic subjects, but rather provide a moral critique of individual conduct in civil society.

Johnson proceeds to develop the theme of anger not through classical anecdotes about the havoc wrought by the ire of despots, but through the "character" sketch of a contemporary type, the self-styled "passionate" man. Johnson sees this label as simply a euphemism, and hence a licence, for displays of anger which ought to be repressed. Having characterized themselves in this way, irascible people "imagine themselves entitled by that distinction to be provoked on every slight occasion, and to vent their rage in vehement and fierce vociferations, in furious menaces and licentious reproaches" (3:58; *R* 11). These figures are guilty of disproportion in their responses to events; as we would say, they constantly overreact. "Those sudden bursts of rage generally break out upon small occasions; for life, unhappy as it is, cannot supply great evils as frequently as the man of fire thinks it fit to be enraged" (3:59; *R* 11). With his usual psychological acuity, Johnson sees anger as an attempt to overcome a sense of insignificance or lack of accomplishment. This attempt at compensation for inadequacy inevitably fails, since it can only exact the appearance of respect, not the reality.

Balance, as Hazlitt saw, is the key to Johnson's psychology of the individual as well as to his social morality. Anger, in this example, originates in pride, and "pride, like every other passion, if it once breaks loose from reason, counteracts its own purpose" (3:58; *R* 11). Johnson's essays are at their most skillful in articulating with clarity the self-contradictions of uncontrolled passions. The irascible man becomes unable "to proportion his anger to the cause, or to regulate it by prudence or by duty" (3:60; *R* 11). His frequent offending of others has to be balanced by a corresponding number of attempts to make amends, trapping him on a moral see-saw: "He spends his time in outrage and acknowledgement, injury and reparation" (3:61; *R* 11), until old age dilutes his anger into mere peevishness. Having failed to maintain his individual moral equilibrium, where emotional responses are proportionate to their causes, the Angry Old Man is forced into isolation and contempt.

The Johnsonian essay itself performs a process of readjustment, between passion and reason, the individual and society, the general and the particular. For Johnson, essaying leads into "righting"; it is a corrective reaction to a perceived imbalance in the moral sphere. The process of readjustment is endless, since passions are always overcoming individuals, and individuals are always making excessive claims on society. In many cases these excesses are self-correcting, in that they bring self-defeat or social punishment, and the moral essayist merely clarifies the workings of this process, perhaps to save his readers from avoidable errors. Partial perspectives are corrected by placing them within a wider, impartial view. Individual behavior can only be judged relative to others' behavior. Our own qualities act within a kind of moral economy: "Neither our virtues nor our vices are all our own. If there were no cowardice, there would be little insolence; pride cannot rise to any great degree, but by the concurrence of blandishment or the sufferance of tameness" (5:186; *R* 180).

The self cannot be understood or judged in isolation; nor, for Johnson, can it be fulfilled in that state. Paradoxically, however, the idea of fulfillment in solitude is a popular commonplace. In *Adventurer* 126, Johnson mounts an attack on this *topos* by defining various character types who are prone to its illusions, and showing how each is disabused. The arrogant man wants to retreat because he is tired of adapting to others and taking account of their criticism of him; but he finds in isolation that he has also lost touch with his flatterers. The perfectionist shuns the moral corruption of the city only to find that his own faults occupy his mind, and he soon returns to the original objects of his scorn. The literalist believes what he has read in books about the joys of solitude, forgetting that the writers may have had much greater personal resources or previous achievements than he has. The scholar flees from the distractions and annoyances of the city, but thereby can no longer use or communicate what he learns. Religious hermits fail to let their righteous example be seen in society, where it is needed. Johnson arranges these examples in order of increasing merit of motive, from arrogance to religious devotion, but finds that in each case the result is the same: the purpose of retirement, however worthy or unworthy, is defeated. The only difference is that in the unworthy cases the individual defeats his *own* ends, while in the others (the scholarly and the devout) the social ends of their activity are defeated, even if the individual ones are attained. Thus the scholar may indeed accomplish his end of reading more; it is only from a social viewpoint that his project can be judged a failure. "He has learned to no purpose," says Johnson, "that is not able to teach" (2:474; *A* 126).

But this, of course, was not the scholar's original purpose; half-way through the series of examples, Johnson shifts his criteria from individual to social. He thus reveals his underlying assumption that all human conduct, whether vicious or virtuous, has its full meaning only in society. Even the arrogant and scornful, however they complain, are happier in society than out; the learned and devout, though, even if they are happier outside society, are of less use. If they choose seclusion, they are guilty, in Johnson's view, of a kind of higher selfishness. He demolishes the commonplace of solitude first on empirical psychological grounds, showing that it fails to deliver the anticipated benefits to the individual, and then on socio-moral grounds, asserting that it delivers little or no benefit to others. The perspective in which these figures are placed and evaluated widens during the essay, and their partial viewpoints are corrected (one of Johnson's favourite words) by a more general one. Thus the original generality, "the pleasures of solitude," is demystified and replaced by a new sense of "the indispensability of society," by way of a series of individual cases.

How is one to overcome the limitations of an "individual" perspective, and attain a broader and more impartial "social" viewpoint? Society is made up of separate individuals and distinct classes, ignorant to a greater or lesser degree of the others, and hence liable to misunderstand or denigrate them. At first sight it might seem that the moral philosopher, relatively detached from social competition, would be most likely to provide such a view. But Johnson, typically inclining to skepticism rather than dogmatism, repeatedly refuses to privilege this standpoint. In a wonderful passage of *Adventurer* 128, he quotes La Bruyère's story of watching from his window the most futile imaginable occupation: polishing marble all day. Johnson turns the tables and imagines what the marble polisher might have to say about La Bruyère after watching him sitting at his window all day: "by all this care and labour, he hopes only to make a little book, which at last will teach no useful art, and which none which has it not will perceive himself to want. I have often wondered for what end such a being was sent into the world" (2:479; *A* 128).

Every occupation tends to exalt itself at the expense of others; and writers have the added advantage of rhetorical skills in putting forward their claims and complaints of neglect. Johnson states in *Rambler* 77:

> The miseries of the learned have been related by themselves; and since they have not been found exempt from that partiality with which men look upon their own actions and sufferings, we may conclude that they have not forgotten to deck their cause with the brightest ornaments and strongest colours. (4:39; *R* 77)

Rhetoric itself can easily be the cause of disproportion, belittling or aggrandizing at will: "As it is thus easy by a detail of minute circumstances to make everything little, so it is not difficult by an aggregation of effects to make everything great" (2:478; *A* 128). All the writer can do is to try to correct his own partiality, and use his rhetorical skills to articulate other viewpoints as far as he can, and as Johnson himself visibly tries to do. Especially he must try to express the viewpoint of morality and the general good, even if he himself as an individual fails to live up to its precepts: "He, by whose writings the heart is rectified, the appetites counter-acted, and the passions repressed, may be considered as not unprofitable to the great republick of humanity, even though his behaviour should not always exemplify his rules" (4:41; *R* 77).

Rectification, counter-action, repression: these words, despite the sinister Orwellian or Freudian overtones they have acquired, are good descriptions of Johnson's moral-rhetorical strategies. His moral universe, like Bacon's but unlike Montaigne's, is a closed one within which every movement provokes a compensatory counter-movement. No individual has a perfect inner equilibrium because desire always exceeds actuality. But the moralist can help people regain or at least understand the process of balancing. Desire is always disproportionate, seeking more than it can get. If the individual cannot repress his desires, society will do it for him, or provide some other response to push him back in his place. Only a few of the aspirants to fame, for example, will succeed: "There is never room in the world for more than a certain quantity, or measure, of renown" (5:295; *R* 203). Once this quota has been filled, a new candidate can only become famous by displacing someone else. A kind of collective equilibrium, in this case between the famous and the rest, will always reassert itself. The happiest and wisest are those who understand these laws of proportion and live in accordance with them rather than having them painfully imposed from outside.

For Johnson, human consciousness is caught in an endlessly repeated cycle of anticipation and disappointment; but the moralist can provide a moment of correction and balancing before the next cycle begins. To live is for Johnson necessarily to err; but he does not happily accept this, as Montaigne tends to do. Johnson's "essaying" incorporates and follows human error to the point where its corrective is discovered. But neither the particular course of the error, nor the particular correction it will provoke, is predictable. That is why his essays remain empirical and exploratory, rather than simply being dogmatic applications of fixed principles. For Johnson, experience precedes law, and not vice versa. The correction of an error may lead to a further, though different, error. Precepts can never succeed in governing human behavior completely. Either the individual corrects his errors of passion and partiality himself, or the whole of which he forms part (whether conceived as Society, Nature, or the divinely ordered Universe) will respond by reasserting its dominance. For Johnson as a Christian moralist the individual is by nature errant and in need of moral and rational correction. He is subject to laws, and should try to submit to them willingly and understandingly: "He therefore that would govern his actions by the laws of virtue, must regulate his thoughts by those of reason," he writes in an essay on the dangers of fantasizing (3:46; *R* 8).

Yet this mistrust of the individual viewpoint is balanced by a sense of its value; it is both inadequate and indispensable. Johnsonian morality is not expounded as a system; it is constantly rediscovered on separate "essays" on different occasions and through different means. Johnson was a moralist, but also a stone-kicking empiricist who realized that individuals only learn through their own experiences. The laws of reason and virtue exist, but cannot be abstractly given. They have to be found by trial and error; nor can they be entirely adhered to when found. Thus Johnson's are moral *essays* as well as *moral* essays. The moralist cannot escape "this state of universal uncertainty, where a thousand dangers hover about us, and none can tell whether the good he persues is not evil in disguise" (5:205; *R* 185). Johnson's faith in the ultimate wisdom of God's design does not enable him to be an infallible moral guide. What he *can* do, however, is to dramatize the process of error and correction through the form of the essay. As we saw, Johnson saw this form as being well attuned to the rhythms of daily life, a periodical reflective excursion, a recurrent outing in many different directions which nevertheless always ends in a home truth.

Johnson's sense of the gap between practice and precept, error and correction, is also at the heart of his literary essays. Much of his criticism is not in essay form, notably the "Preface" to Shakespeare and the *Lives of the Poets*. But the *Rambler* does contain a number of important papers of critical theory and practice where we can see the conflict between the claims of empirical observation and moral guidance being worked out in ways reminiscent of the moral essays. His famous treatment of the realism (though of course he does not use this term) of the eighteenth-century novel in *Rambler* 4 is a case in point. The fantasies of Romance Johnson accuses of being "produced without fear of criticism, without the toil of study, without knowledge of nature, or acquaintance with life" (3:20; *R* 4). Romance is too easy, he implies; the work of empirical observation of human behavior is not needed. Realism corrects this defect, since it demands "accurate observation of the living world," and any departure from reality can easily be noted and criticized, since the writers "are engaged in portraits of which every one knows the original, and can detect any deviation from exactness of resemblance" (3:20; *R* 4). Johnson assumes the existence of a common reality, accessible to all through careful study, against which literary representations can be checked for accuracy.

But at this point in the essay a new literary criterion emerges: morality. Romantic heroes and villains, Johnson argues, cannot create moral danger: they are too remote from ordinary experience. Realistic characters, however, with their typical mixture of virtue and vice, are more likely to influence young readers as role models, and lead them to accept lower moral standards. This is an interesting reversal of the post-modernist perspective, which sees fantasy and "invention" as socially "subversive" and realism as socially stabilizing. Johnson believed that exact representation is (1) possible, and (2) dangerous. Thus he wanted romance's inexactitude corrected by realism; but realism's exactitude must in turn be controlled by morality. Realistic art should indeed imitate rather than invent, Johnson holds; but it can and must select objects of imitation which will themselves be worthy of imitation by readers. The concept of imitation does double duty in this essay: art should imitate life, but life will tend in turn to imitate its own artistic imitation. Therefore art must select from life only those aspects which are morally fit for imitation. Johnson goes so far as to say that representation which is not morally selective is pointless; one might just as well be watching real life. Johnson's essay thus offers a double corrective process: of romance by realism, and of realism by morality. The second criterion is the higher; realism never justifies confusing good and evil in the same character. "Vice, for vice is necessary to be shown, should always disgust; nor should the graces of gaiety, or the dignity of courage, be so united with it, as to reconcile it to the mind" (5:24; *R* 4). However, it is hard to imagine the results of this "moral realism," other than by analogy with something like "socialist realism"; Johnson gives no examples, and we are left with the feeling that, while he strongly believes in both realistic and moral criteria, they cannot be fully reconciled in any actual work.

Experience, whether lived or represented in art, is a necessary but finally inadequate guide to Johnson; he does not trust it in the way Montaigne does. But although he will not uphold truth to experience against the claims of morality, Johnson does defend it against authority and convention where the two are in conflict, especially in the realm of literature. Antiquity does not confer authority for Johnson; in fact the reverse is closer to the truth. Inherited precepts can degenerate into unthinking platitudes unless thay are rigorously tested by an unprejudiced intellect. "The accidental prescriptions of authority, when time has procured them veneration, are often confounded with the laws of nature, and those rules are supposed coeval with reason, of which the first rise cannot be discovered" (5:66; *R* 156). This remark, placing reason and nature on the side of the observant and critical individual rather than of tradition, prefaces Johnson's taking on the Baconian task of testing inherited literary precepts and sorting them out: "Some are to be considered as fundamental and indispensable, others only as useful and convenient; some as dictated by reason and necessity, others as formed by accident, or instituted by example, and therefore always liable to dispute and alteration" (5:67; *R* 156). Johnson rejects many of the neo-classical rules for drama by showing that they originated in particular circumstances: the limitation of speaking actors on stage at a given time to three, of the number of acts to five, and the length of represented action to twelve hours, are all rejected as products of historical accident. The unity of action is accepted by Johnson, however, as a permanent necessity of drama, on the grounds that if there are two actions of equal importance, there is material for two plays. Since "practice has introduced rules, rather than rules have directed practice" (5:76; *R* 158), those rules can always be reviewed, modified, or rejected in the light of subsequent experience. Yet, characteristically, Johnson qualifies this pragmatic approach by saying that even successful practice cannot be an infallible guide. The merit of Shakespeare's tragicomedies, for example, does not necessarily validate the genre in theory, and the question of whether tragic feelings are enhanced or diminished by the presence of comic elements is left undecided. In Johnson's literary thought, there is an interplay of theoretical and practical considerations, and the two levels are often mutually corrective.

Johnson also sifted through the accumulated rules associated with the literary pastoral, but here he starts from a theoretical definition of the genre as "a poem in which any action or passion is represented by its effects upon a country life" (3:201; R 37). Thus its scope includes any person or event normally found in a rural setting. The absurdities of some pastoral poems are caused, in Johnson's view, by a kind of literalism or false realism, which defines the genre "as a dialogue, or narrative of men actually tending sheep" (5:201; R 37). From this error come the misguided ideas that the shepherds should show instances of ignorance and should use rustic language from time to time. For Johnson the only defining characteristic of the genre is the rural setting, "and this it cannot lose by any dignity of sentiment, or beauty of diction" (5:204; R 38). The pastoral "realists" have for Johnson made an aesthetic error by failing to accept consistently the artificial conventions of the genre, just as the fictional "realists" made a moral error in mixing virtue and vice in the same character. In each case Johnson offers a corrective from the perspective that has been neglected. In the case of the pastoral, traditional practice (his examples of improprieties are taken from Virgil, Spenser, and Pope) is corrected by independent theory, while in the essay on the dramatic unities theory is corrected by practice.

Thus in literature as in life, authority and tradition are corrected by observation, and that observation is in turn subject to correction. For Johnson, the individual is not self-sufficient, nor even independent, but is caught up among these corrective processes. The self and its observations have a limited validity, but in isolation are doomed to inadequacy, distortion, and partiality by a kind of moral unrealism which makes contradictory and unreasonable demands on life:

> The reigning error of mankind is, that we are not content with the conditions on which the goods of life are granted. No man is insensible of the value of knowledge, and advantages of health, or the convenience of plenty, but every day shews us those on whom their conviction is without effect. (5:174–5; R 178)

The essay offered Johnson a form he could use to enact his view of the individual as caught in the gap between theory and practice, knowledge and action; a form where the thought and experience of the individual could both separate from and reconnect with a wider literary or social sphere. "The apparent insuffiency of every individual to his own happiness or safety, compels us to seek from one another assistance and support" (4:190; *R* 104). This expresses well the social dimension of Johnson's essays, taken over from Addison and Steele, but made much more deeply and seriously ethical.

Where Montaigne saw the subjective world of the individual developing in vital connection with the objective world, Johnson sees a constant misfit between them: "The desires of mankind are much more numerous than their attainments, and the capacity of imagination much larger than actual enjoyment" (4:191; *R* 104). Where for Montaigne every individual perception had some validity, some at least relative truth, for Johnson it is bound to be distorted simply because of the constitution of human nature. Individuals always overestimate their importance, expect too much from the future, blame others for their own shortcomings, and desire more than they can reach or enjoy. The self is not a secure ground, epistemologically or morally. Man is a creature who cannot know or accept his own nature, and thus is doomed to constant illusion and disillusion. We cannot "forbear to wonder afresh at every new failure, or to promise certainty of success to our next essay; but when we try, the same hindrances recur, the same inability is perceived, and the vexation of disappointment must again be suffered" (4:287; *R* 122). In some ways this describes the experience of the typical Johnsonian essay, though here he is using the word in the sense of "attempt." The experiencing, essaying self is always hopeful of some sort of attainment, but the knowing, judging self looks down pityingly at the inevitable failure. For Johnson, the two can never coincide: his essays both articulate the division and hold the balance between them.

5

Hazlitt: ventures of the self

Like Johnson, Hazlitt played an important role in the institutional development of the study of English literature. His evident love of literature was not that of a gentleman amateur, like Montaigne, but of someone who had also to make a living from it. Hazlitt both lectured and wrote about English literature, and the two activities were closely linked in that the lectures were published fairly soon after delivery. In many ways the institution of the literary lecture as it developed in the early nineteenth century played a parallel function to the literary journals in popularizing English literature, a task already begun in *The Spectator* by Addison's series of essays on Milton and on the Imagination. Classical literature was largely left to the universities, while these public lectures were given to a non-specialist audience outside the academic framework. *Blackwood's*, in reviewing Hazlitt's *Lectures on the English Comic Writers* (1819), categorized this audience sneeringly as "aspiring apprentices and critical clerks" (quoted in Herschell Baker, 256). This kind of general lecture on modern literature becomes a cognate and often a preliminary form of the essay at this time, and even when its subject matter was finally drawn into the official university structure as a "discipline," it continued to occasion some of the most attractive, informal, and essayistic criticism in the hands of practitioners like Lionel Trilling or Frank Kermode. (Emerson's essays are, of course, nearly all revised versions of "addresses" made to general audiences.)

Hazlitt's lectures and essays respond to the pressures of the literary marketplace in which he had to earn his living, but also to political pressures of the time. The period of his greatest involvement in lecturing and essay-writing (from 1810 to his death in 1830) was also a highly politicized one. The era of *The*

Spectator was too, but Hazlitt did not attempt to emulate the detachment of that fictional persona, and in fact dispensed with that device altogether (the main example of it in Hazlitt's day was of course Charles Lamb's Elia, an eccentric whose foibles make an interesting contrast with those of the Spectator). Hazlitt accepted, indeed embraced, the need for taking explicit and personal political positions in his work, while remaining independent of any particular party, especially in his capacity as literary critic. He could pay tribute, for example, to the magnificence of Edmund Burke's style and the honesty and penetration of his thought, while repudiating his conservative conclusions. At other times, however, he produced superb specimens of personal abuse and invective, of precisely the kind that the Spectator would have abhorred. A classic of this genre is his portrait of William Gifford, the editor of the *Quarterly Review* and the author of the Pope imitations, the *Baviad* and the *Maeviad*, in *The Spirit of the Age* (1825). A typical sentence reads: "No statement in the *Quarterly Review* is to be trusted: there is no fact that is not misrepresented in it, no quotation that is not garbled, no character that is not slandered, if it can answer the purposes of a party to do so" (11:124).

Hazlitt's writing career is closely bound up with the politics of journalism of his period. *The Edinburgh Review* (1802–1929), for which he wrote a number of essays, essentially laid down the pattern for all the intellectual reviews of the nineteenth century. It was founded by a circle of Edinburgh Whigs, principally Sydney Smith, Henry Brougham, and Francis Jeffrey, in order to combat the dominance of the Tories in Scotland. Several features distinguished it immediately from the eighteenth-century periodicals, which had continued roughly in the mould of *The Tatler* and *The Spectator*. It was published quarterly, and thus set less store by novelty than the earlier daily or weekly periodicals. The contributions were fewer and longer, and tended to be more thoroughly pondered, heavier in tone, and more severe in judgment. The politics were liberal rather than strictly Whig, and even the Tory Walter Scott contributed before 1808. In that year, however, *The Edinburgh* attacked the war effort against France, and this hastened the founding of a rival Tory journal, the *Quarterly Review*, by Scott, the publisher Murray, and the politician Canning, with Gifford as the editor.

The new journal savaged Hazlitt's *The Round Table* (1817), his

Characters of Shakespeare's Plays (1818), and his *Lectures on the English Poets* (1818), and after 1817 it was joined by another Tory organ, *Blackwood's Magazine*, where Lockhart, Walter Scott's son-in-law, infuriated his victim by referring to "pimpled Hazlitt's coxcomb lectures" (quoted in Herschel Baker, 372). Hazlitt himself mainly published in *The Examiner* (1808–81), a weekly edited by John and Leigh Hunt, and the *London Magazine* (1820–9), where Lamb's "Essays of Elia" appeared as well as Hazlitt's "Table Talk." But despite these links to the "Cockney School" (including Keats), Hazlitt's political stands managed to make him unpopular, or at least suspect, in every quarter, in a way reminiscent of Orwell. His main battle was against the Tories, but he also had hard things to say about the Whigs, the Reformers, and the Radicals, as well as a worrying habit of turning on his friends and allies. He excoriated Wordsworth and Coleridge for abandoning their youthful libertarian views in favor of Toryism, but himself clung to a quixotic worship of Napoleon, whom he persisted in seeing as the incarnation of the French revolutionary spirit. Hazlitt continued with this isolated view even after 1815, when his hero's defeat plunged him into a weeks-long depression.

Hazlitt's sketches of Gifford and Jeffrey in *The Spirit of the Age* give a vivid account of the battles of the journals in the early nineteenth century. But he also gave a clear view of the earlier history of the essay form and its contexts in his Lecture "On the Periodical Essayists" (Lecture V of *Lectures on the English Comic Writers*). Essay-writing he defines as

> applying the talents and resources of the mind to all that mixed mass of human affairs, which, though not included under the head of any regular art, science, or profession, falls under the cognizance of the writer, and "comes home to the business and bosoms of men". (6:91)

The reference is, of course, to the preface to Bacon's *Essays* (which Hazlitt quotes without source, a habit of his), although oddly enough he does not discuss that work. Having defined the subject matter of the essay as human life seen independently of science, philosophy, or religion, he indicates the appropriate method of treatment: "It is in morals and manners what the experimental is in natural philosophy, as opposed to the dogmatical method" (6:91).

Hazlitt acknowledges Montaigne as the founder of this way of writing:

> In treating of men and manners, he spoke of them as he found them,

not according to preconceived notions and abstract dogmas; and he began by teaching us what he himself was. . . . He was, in a word, the first author who was not a book-maker, and who wrote not to make converts of others to established creeds and prejudices, but to satisfy his own mind of the truth of things. (6:92–3)

This emphasis on the essay's independent viewpoint, its essential resistance to political or religious ideology, carries through Hazlitt's treatment of the English practitioners of the form: Cowley and Temple, Addison and Steele, and finally Johnson and Goldsmith, though, as we have seen, he found the impersonal, impartial tone of Johnson's essays unsympathetic. Hazlitt's criteria for the essay are clear: the essay should be personal and informal in tone, and uncommitted to any aesthetic or political orthodoxy. His own writing certainly lives up to the first criterion, and to a great extent to the second: his volume of *Political Essays* would be, like Orwell's, more accurately called *anti*-political essays, in that they attack the absurdities and iniquities of established ideologies and parties without putting anything positive forward in their place. Both respond to political issues in a politicized context, but in an unpredictable way. But for Hazlitt, Johnson fails both tests (of independence and individuality) because of his fixed aesthetic-moral views and his stilted prose.

What use does Hazlitt himself make of the essay form? As far as length is concerned, he accepted the constraints of periodical publication. But in his day this provided more variety than the set format of *The Spectator*, whose daily sheets occupy about four pages in book form. Hazlitt's *Round Table* essays, first published in *The Examiner*, are around twice as long. Nevertheless, Hazlitt seems to improvise happily until the end of his allotted space, whatever that might be, and to make the result sound as spontaneous as Montaigne, who of course did not have any particular constraints of length to obey, or any editors or deadlines to worry about. Hazlitt's arresting first sentences rival those of Bacon, but he does not follow them with a formal division of the topic. In fact, sometimes, as if glimpsing the end of his space, he abruptly recalls himself to the topic after apparently forgetting it during a long digression. Generally the essays are held together by little more than a broad contrast, either announced in the title, as in the "double topic" essays such as "On Thought and Action," "On Vulgarity and Affectation," and "On the Picturesque and the Ideal," or developed in the course of the essay.

Hazlitt's topics are varied, but the constant central element is the experience of the individual self, not defined in the abstract but through relationships: with nature, with other individuals, with society, with art and literature. In all of these relations, the value of experience comes through wholehearted involvement, rather than the detached appraisal typical of the Spectator. Quite different experiences can enrich the self at different times provided it is willing to embrace them fully. The main point of Hazlitt's classic essay "On Going a Journey" is this need for experience to be whole and undivided. The relations of the self to nature and to society cannot be combined (in his particular case, anyway) without distraction and hence dilution. "One of the pleasantest things in the world is going a journey; but I like to go by myself" (8:181). The reader's expectations of an elaboration of the first statement are abruptly cut across by the blunt expression of preference for solitude. To allay this antisocial impression, Hazlitt continues: "I can enjoy society in a room; but out of doors, nature is company enough for me" (8:181). He wants his activities pure and unmixed: "I cannot see the wit of walking and talking at the same time. When I am in the country, I wish to vegetate like the country. . . . I go out of town in order to forget the town and all that is in it" (8:181). Within a few casual sentences, Hazlitt has built up a series of antitheses (society vs. nature, town vs. country, talking vs. walking, company vs. solitude) that seem to reinforce the appropriateness of his choice of being alone, which seemed odd and unsympathetic at first. Even the best company, he goes on to argue, is a constraint on spontaneity. Walking alone, your thoughts, memories, and observations can follow their own rhythm with a freedom that cannot be shared if you have to explain or defend them.

The experience of the self that is provided by solitary travel is not, however, the reaffirmation of a fixed entity. Hazlitt's desire to be alone is not for the purpose of "being himself" in the sense of returning to a normative state, but in order to better escape that fixed identity. The role one is accustomed to play with even a close friend inhibits this free play of the self in the world. For Hazlitt, this freedom from constraint is first of all physical: the pace of walking, the pauses, the side-tracking do not have to be agreed on. The solitary walker is as free as a child: "It is hard if I cannot start some game on these lone heaths. I laugh, I run, I leap, I sing for joy" (8:182). Similarly, his thoughts run on without the need to express or criticize them, even to himself: "I am content to lay in a stock of ideas, and to examine and anatomize them afterwards. . . . For once, I like to have it all my own way; and this is impossible unless you are alone, or in such company as I do not covet" (8:183). Hazlitt calls this "the integrity of fancy" (8:185), and he wants to safeguard it even at the inn where he stays the night. If it is interrupted, he would prefer it to be a stranger rather than a friend, because the impression of the stranger will form part of the local experience, not an exception to it. But ideally, he retains his incognito, as simply "the Gentleman in the parlour" (8:185), and spends his evening reading. These associated memories of walking and resting, eating and reading, can be extraordinarily specific and vivid. With a characteristic switch from generalized speculation to detailed recollection, Hazlitt recreates this occasion: "It was on the tenth of April, 1798, that I sat down to a volume of the New Eloise, at the inn at Llangollen, over a bottle of sherry and a cold chicken" (8:186). This intensely localized moment (he even tells us which letter from Rousseau's novel he read) becomes a kind of epiphany (in the Joycean sense) of his youth.

The experience of solitary travel is the core of Hazlitt's idea of the self, whose identity is simultaneously enriched and endangered by immersion in new surroundings. He sees experience as radically discontinuous, and stresses the limits of the imagination to transcend it:

> There is hardly any thing that shows the short-sightedness or capriciousness of the imagination more than travelling does. With change of place we change our ideas; nay, our opinions and feelings. We can by an effort indeed transport ourselves to old and long-forgotten scenes, and then the picture of the mind revives again; but we forget those that we have just left. It seems that we can think but of one place at a time. (8:187)

We cannot imagine Hazlitt writing about experience in general, like Montaigne, since for him there are only experiences in the plural: vivid, pure, without distraction. "In travelling through a wild and barren country, I can form no idea of a woody and cultivated one. It appears to me that all the world must be barren, like what I see of it" (8:187). This temporary universalizing of the particular is the key to Hazlitt's idea of the imagination as powerful but limited, the power being due to the limitations. For him, it is an *exclusive* faculty: each new or newly recalled impression effaces all the preceding ones for the time it lasts. This may partly account for the characteristic texture of Hazlitt's writing: its alternation, or even struggle, between intensely particularized description and abstract thought, between the painterly and the philosophical.

One problem which this creates is a sometimes unnoted shift between the particular "I" of the writer and "the self" or "the mind" in general. In "On Going a Journey," the preference for solitary walking is at one point presented as a personal foible, as opposed to the example he gives of Coleridge happily walking and talking together for hours, and at another point as the basis for a general theory of the imagination. At times, too, Hazlitt seems to make fun of himself, as when he quotes Cobbett's dictum "that an Englishman ought to do only one thing at a time" (8:182). He also hedges his preference for being unaccompanied when it is a case of sight-seeing, or of trips abroad, where he remarks with apparent seriousness, "There is an involuntary antipathy in the mind of an Englishman to foreign manners and notions that requires the assistance of social sympathy to carry it off" (8:188). Hazlitt's essay offers no overall unity of attitude or argument: he adds exceptions casually, shifts his tone and perspective freely, and seems to quote almost at random with no more justification than the line having occurred to him. It is as if each paragraph provides a separate experience, like Hazlitt's "one thing at a time" theory of the imagination. Within ten pages we have the 40-year-old Hazlitt shouting and jumping on a heath, and the 20-year-old dining at the inn in Llangollen; Coleridge rambling endlessly on foot and in words, and Hazlitt as a well-organized tour guide to Stonehenge or Oxford; images interspersed by a sporadic attempt to decide when company is appropriate and when it isn't. The reader of the essay could be seen as a companion on an imaginary walk, sometimes directly addressed, sometimes left behind. The experience is not an orderly one, but there is a persistent effort at understanding that the reader is invited or forced to share. The thinking process is intermittently thrown off track by new objects which deflect and absorb it, in a way that reproduces the typical rhythm of a walk. "On Going a Journey" is the classic peripatetic essay, a status accorded to it in Robert Louis Stevenson's "Walking Tours," which conducts a continuous dialogue with the opinions and preferences expressed in Hazlitt's piece.

Hazlitt's gift is for recreating mental states rather than assessing them or relating them to each other. Where Montaigne is able to put youth and age into the same framework and compare them, to Hazlitt they are incommensurate and mutually exclusive. The essay "On the Feeling of Immortality in Youth" explores these incompatible perspectives: for youth,

> Death, old age, are words without a meaning. . . . We look round in a new world, full of life, and motion, and ceaseless progress; and feel in ourselves all the vigour and spirit to keep pace with it, and do not foresee from any present symptoms how we shall be left behind in the natural course of things, decline into old age, and drop into the grave. (17:190)

But age is capable of recollecting youth, and on the theme of memory Hazlitt's thought is closest to Wordsworth's. He makes the autobiographical essay into a prose genre equivalent to "Tintern Abbey" or to the episodes of the *Prelude*, except of course that they remain isolated episodes. Hazlitt's reflections on his own life divide it very sharply between youth and maturity.

The division is also a political one in the case of his own generation between the radical decade of the 1790s and the later Tory reaction. "For my part, I set out in life with the French Revolution, and that event had considerable influence on my early feelings, as on those of others. Youth was then doubly such" (17:197). After evoking the atmosphere of that revolutionary decade, Hazlitt turns from it with a quotation from "Tintern Abbey" (ironically, since he saw Wordsworth and Coleridge as the chief recreants from the ideals of that age): " 'That time is past with all its giddy raptures.' Since the future was barred to my progress I have turned for consolation to the past, gathering up the fragments of my early recollections, and putting them into a form that might live" (17:197). Hazlitt claims a continuity of political principle as the unifying element in his life across the disunity of his experiences. Time brings pure unconsolable loss, both perceptually, in the waning power of impressions, and politically, in the loss of hope for progress in society. Both for objects and for people, "first acquaintance" is the best. "Objects, on our first acquaintance with them, have that singleness and integrity of impression that it seems as if nothing could destroy or obliterate them, so firmly are they stamped and rivetted on the brain" (17:196). The same is true in

Hazlitt's autobiographical classic "My First Acquaintance with Poets" (first published in *The Liberal* in April 1823), where, looking back on his visit to Alfoxden twenty-five years after the event, he breaks off with another exclamation of regret for lost intensity: "As we taste the pleasures of life, their spirit evaporates, the sense palls; and nothing is left but the phantoms, the lifeless shadows of what *has been*!" (17:117).

At issue here are more than the traditional commonplaces about youth and age: there is a sense of the radical discontinuity of the self across time (travel produces a similar experience in space). Hazlitt's greatest essays (and indeed most of his total output of writing) were mostly written in the last fifteen years of his life (1815–30). By then he had acquired his famous fluency with the pen, and, given the contrast with the years it took him to produce his philosophical "Essay on the Principles of Human Action," and the contrast of his youthful optimism and later bitterness and disillusion, it is tempting to assign his fluency to a kind of recklessness or even indifference, as well as to nostalgia. For Hazlitt (to adapt Wordsworth) writing is the recollection of powerful feelings and impressions, and also an effort to understand them, which takes place across a chasm of efface-ment and oblivion, a theme which usually accompanies that of memory in his writing. The two moments, one of recalling, analysing, and writing, the other of the original experience, remain radically distinct, yet always potentially about to interrupt each other.

The essay "On Living to Oneself" is a good example of these juxtapositions. Hazlitt sets the writing scene as one that harmonizes well with his subject:

> I never was in a better place or a better humour than I am at present for writing on this subject. I have a partridge getting ready for my supper, my fire is blazing on the hearth, the air is mild for the season of the year, I have had but a slight fit of indigestion to-day (the only thing that makes me abhor myself), I have three hours good before me, and therefore I will attempt it. (8:90)

The detail is reminiscent of the chicken supper at Llangollen, but here the meal (which will be done in three hours) delimits the time available for writing as well as coloring the moment's mood. Hazlitt notes, as if speaking to himself, "It is as well to do it at once as to have it to do for a week to come" (8:90), and it is quite plausible to imagine the essay as resulting from three hours' improvisation. He begins by building up a character type, much like the general figure of the "essayist" discussed in Chapter 1: "He who lives wisely to himself and to his own heart, looks at the busy world through the loopholes of retreat, and does not want to mingle in the fray" (8:91). But soon, warming to his subject, Hazlitt puts himself in the place of this personification: "For many years of my life I did nothing but think. . . . I used to write a page or two perhaps in half a year" (8:92).

After developing this idyllic-sounding phase of his own existence, Hazlitt goes on to another type, the person who lives for the good opinion of others rather than for himself. The "others" who endanger one's self-sufficiency even include friends, and here Hazlitt rejects the essayistic praise-of-friendship tradition that descends from Montaigne: "Most of the friends I have seen have turned out the bitterest enemies, or cold, uncomfortable acquaintance. Old companions are like meats served up too often that lose their relish and their wholesomeness" (8:95). This loss of taste, of course, is the inevitable sequel to the cult of "first acquaintance", as novelty declines into staleness (the food imagery may be connected with the indigestion of which Hazlitt complains at the start of the essay). From individuals, Hazlitt turns to attack society at large in his famous tirade against the Public: "There is not a more mean, stupid, dastardly, pitiful, selfish, spiteful, envious, ungrateful animal than the Public" (8:97). Gradually, in characteristic style, the invective gets more and more personal: first Hazlitt himself and then Keats are presented as victims of the Public's deference to the reviews:

> Taylor and Hessey told me that they had sold nearly two editions of the Characters of Shakespeare's Plays in about three months, but that after the Quarterly Review of them came out, they never sold another copy. . . . A crew of mischievous critics at Edinburgh having fixed the epithet of the *Cockney School* to one or two writers born in the metropolis, all the people in London became afraid of looking into their works, lest they too should be convicted of cockneyism. (8:99)

Having worked himself into a rage Hazlitt has consciously to calm himself to end the essay and presumably turn to his partridge: "Enough: my soul, turn from them, and let me try to regain the obscurity and quiet that I love" (8:100). The trouble is that he has amply demonstrated his own incapacity to live to himself: his own involvement in the London literary world he decries is amply demonstrated by the fact of the essay being destined for periodical publication, and by his own abundant gift for personal and general abuse. In this way (typical of his essays) the counter-subject overcomes the announced subject, the moment of writing is overwhelmed by the moment written about, and the recaptured past mood effaces the present one. The mutual interruption of memory and analysis, description and reflection, gives a dramatic, improvised quality quite different from the judicious tone of Johnson and his steady, consistent frame of values. Johnson remains judicious and even-tempered, where Hazlitt constantly "gets carried away," following his train of thought impetuously until it runs out and a contrary or divergent one takes its place.

This instability of the self, and the consequent difficulty of knowing or judging it, applies in Hazlitt with added force to other selves. Throughout his life, both as an artist and as a writer, Hazlitt was fascinated by the portrait, and his most successful paintings are in that genre: the studies of his father and of Leigh Hunt (the latter is in the National Portrait Gallery, and Hazlitt's *The Spirit of the Age* is in some ways a literary anticipation of that institution, whose founding aim was to provide a collective picture of the Victorian and earlier ages through portraits of great individuals). Besides practicing the literary character sketch, Hazlitt also often considered the theoretical issue of how, and to what degree, one can know others. The *Table Talk* essay "On the Knowledge of Others" is the most thorough of these meditations, but the conclusions are so negative that the title would have read more accurately as "On the Ignorance of Others." Perhaps because of his experience as a visual portraitist, he holds that the truest knowledge is obtainable through that art: "A man's whole life may be a lie to himself and to others: and yet a picture painted of him by a great artist would probably stamp his true character on the canvas, and betray the secret to posterity" (8:303). The contradictory evidence about historical figures like Charles V or Ignatius Loyola is resolved instantly and intuitively on seeing their portraits by Titian, Hazlitt tells us.

In ordinary life the nearest we can get to this is once again first acquaintance: "First impressions are often the truest. . . . A man's look is the work of years, it is stamped on his countenance by the events of his whole life" (8:304). The

81

observer seizes this configuration at once, but later familiarity
blurs it, especially signs of latent, disavowed characteristics.
Hazlitt takes as his example (without naming her) Sarah
Walker, the daughter of his London landlady, with whom his
disastrous involvement is recorded with painful immediacy in
the confessional *Liber Amoris* (1823):

> The greatest hypocrite I ever knew was a little, demure, pretty,
> modest-looking girl, with eyes timidly cast upon the ground, and an
> air soft as enchantment; the only circumstance that could lead to a
> suspicion of her true character was a cold, sullen, watery, glazed look
> about the eyes, which she bent on vacancy, as if determined to avoid
> all explanation with yours. I might have spied in their glittering,
> motionless surface the rocks and quicksands that awaited me below!
> (8:305).

This allusion of course destroys any claim Hazlitt might have
had to be a judge of character in practice! The discordant feature
or habit, noted at first but ignored later, often indicates a
potential reversal of the apparent nature of a person. Although
at times Hazlitt uses the Renaissance language of dissimulation
(the image of a mask covering up "true" character), his actual
model is more often a dynamic or conflictual one, in some ways
anticipating the Freudian theory of repression: "Extremes meet;
and qualities display themselves by the most contradictory
appearances. Any inclination, in consequence of being generally suppressed, vents itself the more violently when an opportunity presents itself; the greatest grossness sometimes accompanies the greatest refinement, as a natural relief, one to the
other" (8:306). Already character is coming to seem less and less
knowable, and the form of the essay makes Hazlitt's point: the
first impression is probably as accurate a picture as one can get,
and the more evidence you accumulate, the more complex and
difficult it gets.

Besides the basic gap between any two individuals, there are
other divisions – of culture, class, age, and sex – across which
knowledge of others becomes even harder to attain. National
character, like individual character, is a favorite essay topic,
perhaps because it is not really amenable to any kind of
scientific or quantitative approach, while remaining an un-
doubted reality in most people's experience. Hazlitt launches
into a comparison of the French and the English, only to reveal
that this cannot be done in a straightforward manner since each

national character itself has internal contradictions. The English, he maintains, are both more reserved and more confiding (once the reserve has been broken) than the French, who are more casually and consistently intimate. The French are both more serious (in their taste for system) and less serious (their liking for intellectual play) than the English. The potential for cultural misunderstanding is immense, and it is not diminished by travelers from either side: "They go abroad with certain preconceived notions on the subject, and they make everything answer, in reason's spite, to their favourite theory" (8:307).

The same applies to the other divisions Hazlitt deals with. People have little notion, beyond certain stereotypes, of the character of people from another class, another generation, or the other sex. Hazlitt implicitly exempts himself from this ignorance (despite his misjudgment of Sarah Walker!) and goes on to deliver a long diatribe against the servant class (8:307–10) – worthy of comparison with his attack on the metropolitan literary public quoted earlier (8:97–100) – where he describes the typical servant's deceitful and resentful consciousness as if it was accessible to him. Intimacy with another might seem to provide evidence for a true judgment, but actually the reverse is the case, Hazlitt maintains: "Familiarity confounds all traits of distinction: interest and prejudice take away the power of judging .... We do not see the features of those we love" (8:311). The harder and longer you look, the more impossible it becomes to attain knowledge of others: "Real character is not one thing, but a thousand things; actual qualities do not conform to any factitious standard in the mind, but rest upon their own truth and nature" (8:313). Hazlitt reaches a point of extreme skepticism about human capacity to know, not only other humans, but reality in general. The mind's lazy, reductive way of working makes firm knowledge practically unobtainable (the theme of human impercipience, like other Hazlitt themes, is later taken up by Orwell).

But this epistemological pessimism did not deter Hazlitt from offering character sketches; in fact it may have challenged him to seize the first impressions and intuitions, the discordant notes and signs of conflict, that energize his portraits. As a portraitist, Hazlitt lends his own propensity for internal and external struggle to his subjects. He sees them as embattled, pitted against themselves, or others, or himself, as in the attack on William Gifford; he arranges his figures in aspects or situations that resemble his classic narrative essay "The Fight." The "Character of Cobbett" in *Table Talk* sets him literally in the stance of a prize fighter: "People have about as substantial an idea of Cobbett as they have of Cribb [a contemporary pugilist]. His blows are as hard, and he himself is as impenetrable" (8:50). Undeterred, Hazlitt squares up to his pugnacious subject as much like an opponent as a portraitist. And indeed, though this is not an attack on Cobbett, the essayist aims to "capture" him, or "pin him down" on paper, in an almost pugilistic sense. But he begins by putting another man in the ring, as it were, through a long point-for-point comparison with Paine, including contrasts in terms of the same simile. For example, Hazlitt conveys the scattered quality of Cobbett's writing thus: "Paine tries to enclose his ideas in a fold for security and repose: Cobbett lets *his* pour out upon the plain like a flock of sheep to feed and batten" (8:52). This set comparison of two authors is a fairly traditional device: other examples of it are Montaigne's pairing of Plutarch and Seneca in "On Books," and Johnson's comparison of Dryden and Pope in the life of the latter in *Lives of the English Poets*. But where Montaigne and Johnson adopt an aloof and impartial tone, Hazlitt sounds like an excited spectator at a fight. Cobbett is seen as a superb fighter, but one who is always liable to round on his own side: "not only no individual, but no corrupt system could hold out against his powerful and repeated attacks, but with the same weapon, swung round like a flail, that he levels his antagonists, he lays his friends low, and puts his own party *hors de combat*" (8:54).

These rapid shifts of external allegiance Hazlitt attributes to Cobbett's hatred of anything established, even in his own mind: opposition is a necessity for him. "I might say that Mr. Cobbett is a very honest man with a total want of principle, and downright earnest in what he says, in the part he takes at the time; but in taking that part, he is led entirely by headstrong obstinacy, caprice, novelty, pique or personal motive of some sort, and not by a steadfast regard for the truth, or habitual anxiety of what is right uppermost in his mind" (8:55–6). This political and intellectual instability shows in his writing as a quality of immediacy and spontaneity: "We see his ideas in their first concoction, fermenting and overflowing with the ebullitions of a lively conception. We look on at the actual process" (8:56).

Hazlitt in his portraits seeks the vital principle of the

individual, and finds and characterizes it through conflicts, which he embodies in metaphors and patterns rather than trying to produce a harmonized or unified overall effect. His characters are, like his sketch of Cobbett, perpetually in process, energetically elusive. What unity they possess is largely due to their being *his* (Hazlitt's) characters, to the configuration of one character by and with another. Hazlitt himself is recognizable in all his portraits, so that what we have in this particular essay is recognizably "a Hazlitt" as much as a "Cobbett" (one tends to identify a portrait by the artist – as "a Gainsborough," for example – as much as by the sitter). The two "characters" articulate each other in the way that dramatists aim at in dialogues, where successive interactions reveal the differences between the characters. With Hazlitt, the essayistic "character," which began as a "type" with Theophrastus and later Overbury, and went on to the "fictional" figures of Addison and Steele, enters a new phase: the "portrait" of an actual (and often living) individual. Journalistic "profiles," of the type found in the *Observer*, for instance, are current versions of this form.

All of Hazlitt's essays can be seen as "characterizations" of one kind or another. They result from an encounter between himself and another character, or a work of art, an idea, a scene, or an event. The encounter may be emotional or intellectual, positive or negative, but is usually a mixture of both. Antipathy is as strong and insightful as sympathy; both are necessary to Hazlitt's emotional economy. In his essay in *The Plain Speaker* "On the Pleasure of Hating," he writes: "Nature seems (the more we look into it) made up of antipathies: without something to hate, we should lose the very spring of thought and action" (12:128). In reflections that seem to anticipate Freud's late theory of culture as being bought at the expense of repressing natural drives, Hazlitt avers that we have only given up the physical expression of hatred, not stopped feeling it. The appeal of Scott's historical novels is precisely to this repressed violence: "As we read, we throw aside the trammels of civilization, the flimsy veil of humanity. 'Off, you lendings!' The wild beast resumes its sway within us" (12:129). After reminding us of Freud, Hazlitt recalls Dostoyevsky's Underground Man mocking Utilitarianism:

Here are no Jeremy Bentham Panopticons . . . no long calculations of self-interest – the will takes its instant way to its object; as the mountain torrent flings itself over the precipice, the greatest possible good of each individual consists in doing all the mischief he can to his neighbour. (12:129)

Hazlitt refuses the temperate, benevolent maturity that is the traditional mood of the essay: maturity, in his account, is predominantly malevolent, in himself and in others. Love burns itself out, but hate lasts as long as life. In a kind of profanation of the traditional essay themes, he writes: "We hate old friends; we hate old books; we hate old opinions; and at last we come to hate ourselves" (12:130).

Having run through the first three objects of hatred, Hazlitt fuses them with self-hatred in a misanthropic diatribe worthy of Hamlet, ending with a conceit worthy of Donne: "have I not reason to hate and despise myself? Indeed I do; and chiefly for not having hated and despised the world enough" (12:136). The philanthropy of Hazlitt's revolutionary youth gives way to the misanthropy of the disillusioned radical in a way that was to become typical of later history. But because of Hazlitt's gift of recalling his impressions and early memories, the overall mood of his essays is not one of unrelieved gloom. There is a mixture; but both moods are passionate. To use his own term, his essays have gusto: "Gusto in art is power or passion defining any object" (4:77). This formulation equates subjective expression and objective definition. Passion (whether love or hate) is necessary to penetrate and animate the object from inside. For example, Van Dyke's flesh colour is inferior to Titian's because, "It has not the internal character, the living principle in it" (4:77). The criticism of works of art, too, should consist of "transfusing their living principles" and should "reflect the colours, the light and shade, the soul and body of a work" (8:217), Hazlitt maintains in his essay "On Criticism." This emphasis on animation rather than judgment is what distinguishes Hazlitt's critical writing from that of the eighteenth century, and it applies to his other writing equally well. Love and hate never subside into a calm and settled judgment, and Hazlitt's impetuous philosophical ventures on abstract topics rarely reach any firm conclusions. He does not have the patience of the good philosophical writer, the careful marking of the stages of argument, the orderly summaries, the sense of calm and order. The concrete and the abstract in his essays interrupt each other as often as they support each other. The phrase "the living principle" embraces both dimensions, and it well describes the goal of the essays, but there is often tension between the concrete "life" and the abstract "principle."

Hazlitt's essays are made up of a series of "movements," long paragraphs sometimes running to two or three pages, which state an initial idea in a compact and often arresting first sentence, and then develop and expand it until the momentum seems to have spent itself and some kind of counter-movement gets under way. Often these long paragraphs are made up of similarly structured sentences, perhaps beginning with the same pronoun each time, "characterizing" the subject through a number of instances or aspects. These are not simply expressions of feeling, but of a passionate intentness on the object or issue at hand, an unwillingness to relinquish it until the particular aspect has been exhausted. Eloquence for its own sake is anathema to Hazlitt; for him, language should be plain and transpicuous. His essay "On Familiar Style" in *Table Talk* makes this distinction: "The florid style is the reverse of the familiar. The last is employed as an unvarnished medium to convey ideas; the first is resorted to to conceal the want of them" (8:246). The florid style consists of a self-referential verbal construct: "Objects are not linked to feelings, words to things, but images revolve in splendid mockery, words represent themselves" (8:247). This does not mean that the florid writers are more creative than the plain ones; on the contrary. "Scorning to imitate realities, they are unable to invent anything, to strike out one original idea" (8:247). Instead they are thrown back on clichés, of which Hazlitt provides a list reminiscent of Orwell's "Politics and the English Language." Also like Orwell, he holds that the plain style is harder because it demands flexibility and precision: "it is easy to affect a pompous style, to use a word twice as big as the thing you want to express; it is not so easy to pitch upon the very word that exactly fits it" (8:243). Both writers firmly believe in striving for an "exact fit" between language and a pre-existing reality, in sharp contrast to the view current in much literary theory now, that language "constructs" rather than "describes" reality.

In aesthetics Hazlitt is emphatically a mimeticist. For him the point of artistic representation is an increased awareness of reality: in the *Round Table* essay "On Imitation" he writes, "Imitation interests, then, by exciting a more intense perception of truth, and calling out the powers of observation and comparison" (4:75). The object and the artistic image reciprocally sharpen awareness of each other:

> One chief reason, it should seem then, why imitation pleases, is, because, by exciting curiosity, and inviting a comparison between the object and the representation, it opens a new field of inquiry, and leads the attention to a variety of details and distinctions not perceived before. (4:73)

Hazlitt speaks mainly as a painter here, but his contention that painting, and (secondarily) looking at painting, teaches you to see, holds good for his theory of language as well. The aesthetic and the realistic are one and the same: "to the genuine artist, truth, nature, beauty, are almost different names for the same thing" (4:75). The value of art is the knowledge it provides. But Hazlitt adds, perhaps thinking of Bacon's equation of knowledge and power: "Knowledge is pleasure as well as power" (4:75). Hazlitt uses this saying again in the *Table Talk* essay "On the Pleasure of Painting" (8:16), where painting becomes an ideal exemplification of passionate objectivity: "Every stroke tells, as the verifying of a new truth; and every new observation, the instant it is made, passes into an act and emanation of the will" (8:11). Empirical knowledge and artistic recreation become parts of a single activity.

For Hazlitt, painting becomes a model for active awareness, which fuses creation and perception, art and knowledge. It also in practice demands a unity of mental and physical skills, of the mechanical and liberal arts, whose separation Hazlitt lamented in the classic essay "The Indian Jugglers." This affects the painter's whole nature in a positive way: "they are the most lively observers of what passes in the world about them, and the closest observers of what passes in their own minds" (8:10). Objective and subjective awareness reinforce each other and produce an ideal perceiver for Hazlitt. The painter

> applies the same standard of truth and disinterested spirit of inquiry, that influences his daily practice, to other subjects. He perceives form; he distinguishes character. He reads men and books with an intuitive glance. He is a critic as well as a connoisseur. The conclusions he draws are clear and convincing, because they are taken from actual experience. He is not a fanatic, a dupe, or a slave: for the habit of seeing for himself also disposes him to judge for himself. (8:10)

This ideal of the painter may be a compensation for Hazlitt's disillusion with the literary world, but it could certainly serve as a description of his ideal as an essayist, one which his best work triumphantly lives up to.

6
Henry James: patterns of art and life

After the middle of the nineteenth century it became common practice for novelists and poets to supplement their fiction and poetry writing with essays. The figures we will treat here after James – Virginia Woolf, T. S. Eliot, and George Orwell – were typical in this respect, for one could cite also George Eliot, Stevenson, Wilde, Yeats, Lawrence, Forster, or Aldous Huxley. The poet, novelist, and dramatist became increasingly the poet-essayist, the novelist-essayist, and the dramatist-essayist, participating in the literary culture on two levels, in creative writing and critical and social commentary. Few essayists from this period (1850–1950) who were *only* essayists have survived in reputation as well as Hazlitt, Lamb, or Montaigne. The essays which have remained a vital part of the culture tend to be signed by a name famous for achievement in a different, "major" genre. Thus these essays are usually treated as an adjunct to the main work, an aid to its better understanding through knowledge of the author's critical or social views. Critical essays may be seen as adjuncts to the works discussed in them, or as documents in the history of taste or "reception." And certainly it is a fascinating exercise to compare a writer's novelistic or poetic patterning of experience to his essayistic patterning of it. Also it is undoubtedly helpful in some cases to have a writer's personal "map" of literature providing a context for his major texts. But there is also a need to study essays in their own terms.

In Henry James's "case" (to use his own favourite term for studies of writers) the links between fiction and essays are abundant and clear. He wrote prolifically in both forms all his life, and the main subjects of his essays, travel and art, bulk large in his fiction as well. However, the moral concerns of the fiction do not find expression in explicitly moral essays: there are no pieces entitled "On Innocence" or "On Trust," for example. James does not deal with these issues in a general way in his essays, but in relation to a particular cultural environment. Morals and manners interact in as complex ways in his essays as in his novels, and James's "vision" is recognizable in both.

The original audience of James's essays was the cultivated American middle class, to whom he aimed to interpret European culture through the record of his travels and his reading in contemporary literature. Although he occasionally contributed to English reviews, the bulk of his essays appeared in American periodicals such as *The Nation, Harper's Weekly, Lippincott's Magazine,* and *Atlantic Monthly.* Even the late travel pieces collected in *The American Scene* (1907) were written for an American audience and published in the *North American Review, Harper's,* and the *Fortnightly Review* – here the interest was in the half-European viewpoint of a long-term expatriate returning to his native land, rather than a traveler's report for the benefit of other travelers, like his earlier work. Thus even here cultural displacement (partly his, partly his audience's) conditions James's basic perspective. The same is true of his literary essays where his aim is to provide a sympathetic introduction to the possibly alien modes of feeling and aesthetic form, largely in French, but also in Russian and English literature, which form a vital context for the true appreciation of his own fiction. James as essayist takes on the role of guide and interpreter, sending advance reports to those who might plausibly venture after him in their readings of their travels.

The travel essay arises from the convergence of two factors in the mid-nineteenth century: the proliferation of periodicals and the rise of international tourism. The earlier literature of travel consisted mainly of explorer's records of their travels, and the emphasis was on the extraordinary and marvelous and often dangerous quality of the experience. Also the length of the journey usually meant that its recording demanded the length of a book. This kind of "adventure" travel has of course persisted to the present day, though the world-wide spread of tourism has meant that dangers and marvels are harder and harder to come by, as Robert Louis Stevenson was already complaining in the 1870s. Sometimes the means of travel can provide the focus of excitement, as in Stevenson's *Travels with a Donkey in the Cévennes* or Paul Theroux's *The Great Railway Bazaar*. But in quantity, at any rate, "cultural" travel, focused on cities and historical monuments, has displaced "adventure" travel, centered on wilderness and hardship. Formerly the privilege of the aristocracy, in the shape of the Grand Tour for instance, travel as a means of aesthetic and historical education became available to the European and American middle classes, or at least their more prosperous members. This provided a large and lucrative market in the reviews for travel essays (often, of course, reprinted in "travel books" but generally occasioned or commissioned for the periodical press). These pieces are pitched between systematic treatments of a nation's or city's history, geography, and social structure on the one hand, and the kind of practical information contained in the Baedeker guides and their many successors, on the other.

The essay proved ideally adaptable to this task of preparing a traveler for a visit, reminding him of a previous one, or providing a vicarious experience where an actual trip was impossible. There is a mixture of shared (or potentially shared) experience with the writer through visiting the same public places, but also a consciousness of differences created by different times and circumstances of the visit and the distinct personality of the writer. Travel pieces by well-known writers are highly marketable, not only because of the recognition of the name, but because of the reader's desire to revive or prepare for his own "impressions" (to use the common nineteenth-century term) through those of an established sensibility. The reader has the opportunity to sharpen and distinguish his own impressions by reference to the writer's. The ideal result is the same as one would get from a good critical essay on a book one had read: an experience partly shared and partly distinct. The bored and unappreciative traveler needs the same kinds of help and stimulus as the bored and baffled reader. In each case the essayist offers to enhance enjoyment and improve taste by example rather than by authority.

The essence of James's travel essays is conveyed by the title of his first collection of them: *Portraits of Places* (1884). In an image we have used before, James is seeking a "likeness" of the places he is writing about, an intuition of their essential character. This character is analogous to that of a human individual: of Venice he writes, "The place seems to personify itself, to become human and sentient and conscious of your affection" (14). At the same time, there is also a likeness of James himself. In his best travel essays, there is a convergence between place and self, expression and impression, the passive surrender to the environment and the active, conscious quest for what will be for him its symbol, its essence. For example, in "Venice," the first essay in *Portraits of Places*, there is a progressive merging of qualities between the "Jamesian" and the "Venetian," so that the two reveal and complement each other. The essay, based on James's stay in Venice in April-June 1881, offers some intriguing resemblances to Thomas Mann's story of thirty years later: the isolated central figure of the writer and his ambivalent delight at "staying on," the visit to the Lido, the serenading, the raucous chatter of the gondoliers, and so on. Naturally many of the motifs would be common to any account of Venice, but the delight and energy of James's orchestration are quite different from Mann's thematics of moral decadence and physical exhaustion.

The problem of writing about Venice is of course how to say something new about a place so much visited and so much described. James begins his essay with a disclaimer of having something new to offer, and he can only plead love of the subject as his excuse for writing. But this disarming modesty, as if to forestall the bored complaint about yet another piece on Venice, actually masks a desire to possess the city in his own way and to make his own image of it. As an English-speaker (or "Anglo-Saxon" in the terminology of the day) the key presence he has to displace is Ruskin's, to whose love of Venice James pays tribute while criticizing the "angry governess" tone of his late writing about the city. Ruskin has to be set aside like an old and querulous suitor as James presents himself as a fresh and more indulgent lover. Of the pleasures of getting to know Venice, he writes,

> Reading Ruskin is good; reading the old records is, perhaps, better; but the best thing of all is simply staying on. The only way to care for Venice as she deserves it, is to give her a chance to touch you often – to linger and remain and return. (5)

The city's seductive spell has the same effect on him as on Mann's Aschenbach: to discard, or at least defer, literary tasks in favor of direct sensory experience: "The effort required for sitting down to a writing-table is heroic, and the brightest page of MS. looks dull beside the brilliancy of your *milieu*" (17). For the time being, under the spell of this environment, life completely eclipses literature, and the literary reckoning has to come later.

This is not true of visual art, however. For James, the reason for deferring the literary moment is not to enjoy the absence of art, but to enjoy its superabundance. Literature's reflective function is already played by painting, the Venetian art *par excellence*, which in turn often mirrors the splendors of its architecture.

> Nowhere . . . do art and life seem so interfused and, as it were, so consanguineous. All the splendour of light and colour, all the Venetian air and Venetian history, are on the walls and ceilings of the palaces; and all the genius of the masters, all the images and visions they have left upon canvas, seem to tremble in the sunbeams and dance upon the waves. (24)

For James, Venice is a fascinating "case" of the relation between art and life, the same theme that preoccupies him in his literary "cases." In Venice the relation is of the maximum possible interpenetration, so that art comes to life and life becomes artistic.

> You don't go into the churches and galleries by way of a change from the streets; you go into them because they offer you an exquisite reproduction of the things that surround you. All Venice was both model and painter, and life was so pictorial that art could not help becoming so. (24)

Venice is still for James a *social* work of art, a setting for human interaction, and specifically conversation: its accoustics, he notes, are conditioned by the water and by the absence of the traffic noise (train and horse-and-carriage) typical of other nineteenth-century cities. The exceptionally clear soundscape provides the setting for a unique social and musical work of art going on through the day and night: "It is all personal, articulate sound" (20). Gondoliers and tourists, actors and audience, mingle freely on the stage.

Venice is also an *elemental* work of art in James's vision. The elements of water and air flow through and around the architecture as constantly as the human life. As a tourist you become part of this three-way interaction, for example, as you go on a gondola outing "with perpetual architecture above you and perpetual fluidity beneath" (25). James's imagery constantly fastens on interactions between art and life, solid and liquid, figure and ground, object and setting, weaving his essay together out of these connections and interfusions of opposites. Examples can be found on almost any page. Near the end he notes the fishermen's "cheeks and throats as richly brown as the sails of their fishing-smacks – their sea-faded tatters which are always a 'costume'" (37), where the elements themselves take the function of operatic stage designers.

But the most striking artistic effects of the elements are of light and color. In the fourth section of the essay, James sets out first on a quest for an abstraction: the essential color of Venice (later he finds the essential sound in the voices of the gossiping gondoliers carrying over water). "It is a faint, shimmering, airy, watery pink; the bright sea-light seems to flush with it, and the pale whitish-green of lagoon and canal to drink it in" (15–16). The mental picture called up for him by the name Venice (this idea is strongly reminiscent of Proust's "Nom de pays: le nom" section in *A la recherche du temps perdu*) consists not of a grand prospect but what is almost an abstract: "a patch of green water and a surface of pink wall" (16).

Having announced this dominant color-theme, James goes on to play variations on it. Noting the changes from spring to early summer during his stay, he presents them like the birth of a work of art (in a way reminiscent of Mann, though with a different result). In April, "it was all cold colour," though with "charming cool intervals, when the churches, the houses, the anchored fishing-boats, the whole gently-curving line of the Riva, seemed to be washed with a pearly white" (17). The choice of "washed" is deft, since it suggests the actions of cleansing, of the sea, and of a brush on a water-color painting, the latter being itself a perfect description of James's own combinations of "water" and "color." But in mid-May the whole color-scheme modulated into a more intense brightness:

> The sea took on a thousand shades, but they were only infinite variations of blue, and those rosy walls I just spoke of began to flush in the thick sunshine. Every patch of colour, every yard of weather-stained stucco, every glimpse of nestling garden or daub of sky above a *calle*, began to shine and sparkle – began, as the painters say, to "compose." (18)

Through James's careful mixture of terms suggestive to both, the scene seems to come to life and to become art in the same process. The colors and textures, in a characteristic Jamesian way, are abstracted or excerpted from their objects as samples, as a "patch," "yard," "glimpse," or "daub," and then composed as a representative image like the earlier "patch of green water and . . . surface of pink wall" (16).

Since this is living composition rather than a still life, it never reaches permanent form but is incessantly recomposed. The final transformation of Venice comes at the end of the essay, with the month of June and the climax of James's stay. "Then Venice is rosier than ever in the morning, and more golden than ever as the day descends. It seems to expand and evaporate, to multiply all its reflections and iridescences" (35). The temporary balance of light and form, shape and reflection, dissolves into a multiplicity too overpowering to hold in an artistic pattern. The "sentimental tourist," as James calls himself repeatedly, flees the city for the Lido and the fishing villages, and the final image of the essay is of surfeit: the replete traveler leans on his balcony on a June night looking down at the lights and reflections and boats on the canal, and, saturated, turns away to the refuge of his apartment.

The Venice essay is a triumph of James's poetics of description, where the observed detail gains its power from an intent but unobtrusive analytic process, a quest of the "figure in the carpet," the essential core of identity of a place and its life. He is seeking its distinctive culture, not by any set artistic or intellectual method, but by sensibility and intuition, refining the "impressions" he has collected and then finding or letting them find a pattern which will for him be the "figure" of that place. The essayistic "portrait" which results constitutes the "place" as a unique aesthetic and cognitive object, an artistic rather than an historical or sociological construct. The materials of this kind of essay are partly provided by chance (the weather, the people encountered, the local events which happen to coincide with the visit), and this in itself would invalidate any kind of "scientific" conclusion. The ability to pattern this partly chosen and partly adventitious material into a whole is the gift of the greatest travel essayists (one thinks of Jan Morris as James's successor in this at the present day).

The object of James's quest in this kind of writing is to find the essence of the local culture: he very rarely writes about wild or uncultivated nature. There is an implicit concept of culture here, though it is nowhere defined in the abstract. It consists of the peculiar accommodation reached between a given physical setting and the life it contains, perceived through the evolving history of that relationship evident in buildings, gardens, ruins, and so on. James's object might be called a "settlement" in various senses: a settlement of man in nature, or *between* man and nature, a settlement between past and present, between art and life, and his descriptions fasten on the meeting point of these dimensions. James's landscapes are always social, whether he is describing the "perpetual comedy" (35) of Venice, or the quite different rural landscape of England, as in the second of the *Portraits of Places* I want to discuss, "In Warwickshire." Here the cultural essence he is seeking is not simply of this county, but of England. Warwickshire, he announces, "is the core and centre of the English world; mid-most England, unmitigated England. The place has taught me a great many English secrets; I have interviewed the genius of pastoral Britain" (247). Unlike the Venice essay, James does not deal here with the most obvious tourist sights; he describes a series of castles and houses in the area of Stratford, omitting the central Shakespearean attractions, though the spirit of the poet is present throughout.

The dominant theme is not so much the cultivation of nature as its *domestication*. The outdoors is described in terms of the indoors, and fields in terms of gardens: we hear of a "cushiony lawn" (251), a "carpet of turf" (261), and "lawn-like meadows" (248). In James's eyes "the coat of nature" in Warwickshire is "so prettily trimmed" (261) that it has almost become a polite participant in society; in one garden, the lawns touch the river with a line "as even as the rim of champagne glass" (262). As in the "Venice" essay, James abstracts the qualities and textures of the place; again the components are pairings of art and nature, but the role of light is here played by the vegetation largely missing in Venice. The elements of the composition are "a happy mixture of lawn and river and mirrored spire, and blooming garden" (263), or in another typical scene, "ivy-smothered brickwork and weather-beaten gables, conscious old windows and clustered mossy roofs" (267). The abstract effect of the plurals and the detachment of the features from a specific object makes them into a kind of repertoire for imaginative recomposition; yet at the same time they are highly concrete, a combination suggestive of Cézanne's painting.

But the dominant art form here is literature rather than painting: in this essay Shakespeare and George Eliot (both local authors whom it would be hard to imagine together in any other context) play a similar role to Carpaccio, Tintoretto, and Veronese in "Venice." With Shakespeare, the tourist is always conscious of "these densely verdant meadows and parks having been, to his musing eyes, the normal landscape" (260). With George Eliot, this awareness of looking at material that has *already* been incorporated into an imaginative vision is even stronger: "the stranger . . . recognizes at every turn the elements of George Eliot's novels" (263). If successful, this kind of literary tourism should enhance one's appreciation both of the landscape and of the novels, and this literary aspect of the travel essay only adds to the process of recombination of life and art.

The landscape is not purely an aesthetic phenomenon, however; the physical layout of the scenery insistently raises the question of property, which it did not in "Venice." But the question is largely kept at a distance through the traveler's detachment. The visual descriptions often include screens, barriers, and enclosures, which symbolize the private character of the paradisal scenes. The wealth of the county (and the country) is protected by woods, walls, hedges, and moats, and its architectural riches are well screened from casual inspection. When James describes the political complexion of the landscape, he reads it as conservative: "the fact seemed written in the hedgerows and in the verdant acres behind them" (257). The protective distance works both ways, in that the observing visitor is not subject to, or complicit with, that politics, and can afford to view it as picturesque, as he did the squalor of the Venetian poor: "Self-complacent British Toryism, viewed in this vague and conjectural fashion – across the fields and behind the oaks and beeches – is by no means a thing the irresponsible stranger would wish away; it deepens the local colour; it may be said to enhance the landscape" (258). Politics appears, only to be reabsorbed by aesthetics; for someone whose main impression of the country is of "a perfect ripeness of civilisation" (264), any protest is likely to be on aesthetic grounds, and indeed the only discordant note in the essay is the "cockneyfication" of tourist sites like Kenilworth Castle. James laments "how I stumbled over beer-bottles; how the very echoes of the beautiful ruin seemed to have dropped all their *h*'s" (248).

That James did not find the patois of the gondoliers in Venice equally grating perhaps suggests a different relation to England than to Italy. Although he stresses the distance between his consciousness and that of the English, especially his surprise and delight at things they took for granted, like the profusion of historic houses in the county, he is after all a fellow Anglo-Saxon. Often he seems to be taking the measure of the "English girl-face" – he approves the "look of being completely and profoundly at the service of the man she loves" (255) – and the English country residence with the eyes of a potential possessor. In one very striking, almost voyeuristic scene, he stands by watching "a young girl who stood in an old oak parlour, the rugged panels of which made a background for her lovely head, in simple conversation with a handsome lad" (255). The beauty of the girl and her setting, rendered like a Dutch interior, is implicitly contrasted with the banality of their talk – James politely hints at stupidity on the part of the young man. The anecdote ends without an explicit point, with an image through the window of the moat and the old walls. This suggests, below the contrast between the conscious outsider and the heedless possessor, that the outsider is barred, the house and the woman are fortified against him, that he cannot walk into his own picture. Yet the desire for possession is there, in uneasy balance with the need for protection and detachment.

Both involvement and detachment are expressed in the phrase "the sympathetic stranger," which James uses to denote himself in this essay (in "Venice" it is "the sentimental tourist," while in *The American Scene* it is "the restless analyst"). James uses a variant on the phrase in his final image, of a moment "when fancy takes her ease in an old English country house, while the twilight darkens the corners of expressive rooms, and the appreciative intruder, pausing at the window, turns his glance from the observing portrait of a handsome ancestral face and sees the great soft billow of the lawn melt into the park" (269). This reverses the final moment in the "Venice" essay, where the writer turns from the exterior to the interior; both are threshold images suitable to an ending, and define the essay spatially as a kind of "room." The dusk provides another "turning-point" in keeping with the turn of the essayist (though the use of the third person more or less converts him into a fictional "character"). Another reversal (worthy of *The Turn of the Screw*) catches the "intruder" between the two frames of the ancestral portrait and the window, symbolizing temporal and spatial possession, historical and territorial authority. For a moment the outside observer is turned into an object of observation, until he joins the ancestor's perspective by looking in the same direction, away across the lawn and park. In so doing he seems to vanish, so that the ancestor can resume his proprietory gaze unobstructed. The visitor becomes a visitant; he, rather than the portrait, seems like a ghost. He has possessed the place, or been possessed by it, like the other places in Warwickshire, but in a spiritual or imaginary way. His appropriation is subtler and less substantial than the actual inhabitants or past owners are capable of, for all their handsomeness and health. Only the intruder can be fully appreciative, only the stranger provide fully conscious sympathy.

In James's last major ventures in the travel essay, collected in *The American Scene* (1907), the element of strangeness results from his twenty-one–year absence from America: he describes himself as "the repentant absentee" (2) as well as "the restless analyst" (e.g. 9, 29, 34) of the changes that have taken place. There is also a new form of sympathy, the revival of his early memories of New York and New England, so that we witness a process of attempted *re*possession of a native heritage. But where the English essays painstakingly penetrate the privacy, even secrecy, of English life behind its protective screens, the American essays show almost a state of shock at the opposite effect. James spends his first afternoon back on American soil by driving around the New Jersey suburbs, and is struck by "the air of unmitigated publicity": "there was no achieved protection, no constituted mystery of retreat, no saving complexity, not so much as might be represented by a foot of garden wall or a preliminary sketch of interposing shade" (9–10). Everything is completely "at the mercy of observation" (7), and the essayist is left disoriented by the lack of difficulty, the lack of need to circle and penetrate the social space.

Later in this essay, "New England: an Autumn Impression" (James apologizes for including glimpses of New Jersey and New York under this heading), he describes at length the behavior of two young women and a young man near whom he sat on top of a coach:

> The immodesty was too colossal to be anything but innocence – yet the innocence, on the other hand, was too colossal to be anything but inane. And they were alive, the slightly stale three: they talked, they laughed, they sang, they shrieked, they romped, they scaled the pinnacle of publicity and perched on it flapping their wings. (33)

Both here and in the Cape Cod landscape where the young people have been on holiday, the problem for James is the "extreme simplification of the picture." Unlike the ever-changing complexity of Venice, say, the scene has an almost abstract character:

> The simplification, for that immediate vision, was to a broad band of deep and clear blue sea, a blue of the deepest and clearest conceivable, limited in one quarter by its far and sharp horizon of sky, and in the other by its near and sharp horizon of yellow sand overfringed with a low woody shore; the whole seen through the contorted cross-pieces of stunted, wind-twisted, far-spreading, quite fantastic old pines and cedars, whose bunched bristles, at the ends of long limbs, produced, against the light, the most vivid of all reminders. (34)

James produces another brilliant word-painting through his familiar technique of building up a repertory of features and colors, and he goes on to do this for the typical New England village, which he finds equally delightful and equally unvaried. Although there are many vivid pictures in this and the other essays of *The American Scene*, James seems to be left floundering between his impressions of the "simplicity" and "publicity" of American life and manners on one hand, and the methods and expectations developed in his European travel essays on the other. He is thrown back on himself much more, and supplies the complications from his own thoughts, not the environment.

One similarity between James's travel essays and his critical essays is the resemblance they both bear to ghost stories, particularly of course to his own. The common element is a scrupulous attention vigilantly focused on something very hard to define. With the travel essays the goal is some kind of essence of place and local culture, something which can be sought, but which also appears unsought, like a ghost; with the critical essay it is the mystery of creativity, as manifest in the particular instance he is discussing. The essays are also like detective stories, as James himself implies with the persistent use of the word "case" to describe his later critical studies. They are like a literary equivalent of Conan Doyle's *The Casebook of Sherlock Holmes*; the essayist becomes a detective of creation rather than crime, but shows the same careful investigative, but also intuitive, approach. But the solutions lack the neatness of Sherlock Holmes's, and there is a residue of mystery at the end quite often. The essays thus hover between the ghost story and the detective story, the insoluble and the triumphantly solved. James's own fictional equivalent of the critical essays is of course "The Figure in the Carpet," where the nature and even the existence of a unifying pattern in a writer's work remains uncertain to the obsessed critic-detective. The Lukácsian ideal of the essay as "a supreme literary portrait, a kind of critical Vandyke or Velásquez" (*Soul and Form*, 80) is never achieved in the story, but it provides a clue to what James was attempting in his own critical work.

James wrote critical essays throughout his long career, and nearly all of those he preserved in volume form are worth re-reading today, despite the occasional *longueurs* of the full-length Victorian review. He published four collections in his lifetime: *French Poets and Novelists* (1878), *Partial Portraits* (1888), *Essays in London and Elsewhere* (1893), and *Notes on Novelists* (1914). Since my view of James's essay output is that the earlier travel essays and the later critical essays are more interesting (perhaps reflecting James's more sedentary life or more contemplative nature in middle age), I want to focus here on the great triptych on the nineteenth-century French novel, written in 1902–3 and collected in *Notes on Novelists*: "Honoré de Balzac," "Gustave Flaubert," and "Emile Zola;" I will use his preface to *The Tempest* (1907) as a tailpiece (all these texts, with a good selection of the earlier work, are conveniently gathered in *Henry James: Selected Literary Criticism*, ed. Morris Shapira, intro. F. R. Leavis, the edition cited here). The reasons for this focus are that the three essays form a mature assessment (though he had written on all three French authors on various previous occasions) of the writers James saw as his peers in the art of the novel, and who formed his own vital enabling context; that James's significance as an interpreter of the French novel to an Anglo-American audience can be fully appreciated; and that the three novelists taken together are constituted by James as a classic historical and comparative "subject" for criticism, later taken up by such critics as Georg Lukács and Harry Levin.

The autobiographical element is another link between the travel essays and this critical triad. Experiences of reading are woven into one's life like experiences of travel; revisiting books can revive memories as strongly as revisiting places. Sometimes the two experiences overlap, as in Thomas Mann's classic "Voyage with Don Quixote" (from *Essays of Three Decades*), where the transatlantic crossing is interwoven in diary form with the novel-reading. At the end of the Zola essay James recalls the setting of his reading of *La Débâcle* (1892): "It was early in the summer; I was in an old Italian town; the heat was oppressive, and one could but recline, in the lightest garments, in a great dim room and give one's self up" (264). A much earlier instance of this combination of text and context involves Flaubert; when *Madame Bovary* was being serialized in the *Revue de Paris* the young James (he cannot have been more than 13) read and clearly remembered one of the episodes:

> present to me still is the act of standing before the fire, my back against the low beplushed and begarnished French chimney-piece and taking in what I might of that instalment, taking it in with so surprised an interest, and perhaps as well such a stir of faint foreknowledge, that the sunny little salon, the autumn day, the window ajar and the cheerful outside clatter of the Rue Montaigne are all now for me more or less in the story and the story more or less in them. (220)

Place and text fuse together in the recollected act of reading, which becomes not only part of the reader's life, but for him part of the work as well. In the Balzac essay, James writes of rediscovering the well-known work: "it is all overscored with traces and impressions – vivid, definite, almost as valuable as itself – of the recognitions and agitations it originally produced in us" (191). Previous readings, and their accompanying feelings, are inscribed in the work, so that to re-read is to re-experience an earlier self. For James, the process of turning life into art is mirrored by its reverse, as the work of literature enters the life of its reader. If the reader is a writer as well, the process continues as the reading becomes an element in a new creation. With the three French authors, James is bringing a lifetime of reading and writing into play.

Meeting an author is of course a second way of forming an "impression" of an author (the "impression" – his term – is the basic constituent of James's criticism as of his travel writing). Even given James's precocity as a child, he was too young to have met Balzac, but his personal memories of Flaubert and Zola intervene in vital ways in these late essays devoted to them. The personal anecdote about Flaubert is part of an account of his social life in Paris as a contrast to his hermit-like existence at Croisset. James once happened to visit his salon and find Flaubert alone; perhaps to cover a certain awkwardness, the Frenchman read him a poem of Théophile Gautier as an example of something quintessentially and uniquely French. The focus of the anecdote, however, is not the putative Frenchness of this text, but Flaubert's voice, to which James applies the terms "spout," "bellow," and Flaubert's own word, *"gueuler"* (217). Flaubert's physical presence, "huge and diffident, but florid too and resonant" (216), seems oddly out of keeping with the delicacy of his literary taste, though James does not comment on this, or connect the "impression" directly with the essay's train of thought; the "impression" is simply "left" with the reader. As in a detective story, the evidence is built up, but not patterned until the end.

The anecdotal figures more largely in the Zola essay; since the two writers were contemporaries, James knew Zola over a longer period than he did Flaubert, and their careers were parallel but contrasting. With regard to two of the anecdotes, James admits that they have little to do with the "critical spirit," and appeal rather to the "romantic" idea of the "evolution of a classic," like the story of the early reading of *Madame Bovary* during its serialization. Here the classic is *L'Assommoir*, and we glimpse the work in progress at two points, both ironically contrasted with its eventual critical success and acceptance. Both are set in Sunday afternoon literary salons: the first shows Zola discussing his next novel and his preparatory collection of popular profanities and obscenities for use in it. James comments: "I was struck with the tone in which he made the announcement – without bravado and without apology . . . just as I was struck by the unqualified interest that his plan excited" (249). The second story recalls "the chorus of contempt" (249) expressed in Zola's presence for the magazine editors who halted the serial publication of *L'Assommoir* midway. James justifies the inclusion of these impressions as illustrations of the "drama of romantic interest" (250) constituted by the early struggles of a masterpiece; but the reader is left feeling that the full meaning, the true point, of the tale has been deferred, and that the ostensible point isn't all there is to the matter.

So far James has shown us the reader reading (himself, between the 1850s and the 1890s) and the writer talking (except Balzac). What of the writer writing? Or the writer living? These are the central mysteries. What access can the reader have to them? One answer is of course through the writer's letters, and

James makes use of this third perspective when it is available. He wrote a review of "Balzac's Letters" (included in *French Poets and Novelists*) and his 1893 essay "Gustave Flaubert" (included in *Essays in London and Elsewhere*) is a review of Flaubert's correspondence. Zola's letters, as he was James's contemporary, were not yet available – James's essay is written on the occasion of Zola's death and the publication of his last book, *Verité* (1903) – and the added anecdotes may be there to compensate. The fascination of writers' letters for James was clear: the opportunity to see the writer writing, but off duty at the same time, *writing as a means of carrying on life*. Here potentially is evidence of the writer's personality prior to and aside from his work. But what does James find in these cases? Of Balzac he comments: "His published letters . . . are . . . almost exclusively the audible wail of a galley-slave chained to the oar" (204). In other words this window onto the life only shows us the work again. James went to the letters to find out how Balzac lived, apart from his work. The answer is: "He did *not* live – save in his imagination . . .; his imagination was all his experience; he had probably no time for the real thing" (205). Balzac, of course, produced in the *Comédie humaine* a prodigious amount of work, while Flaubert's finished œuvre was relatively tiny. Yet the relation to the life was the same: both did nothing but write. To borrow a phrase from the 1893 essay on Flaubert's letters, they "show us the artist not only disinterested but absolutely dishumanized" (140). And in the 1902 essay: "Flaubert's life is so exclusively the story of his literary application that to speak of his five or six fictions is pretty well to account for it all" (212). With Zola we get a "direct impression" (243), not an epistolary one (Flaubert, as the central figure in the triptych, is the only one where we get both):

> It consisted, simply stated, in his fairly bristling with the betrayal that nothing whatever had happened to him in life but to write *Les Rougon-Macquart*. It was even for that matter almost more as if *Les Rougon-Macquart* had written *him*, written him as he stood and sat, as he looked and spoke, as the long, concentrated, merciless effort had made and stamped and left him. (243)

The man is a pale shadow of the work, a ghostly creation of his own text.

The three avenues of approach James has followed in these essays – reading the writer's work, talking to him, and reading his letters – do not seem to converge as we follow them. Instead there is a sense that they stop disappointingly short of the goal. Or, to change the metaphor, the strands still await integration into a single fabric. There seems to be a kind of blank at the center, an unexplained discrepancy, an unanswered question: how *did* those works get written? There is a gap between the man and the work, sometimes seeming so wide that James almost asks *who* wrote them. The doer and the deed don't match, so that these essays are almost "whodunits." In all three of them, but especially the Zola piece, the verb "do" is repeated often, put in quotation marks, and loaded with a freight of implication. For an artist contemplating the work of a fellow artist the question is "How after all does it so get itself *done*? – the 'done' being admirably the sign and crown of it" (259). James is like a detective trying to catch his writers *in the act*. He searches for the vital clue connecting the supposed author to his work; he watches them stand alongside it with a suspicious air of innocence, waiting for them to betray their guilt. The figure of the writer hovers for James between that of the "criminal" who can be caught, and the ghost, who can't. Thus, unlike Sherlock Holmes, he might have to leave the mystery unsolved. There is even an air of voyeurism, as if the critic is trying to glimpse some primal scene of procreation that will explain the hidden connection between parent and offspring.

James fails to catch his writers in the act of creation; that remains an inaccessible secret. But he does catch them out in a crucial failing, and the center of his essay-texts becomes a lack, an absence, in *their* fictional texts. Only through this failing, which is perceptual, moral, and aesthetic, can the life and the work be connected. The negative link is the only possible one; the positive one seems to be unattainable. Unlike Arnold's, James's touchstones are faults, in the moral and the geological sense. This idea of the "break" or "gap" in the text sounds at first akin to deconstructive or ideological criticism, but James's concern with what he calls "the fatal break of 'tone'" (195) is both moral and perceptual: when James pounces on his suspects they seem unaware that they are doing anything wrong:

> This is Balzac caught in the very fact of his monstrous duality [as artist and scientist], caught in his most complete self-expression. He is clearly quite unwitting that in handing over his *data* to his

twin-brother the impassioned economist and surveyor, the insatiate general inquirer and reporter, he is in any sort betraying our confidence. (195)

With Flaubert the fatal giveaway is his treatment of Mme Arnoux in *L'Education sentimentale*, his one attempt to show "beauty of character and life" (225). Instead, according to James, he shows her only through the worthless medium of the hero's consciousness, without even realizing how inadequate that viewpoint is. What shocks James is "the unconsciousness of error in respect to the opportunity that would have counted as his finest. We feel not so much that Flaubert misses it, for that we could bear; but that he doesn't *know* that he misses it is what stamps the blunder" (226). In other words, there is a fatal blind spot in Flaubert's sensibility, an aesthetic lapse pointing to a moral lack. Nor is this just an isolated instance; it is simply the essential clue of an absolutely fundamental objection to Flaubert's entire work, which for James is radically flawed.

James's third and most decisive "pounce" is on Zola. The twenty-volume series of *Les Rougon-Macquart* had been appearing throughout the 1870s and 1880s, and for James's generation Zola had always somehow been "there." He mentions reading *La Conquête de Plassens* at the start of Zola's "Natural and Social History of a Family under the Second Empire," and *La Débâcle* at the end; Zola was a continuous presence in James's own literary life. But he only began to focus on Zola's "presumption" during the appearance of *The Three Cities* trilogy in 1894–8. Here he wanted not just to recognize the same, tired Zola formula, but

> really to give the name to the particular shade of blindness that could constitute a trap for so great an artistic intelligence. The presumptuous volume [*Rome*] . . . betrayed or 'gave away' . . . the state of mind on the author's part responsible for its inflated hollowness. To put one's finger on the state of mind was to find out accordingly what was, as we say, the matter with him. (254)

This revelation occurred during the publication of the third volume of the unfinished *Les Quatre Evangiles* in 1902–3: "these three productions joined hands at a given moment to fit into the lock of the mystery the key of my meditation" (254).

This unlocking of the mystery seems to coincide with the locking away of the guilty party (all three essays are full of images of judicial process: weighing, scales, cages, and bars).

Zola has been caught: he is guilty of lack of taste. As he with Flaubert, it is not a case of an occasional blemish (here the imagery switches to disease): "the misfortune of being tasteless . . . does not merely disfigure the surface and the fringe of your performance – it eats back into the very heart and enfeebles the sources of life" (255). Exposed and ashamed, Zola's figure seems to wither and die in front of your eyes. His absence of taste (rather than defiance of established taste) was, of course, the delayed point of the earlier Zola anecdotes. James has discovered, not the source of creative energy, but the canker that destroys it. Here, finally, is what is "'the matter with' Zola" (254). The bad work reveals the limitations of the good, by reference to the character of its author; but the other mystery, the life-source of the good work, remains.

Accordingly, James feels he has solved the riddle of Zola's failure, but not that of his success. Near the end of the essay, James is still asking: "How, all sedentary and 'scientific,' did he get so *near*? By what art, inscrutable, immeasurable, indefatigable, did he arrange to make of his documents in these connections, a use so vivified?" (259–60). This aspect of the problem goes back to the essay's first "direct impression" of Zola's "inexperience of life" (243), and is illustrated later by personal anecdote. Meeting Zola in London just after the completion of *Les Rougon-Macquart*, James asked him whether he had traveled in Italy. Zola replied that he had always been too busy to travel outside France (James implies that the almost exclusively French context of all three writers is a limitation in them), except for a brief excursion across the border to Genoa. Zola next announces his project on the three cities, one of which is Rome. James is staggered by this man, who "stating in one breath that his knowledge of Italy consisted of a few days spent in Genoa, was ready to declare in the next that he had planned, on a scale, a picture of Rome" (253).

Previously, James believes, Zola's methods of documentation and research had worked, because "the process, to my imagination, became vivid and was wonderfully reflected back from its fruits" (254). Yet even then, there is something fatally second-hand and impersonal: "his whole process and its results . . . constitute together perhaps the most extraordinary *imitation* of observation that we possess" (261). James calls Zola's research methods "his magnificent treadmill of the pigeon-holed and documented – the region we may qualify as that of experience by imitation" (262). James's contrast between methodological fiction and fiction that comes out of personal experience and observation corresponds to our earlier distinction between disciplinary writing and the essay. Zola is able to overcome this fundamental inauthenticity until *Rome* decisively unmasks his presumptuousness, and simultaneously reveals his lack of true (i.e. personal) experience as well as his lack of taste. Such a disaster never befell Balzac, according to James; his "scientific" pretensions never strangled his imaginative vitality in this way.

The "process" of James's critical essays (to use the word he applies to Zola) enacts the values he finds crucially lacking in his three subjects, despite the praise he lavishes on them as true artists of the novel. The essays recreate a process of intent inquiry in which the critic's personal experiences (reading, meetings, discussions, etc.) are carefully presented and used as the basis for judgment. Both the evidence and the verdict involve a unity of the perceptual, moral, and aesthetic, and it is against this unity that the writers are judged and found wanting at one or more crucial points. Although James is often now presented as an aesthete, or a self-referential textualist, he never abandoned the moral criterion – "the deepest quality of a work of art will always be the quality of the mind of the producer" (66) – and the realistic criterion – "the air of reality (solidity of specification) seems to me to be the supreme virtue of a novel" (57) – first advanced in 1884 in "The Art of Fiction." He seems to demand of good fiction some of the same qualities as good essay writing. Conversely, some of his "fictional" forms are used effectively in his essays. One example would be the interaction of a problematic set of discrepant impressions and a consciousness intent on unifying them, a structure typical of his short stories. Some of the themes are the same, especially the relation between moral, perceptual, and aesthetic integrity, and the need for attentiveness in all three areas, the importance (in reading as in living) of not "missing the point," especially when the point is that someone else has missed the point. The central notion of "The Figure in the Carpet," James's indispensable "critical-detective" short story, is the possibility that *every* reader might miss the point. Thus he astonishingly remarks, after "catching" Flaubert on his treatment of Mme Arnoux, "It is the only stain on his shield; let me even confess that I should not wonder if, when all is said, it is a blemish no one has ever noticed" (226).

Thus if James the essayist sets out looking for the "whole-ness," the figure in the carpet, of his literary subjects, he usually ends up with the fatal flaw, the crack in the golden bowl, discovered through connecting the aesthetic quality of the work with the moral nature of the producer. The triumphant exception to this is the late essay on *"The Tempest"* and the "strange case" (305) of Shakespeare's abrupt retirement – the phrase may echo the title of *The Strange Case of Dr Jekyll and Mr Hyde* by James's friend, Robert Louis Stevenson. The echo, conscious or not, is highly apposite here, for James the literary detective is now confronting "the eternal mystery, the most insoluble that ever was, the complete rupture, for our under-standing, between the Poet and the Man" (306). The collateral evidence about the lives of Balzac, Flaubert, and Zola is abundant; with Shakespeare it is almost entirely lacking, and what there is of it points, for James, to an utterly commonplace figure, scarcely to be connected by any stretch of the imagina-tion to the author of the plays. Instead of a solution, James creates a miniature Shakespearean (or perhaps Beckettian or Stoppardian) drama. The stage set consists of a tapestry, which represents the Work; the "immitigably respectable person" of the Man sits in front, and somewhere behind hides the "undetermined figure" of the Poet (the two senses of "figure" are beautifully merged). Enter the Critic, armed with a rapier, tempted by a "vague stir . . . to try for a lunge at the figured arras" (306). Although James is writing about *The Tempest*, and although he compares the Poet's invisibility to Ariel's, this little scene most resembles the scene in *Hamlet* when the hero stabs at the stirring presence behind his mother's arras, only to find he has killed Polonius instead of Claudius.

James has moved from critic as detective or judge to critic as assassin, at the same time implicitly admitting the possibility of killing the wrong man! The violence of the critical approach to identifying the man within or behind the work seems to increase with its fallibility. James leaves his little drama frozen until the end of the essay when he expresses a hope for a "Criticism of the future" whose improved equipment and methods will finally be able to do the job of locating the Poet:

> The figured tapestry, the long arras that hides him, is always there, with its immensity of surface and its proportionate underside. May it not then be but a question, for the fullness of time, of the finer

weapon, the sharper point, the stronger arm, the more extended lunge? (306)

There are strong parricidal implications in this image, not to speak of the damage to the "text" by making this kind of stab at it. But twentieth-century criticism, led by T. S. Eliot, largely turned away from the whole issue of the author's relationship to the text. Eliot the Critic ratified the gap between the Man and the Poet, and successfully hid his creative self behind the arras of the "impersonal" theory of poetry.

7

Virginia Woolf: angles of vision

In 1925, the same year that *Mrs Dalloway* defined her status as a major novelist, Virginia Woolf collected a volume of the literary essays she had written over the previous twenty years, mostly for *The Times Literary Supplement*. She chose the title *The Common Reader*, and was sufficiently attached to it to use it again for her second essay collection in 1932. After her death, Leonard Woolf brought out several further volumes of her essays under different titles, and eventually a four-volume *Collected Essays* (cited here). Finally, in 1976, her autobiographical essays were published under the title *Moments of Being*. But the phrase "the common reader" is the only one she herself chose to group her essays under, and to represent her view of literary criticism. It is taken from Johnson's *Life of Gray*: "I rejoice to concur with the common reader; for by the common sense of readers, uncorrupted by literary prejudices, after all the refinements of subtilty and the dogmatism of learning, must be finally decided all claim to poetical honours" (*Lives of the English Poets*, Everyman edn, London: Dent, 1961, 2:392). The common reader is the natural companion of the essayist, and the essay is, of course, the natural means of expression for such a reader, as Woolf's volumes demonstrate. In her page-long Preface to *The Common Reader* (unfortunately not reprinted in *Collected Essays*) Woolf distinguishes him from the critic or scholar: "He reads for his own pleasure rather than to impart knowledge or correct the opinions of others." But he plays an active, creative role as well: "he is guided by an instinct to create for himself, out of whatever odds and ends he can come by, some kind of whole – a portrait of a man, a sketch of an age, a theory of the art of writing." This gives her own essential aim in her literary essays – a sense of wholeness – and three of her own favourite subjects, to which we might add a fourth as our own starting-point: her theory of the art of reading.

Woolf's approach to reading anticipates in many respects, though in a non-systematic way, the theories of Georges Poulet, current in academic criticism in the 1950s and 1960s, as well as the "reader-response" criticism of the 1970s. The basic ideas of Poulet's "phenomenology of reading" are the complete surrender of the reader's imagination to the "world" of the author, and the subsequent attempt by the critic-reader to reconstitute his experience of the world. Woolf does not use phenomenological terms but her theory in "How Should One Read a Book?" is essentially the same: each great author creates a world. "Yet different as these worlds are, each is consistent with itself. The maker of each is careful to observe the laws of his own perspective" (2:3). Her advice to the reader is also similar to Poulet's: "Do not dictate to your author: try to become him. Be his fellow worker and accomplice" (2:2). For Woolf the reading process has two parts. The first is "to receive impressions with the utmost understanding" (2:8). The second is "to pass judgment upon these multitudinous impressions" (2:8). This means seeing the book as a whole (or, as we would say now, "totalizing" it), and this spatial or simultaneous view constructs a different object from the page-by-page reading process: "the book as a whole is different from the book received currently in separate phases" (2:8).

These distinctions are recognizable in later critical theory; but Woolf uses them while assuming the existence of individual personality in reader and writer, rather than treating them as "subject positions" within a "textual system": for her, as for *essayistic* criticism in general, the goal of reading is the sense of the unique individuality of the author. "If you open your mind as widely as possible, then signs and hints of almost imperceptible fineness, from the twist and turn of the first sentences, will bring you into the presence of a human being unlike any other" (2:2). For her, personality is ubiquitous in writing: "Somewhere, everywhere, now hidden, now apparent in whatever is written down is the form of a human being" (2:29). Reading is the immersion of the self in the created world of another self; the experience of reading takes its place among "the great moments of our own experience," from which "we return to life, feeling it more keenly and understanding it more keenly than before" (2:40).

Woolf's sense of the complex relationships between reading and life are nowhere better expressed than in her essay "Reading" (this was her original title for the collection published as *The Common Reader*). Presumably written in 1919 (that date is mentioned as the present), it was not published in her lifetime, and was found in her papers after her death. It is an unusual but effective mixture of autobiographical and critical elements in an often lyrical style. The setting is an English country house, and the first of the three parts describes the essayist's memories of reading in the library on a fine summer day. This Proustian recollection of reading is related to life on various levels, which Woolf evokes. First, there is the slow development of civilization which made the library possible: the original construction of the house as a protection against nature and human enemies, the gradual increase of wealth, travel, politeness, and taste, the standardization of language, and the collection of the books themselves. Then there is the world outside the library, symbolized by the open window – this was a favourite image of Woolf's, and figures also in "How Should One Read a Book?" (2:5). In "Reading" the girl is sitting by the library window, so that "instead of being a book it seemed as if what I read was laid upon the landscape, not printed, bound, or sewn up, but somehow the product of trees and fields and the hot summer sky" (2:13). Outside, a gardener is working; beyond him, the garden seems to be full of the figures of the great English writers, and classics whose books line the library walls. But there are also lesser works: "Travels, histories, memories, the fruit of innumerable lives" (2:22). These lives continue in the library: "Standing at the window and looking out into the garden, the lives of all these books filled the room behind with a soft murmur" (2:22). The inside and outside, the lived past and the literary past, meet at the window where the girl is reading; the same slow historical process has created both the conditions and the material of her reading, as the two merge in her imagination.

The second part of the essay describes a children's expedition into the woods at night to hunt moths. Flannels soaked in treacle have earlier been fixed to certain trees, and when the children revisit them, their lantern reveals numerous moths feeding drunkenly on the sweetness. They are so struck by one huge moth, with red eyes and crimson underwings, that they let it escape. Whenever the lamp is set on the ground, insects come crowding in out of the darkness. The children go on to a tree in the heart of the wood, where they see and finally capture the splendid crimson moth. Then, in awed silence, they hear a terrible cracking noise: a tree has fallen. Woolf does not clarify the relation between this extraordinarily vivid adventure and the theme of reading. But the general parallel is that imaginative reading can lure past lives out of the huge darkness of history and let them feed for a while in this brief, haphazard light. As his title indicates, a comparable image is used by Walter Benjamin in his essay collection *Illuminations* to describe these Proustian moments of reliving the past.

When we return to the library in the third part of the essay, it is in search of clear and "enlightened" reading suitable to the morning hours, rather than the "voyages and memoirs, all the lumber and wreckage and accumulation of time which has deposited itself so thickly upon our shelves and grows like a moss at the foot of literature" (2:25–6). Instead, we focus on a single writer, Sir Thomas Browne. This exemplary figure – doctor, scholar, and himself the occupant of a small country house – is the type of enlightenment: "In that dark world he was one of the explorers" (2:28). Woolf sees Browne as being, like Montaigne, one of the first authors to discuss and define himself in writing. Yet even he, "humane and tolerant in almost every respect, was nevertheless capable of a mood of dark superstition in which he would pronounce that two old women were witches and must be put to death" (2:30). On the level of style, too, his many dull or obscure passages contrast with what Woolf saw as the relative facility and clarity of modern prose (this in 1919; Orwell in the 1940s held the opposite view). Woolf thus returns to her opening theme of the gradual refinement of a culture from the original isolation of the country houses, through the gradually increasing ease and frequency of communication, up to the modern period. Yet the darkness of the past, and of the human unconscious, still persist; the adult never forgets the night terrors and wonders of the child. Reading is the key process in linking these phases: night and day, past and present, book and world.

Can reading really give knowledge of the past? This question occupied Woolf frequently in her essays, as it does Proust in his novel. How much of what we think we see in the past is simply projected from the present? "One is tempted to impute to the dead the qualities we find lacking in ourselves. There is balm for our restlessness in conjuring up visions of Elizabethan magnanimity" (2:21). She asks the same question of individual authors, such as Cervantes: "How far did he himself know what he was about – how far again do we over-interpret, misinterpret, read into Don Quixote a meaning compounded of our own experience" (2:31). In her essays these moments of doubt often alternate with the moments of confident vision, creating a light and dark pattern, or, to borrow Paul de Man's phrase, a pattern of "blindness and insight." Woolf's intuitions are undercut by suspicion of their validity, and the imaginative recreation of a culture, a period, or an individual, is often followed by skeptical inquiry into how much has simply been invented.

This skepticism is announced even in the title of her essay "On Not Knowing Greek," which was written especially for *The Common Reader*, and which through its early position in the collection serves as an introduction to some of its themes. Woolf did in fact know Greek in the usual sense, as soon becomes apparent from her quoting the original texts (she was taught the language as a girl). The point is that no-one *really* knows Greek, either the language or the culture which produced its classical literature. The attempt to read with understanding confronts an unbridgeable gap, yet we are constantly attracted to it nevertheless. Woolf makes the attempt by giving a picture of a familiar scene (an English village) and then transforming it into an unfamiliar one (a Greek landscape): "We must sharpen the lines of the hills. We must imagine a beauty of stone and earth rather than of woods and greenery" (1:2). Through this contrast of setting, Woolf is able to emphasize the *outdoor* quality of Mediterranean life and culture, so unlike the indoor, private character of the Northern equivalent. This extroverted quality of street life she sees reflected in Greek drama and its need for powerful impact. The dramatists had the challenge of thinking of "something emphatic, familiar, brief, that would carry, instantly and directly, to an audience of seventeen thousand people perhaps" (1:3). She goes on to give a group portrait of Sophocles, Aeschylus, and Euripides, and the different ways they responded to this challenge. The "dramatic" quality of ancient Greek culture she even sees extending to philosophy in the dialogues of Plato, despite the indoor, winter setting in which she sees them. Throughout the essay she tries to characterize by contrast: Greece versus England, outdoors versus indoors, public versus private, oral culture versus print culture.

But the effect of these illuminating pairs of images is undercut by displays of authorial self-doubt. A strain of essayistic skepticism comes to question the lyrically evocative historicism:

> are we not reading wrongly? losing our sharp sight in a haze of associations? reading into Greek poetry not what they have but what we lack? . . . Back and back we are drawn to steep ourselves in what, perhaps, is only an image of the reality, not the reality itself, a summer's day imagined in the heart of a northern winter. (1:11)

For Woolf one of the central aims of reading is to recuperate the past "as it really was" (to cite the historicists' key concept); this takes an act of the imagination, but who is to tell how much is supplied by compensatory fantasy? The only answer for her is a dialectic of intuition and doubt, knowing and not knowing. Acknowledging the fallibility of the imaginative visions sometimes works to enhance them, in fact, as if the reader's possible doubts are drawn in and woven into the essay.

In the case of the great Russian novelists of the nineteenth century, the gap of language and nationality is still present, but the historical gap is much less. Woolf's essay "The Russian Point of View," written in the wake of the 1910s vogue for Russian literature, treats Chekhov, Tolstoy, and Dostoyevsky as almost her own contemporaries. But where "we" were assumed to know some Greek in the earlier essay, "we" are assumed to be in complete ignorance of the Russian language, so that we cannot even be puzzled over it. The result is "that we have judged a whole literature stripped of its style" (1:238). Even without a large historical gap, the differences of language and national character are enough to give the English an odd angle of vision on Russian authors. Woolf uses this metaphor throughout the essay to stress the idea that any "reading" must take place from a specific viewpoint. This viewpoint is bound to distort the response and determine the pattern of blindnesses and insights. The distortion will probably be less, Woolf states, the closer the reader is to the writer in terms of nationality, history, and language (and also, as we will see later, class, sex, and age). After citing the case of Henry James and the sense of cultural distance that, despite his long residence in England, still informs his depictions of it, she writes:

> A special acuteness and detachment, a sharp angle of vision the
> foreigner will often achieve; but not that absence of self-
> consciousness, that ease and fellowship and sense of common values
> which make for intimacy, and sanity, and the quick give and take of
> familiar intercourse. (1:238)

If that supposedly natural understanding is lacking for an
American in England, where there are such strong ties of
history and language and tradition, how much more must it be
lacking between England and Russia?

The "group portrait" we are offered in the body of the essay is
framed by statements about the limited viewpoint from which
it is painted. Woolf ends by practically cancelling her hard-won
"likenesses" of the three novelists (though she takes the "angle"
metaphor from the game of bowls this time): "But the mind
takes its bias from the place of its birth, and no doubt, when it
strikes upon a literature so alien as the Russian, flies off at a far
tangent from the truth" (1:246). Indeed there are definite
limitations on Woolf's responses in the essay. The theme of the
Russians' "formlessness" is reminiscent of James's strictures
about "loose and baggy monsters" and "fluid puddings." The
theme of Russian "soul" was almost a cliché by the time Woolf
was writing. The most interesting element in the essay is how
the characteristics of English fiction emerge by contrast.
"Whether he wishes it or not, there is a constant pressure upon
an English novelist to recognize these [class] barriers, and, in
consequence, order is imposed on him and some kind of form"
(1:244). The moral and aesthetic restraint of their traditions, she
says, leaves English readers ill-equipped for appreciating
Russian fiction. To them "the novels of Dostoyevsky are
seething whirlpools, gyrating sandstorms, waterspouts which
hiss and boil and suck us in" (2:242). For Woolf this Russian
violence affects "our" sense of morality and feeling as well as
form: "We love and hate at the same time. There is none of that
precise division between good and bad to which we are used"
(2:243). For her, Russian literature remains fundamentally
"alien" (a word that she uses repeatedly in the essay).

But literature does not have to be foreign or historically
remote to be alien. The literature of one's own period and
country can be so in different ways: lack of sympathy rather
than lack of understanding might be the problem here. With a
writer, there might be rivalry with contemporaries, and also a
sense of generational solidarity against other living genera-

tions; both these are evident in Woolf's assessments of twentieth-century English literature. The best-known of these is "Mr Bennett and Mrs Brown," often treated as a manifesto of Modernism, though Woolf uses the conventional historical labels taken from the name of the reigning monarch to separate her Georgians (Forster, Lawrence, Strachey, Joyce, Eliot, and implicitly herself) from the Edwardians (Bennett, Wells, and Galsworthy). Here she paints a double group portrait, where the individual differences within each group are outweighed by the generational gap. She presents the Georgians as youthful innovators still in the early experimental stage of their art, but on the verge of tremendous achievements, although she complains about Joyce's "indecency" and Eliot's "obscurity," and sees Forster and Lawrence as partly compromised by continuing some Edwardian attitudes.

Her complaint against the Edwardians echoes James's 1914 essay "The New Novel," where he sees the younger novelists (including Conrad and Lawrence) as being oversaturated in realistic detail. For Woolf, the main criticism is that the Edwardians substitute environmental facts for an inward grasp of a character's viewpoint. Her basic argument is historicist: this attitude and method were suitable to the Edwardian period, but no longer to the Georgian, given the fact that "in or about December, 1910, human character changed" (1:320). This assertion, however, is difficult to reconcile with what she later says about Mrs Brown, the "character" through whom in this essay she symbolizes the novelist's raw material:

> There she sits in the corner of the carriage – that carriage which is travelling, not from Richmond to Waterloo, but from one age of English literature to the next, for Mrs Brown is eternal, Mrs Brown is human nature, Mrs Brown changes only on the surface, it is the novelists who get in and out. (1:330)

This seems to suggest that the novelist's object is constant, but the viewpoint is changing; in other words that artistic technique develops independently of social change. Only *some* people changed in 1910: artistic people. Mrs Woolf did, but Mrs Brown didn't.

The historicist argument is undercut, but Woolf gives two other grounds for preferring the Georgians (besides their being the coming generation); they are aesthetically preferable (more exciting and adventurous than the dull Edwardians) and more realistic (they haven't confused truth with detailed descriptions of material circumstances). Yet at other points, when she is dealing with nationality rather than generation, she posits the equivalence of all viewpoints; none is intrinsically more valid than another. She sketches possible national viewpoints on Mrs Brown as a curious "character" (the English view), a psychological type (the French view), and a "soul" (the Russian view), and then adds: "Mrs Brown can be treated in an infinite variety of ways, according to the age, country and temperament of the writer" (1:325). The tensions and distortions in Woolf's argument can be attributed to her polemical response to Arnold Bennett's criticism that the younger novelists could not create convincing characters. At one point she needs to assume a changed human nature in order to make Bennett look out of date, while at a second point she wants to contest his challenge on its own ground by claiming for the Georgians a more convincing version of an *unchanging* human nature.

From this we can see that Woolf's concept of "viewpoint" is not simply a matter of cultural or historical distance; one's "interest" also enters in. Here her interest was to defend herself and her contemporaries against Bennett's attack, and to sway literary opinion to her side. It is fascinating to compare this paper (originally given to a university audience at Cambridge in 1925) with a less known one, given to the Workers' Educational Association in 1940 and called "The Leaning Tower." In only fifteen years, Woolf has turned from representing the insurgent avant-garde to being seen as a dated relic from a previous era. This, the last of her literary group portraits, is of the young poets of the 1930s: Auden, Spender, and MacNeice. But instead of using "Modernist" or Georgian ideas and values to depict these young men, she turns their own Marxist and Freudian ideas against them. Addressing them at times as if they were disturbed schoolboys and she were the school matron, she fills in the economic, social, and historical forces she sees as shaping their outlook. She avoids discussing the aesthetic merit of their work, but manages to imply that its only interest is as a symptom of sociological and psychological forces.

These forces are summed up in the image of the tower, the tower of economic and educational privilege occupied by the English upper and upper-middle classes without major disturbances from 1815 to 1914 (this second date seems to have replaced 1910 as Woolf's inaugural year for modernity). Perhaps trying to show solidarity with her working-class audience, Woolf takes the viewpoint of one of those excluded from the tower class, though without comparing her own exclusion as a woman with the exclusion of the working class as a whole. Her rhetorical perspective on the tower is from below, while the privileged look down from the battlements. The male English writer, almost always educated at public school and Oxford or Cambridge, "sits upon a tower raised above the rest of us; a tower built first on his parents' station, then on his parents' gold. It is a tower of the utmost importance; it decides his angle of vision; it affects his power of communication" (2:169).

After 1914 the tower of privilege began to lean dangerously. But, according to Woolf, the effects did not really show on the generation who dominated the period 1910–25, and whom we now call the Modernists. Their education was safely over and their outlook on life was still influenced by the period of cultural security and continuity they had known in their youth. But the next generation, which she dates from 1925 to 1939, had spent their formative years in the leaning tower; they had the traditional élite education but were surrounded by war, revolution, and change, mostly, she concedes, in Europe, but close enough to England to be menacing. At this juncture she brilliantly reverses the viewpoint, and imaginatively joins the 1930s writers on their leaning tower. She sketches first the strange view, "not altogether upside down, but slanting, sidelong," and then the feelings provoked by it: "First discomfort; next self-pity for that discomfort; which pity soon turns to anger – to anger against the builder, against society, for making us uncomfortable" (2:171). Woolf sees their class guilt as being projected onto social stereotypes like the retired admiral or the arms manufacturer: "The bleat of the scapegoat sounds loud in their work, and the whimper of the schoolboy crying 'Please, Sir, it was the other fellow, not me'" (2:171). For her, that generation is fatally marred by self-consciousness: "That, perhaps, is why they create no characters" (2:171).

Ironically, this is exactly the same charge that Bennett had brought against Woolf and her generation. Instead of creating characters, she charges, the young writers of the 1930s have been "great egotists" (2:177), and have for that reason produced better autobiographies than poems, novels, or plays. For her, this honesty in facing unpleasant facts about themselves (though this seems to contradict the earlier point about their scapegoat-hunting) will be their major contribution to the next generation, the post-war generation, who she hopes will inherit a classless Britain where the tower of privilege has been razed. Using a similar historicist argument to the one in "Mr Bennett and Mrs Brown," she sees them as a transitional generation whose aesthetic faults are mitigated by their historical situation. This double verdict is created by the crucial reversal of viewpoint in the essay: from looking *at* them to looking *with* them. She gives them both a symptomatic and an apparently sympathetic reading, though the implications of the "sympathy" are almost more devastating. Her general hostility is clearly shown, perhaps in response to attacks on her own fiction as embodying a privileged class outlook. Here she hits back by taking the perspective of the culturally excluded (to which she was entitled by gender, but not in class terms), and she also avoids the charge that she is displaying mere conservative hostility to the younger generation by appealing over their heads to a still younger one: the unborn inheritors of the Welfare State.

This essay, like the "Mr Bennett and Mrs Brown" essay, presents an intriguing mixture of partisanship and detachment. In both Woolf ultimately validates the viewpoint of herself and her generation against the flanking ones of Bennett and Auden (significantly, those two generations never appear in the same survey, perhaps because Bennett and Wells would have upset the "privileged education" hypothesis about English writers). Her technique is to include the alien viewpoint through imaginative reconstruction and quotation (from Bennett's *Hilda Lessways* and MacNeice's *Autumn Journal*), but to frame it with her own more persuasively presented outlook. The historicist arguments appear to be neutral or sympathetic (they encourage us to understand the writer's background in the 1910s or the 1930s) but instead of making the period's literature look better they sometimes make the period itself look worse by merging the works with their drab and unpleasant backgrounds. Instead of historical sympathy increasing aesthetic sympathy, the reverse happens: aesthetic distaste becomes historical distaste. Thus we reject the Victorian Midlands along with Bennett, and 1930s) London along with Louis MacNeice. The only hope is the post-war generation, and Woolf's faith in it was justified to the extent that Bloomsbury and Modernism in general enjoyed a great vogue in the 1960s and 1970s, largely at the expense of the 1930s writers.

Even in these literary polemics, the basic feature of Woolf's essays remains the juxtaposition of viewpoints. She seeks not only to express her own (or, as she often puts it, "our" own) viewpoint, but also to re-imagine the world from another perspective, historical, cultural, or individual. Obviously, it is easier to sympathize when the "other" viewpoint is not a directly threatening rival to one's own, but in those cases other problems created by historical distance loom correspondingly larger. With Bennett or MacNiece, the difficulty is to sympathize; with remoter figures, the problem is to understand. For Woolf, the context of history, class, and culture is necessary for either sympathy or understanding. Yet this context is not an end in itself: the end is the living individual. She does not make a sharp distinction between the vision embodied in a written work and the character of its writer, and often treats the first as an expression of the second. For her, text and context are both relevant largely for the sake of the individual self. All of her essays are basically characterizations, and there is a greater ease and intimacy in her portraits of individuals than in the various group portraits we have been looking at, despite the vital role they play in her critical perspective. For her essays, the justification of history is to produce interesting individuals. The moment of this sudden coming to life, like the sudden coalescence of a likeness in the course of a portrait, is almost magical, and makes all the dullness and alienness of the 1930s writing of the past worth tolerating.

Woolf describes such a moment in "The Strange Elizabethans": "something fitfully and doubtfully emerges from the violent pages, the voluminous arguments – the figure of a man, the outline of a face, somebody who is not 'an Elizabethan' but an interesting, complex, and individual human being" (3:38). This emergence resembles the apparition of the strange and wonderful moths in the light of the children's lamp in "Reading." Here, Gabriel Harvey is the individual who comes to life and steps out of his historical "background" by means of various illuminations that we catch from his commonplace book and other sources. In her essays of this type, on minor historical figures, Woolf takes the viewpoint almost of a naturalist, "finding them off their guard and so becoming at ease with them" (3:33). In her 1939 essay "White's Selborne" she takes the perspective of an ornithologist on the ornithologist himself, to good comic effect, just as she turned the Marxist – Freudian weapons of the 1930s writers back on them to good polemical effect. Here, after quoting White on identifying the distinguishing features of natural species, she writes: "But when the bird happens to be Gilbert White himself, when we try to discriminate the colour and shape of this very rare fowl, we are at a loss" (3:122). This reversal of viewpoints provides the running metaphor for the essay, and by the end Woolf has succeeded in paradoxically identifying him by his very aloofness, his independence from his habitat: "he escapes from Selborne, from his own age, and comes winging his way to us in the dusk along the hedgerows. A critical owl? A parson with the wings of a bird? A hybrid?" She finally identifies him with his own description of a kestrel, once again turning the observer's observation back on to himself. Always she includes another viewpoint; her essay "Lord Chesterfield's Letters to His Son," after spending most of the time on the noble letter-writer, ends with an affectionate sketch of the poor recipient, who began to receive these disquisitions when he was only 7 years old, and failed more or less completely to make the career all this advice should have amply prepared him for.

This sympathy for, and interest in, the ordinary lives of the past, as well as the "great" ones, parallels Woolf's concern for "the common reader" as well as for the great critic. All of these viewpoints have worth, even if not equal worth. Woolf allows that a great deal of reading is motivated by simple curiosity about people's lives in the present and the past. Many of her essays are about very minor figures who have left some written testimony about themselves, for which she would never claim high literary quality. Here, the challenge is quite different from that of the classic, where the reader subjects himself to a fully ordered and fully unified imaginative vision. With minor literature, the challenge is to reanimate the past by seizing on the glimpses it occasionally offers amidst otherwise dull or stilted prose:

> Every literature, as it grows old, has its rubbish-heap, its record of vanished moments and forgotten lives told in faltering and feeble accents that have perished. But if you give yourself up to the delight of rubbish-reading you will be surprised, indeed you will be overcome, by the relics of human life that have been cast out to moulder. It may be one letter – but what a vision it gives! (2:5)

Neglected figures and neglected genres – diaries, letters, biographies, autobiographies, and, of course, essays – are the subjects of more than half of Woolf's essays, and her chronological arrangement of her two *Common Reader* volumes mixes them in with the major writers and genres to produce an effect very different from, say, F. R. Leavis's *The Great Tradition* or T. S. Eliot's *Selected Essays*. Woolf does offer evaluative judgments of major authors, but her delight in the indubitably minor (for which she does not make great literary claims) separates her essayistic approach to criticism from the academic approach, and places her with Lamb and Orwell (both of whom liked to write on "neglected" authors) rather than with Arnold, Eliot, and Leavis. She does not have the canonical urge as a critic; despite her respect for the classics, she has an equally strong "spirit of curiosity" which she sees as going with "a taste for bad books" (2:37), whether of the present or of the past. Ultimately, this is because the great do not have a monopoly on individuality, though they may express it more powerfully and completely. To ignore, as a reader, the vast multiplicity of lesser viewpoints on existence, would be for Woolf a tremendous impoverishment. In some ways, too, the suspension of strict literary value-judgments is a liberation for other kinds of interest in reading. The satisfaction of curiosity about the past is one pleasure of the "common reader" which can be independent of aesthetic value, and it is a pleasure celebrated in some of Woolf's best essays.

Despite the focus on individuality in her vision, Woolf did not see it as something fixed and easily described or felt, either for the individual himself or for the observer. Closeness can blur the picture as much as distance; time brings subtle or dramatic changes. It seems natural that Woolf was drawn to Montaigne and his vision of the self in flux. Her essay "Montaigne" starts from his notion of self-portraiture, its fascination and difficulty, both for its artist and its viewers. Montaigne's self-portrait has taken on aspects of a mirror for those who study it: "As the centuries go by, there is always a crowd before that picture, gazing into its depths, seeing their own faces reflected in it, seeing more the longer they look, never being able to say quite what it is that they see" (3:18). The portrait gives us one self as seen by another, forming a triangle of viewpoints if the spectator is included. But with the self-portrait, the spectator takes the viewpoint of the self-observing self. We catch the look the artist originally cast at himself: hence the uneasy feeling of intimacy it can create, unlike the more social "look" of an ordinary portrait.

Woolf is now no longer simply observing another self, as in her other essays, but observing a *self-observing* self. As if to dramatize this, she personifies Montaigne's "soul" (his self-as-object) as "she," so that Montaigne seems to be looking back at "her" (his "soul" almost seeming to be appropriated by Woolf's female self). Montaigne's tower becomes Woolf's room of "her" own: "But watch her as she broods over the fire in the inner room of that tower which, though detached from the main building, has so wide a view over the estate" (3:20). The tower here, and Montaigne's lordly proprietorial gaze, do not have the negative connotations of "The Leaning Tower." Instead, this tower looks open to all as an ideal of retirement, as Montaigne seems to "advise us to withdraw to the inner room of our tower and there turn the pages of books" (3:20). Yet immediately Woolf identifies a counter-movement in Montaigne's thought: country life is dull, he gets bored reading, he can't remember what he has read. She recapitulates his thinking on a variety of issues through this pattern of movement and reaction: the common people are closer to reality, but on the other hand they are vile and ignorant; freedom is essential, yet so is restraint; and so on. Woolf moves beyond paraphrase and seems to take over Montaigne's voice, expressing his/her views in her own language:

> Observe how the soul is always casting her own lights and shadows; makes the substantial hollow and the frail substantial; fills the broad daylight with dreams; is as much excited by phantoms as by reality; and in the moment of death sports with a trifle. (3:25)

In re-portraying Montaigne's self-portrait, Woolf's self-image seems to merge with his and the picture becomes a mirror; the two selves, and two likenesses, coalesce, and their views of existence briefly merge.

This is an unusually intense moment in her published essays, where the subjective lyricism is usually contained by a basically urbane conversational manner. A quite different tone, or range of tones, characterizes her autobiographical essays, published posthumously in the collection *Moments of Being*, though some of the papers published by Leonard Woolf in the four-volume *Collected Essays* could be considered semi-autobiographical

("Reading," for example, the essay discussed earlier). The difference of tone could be expressed socially as "Mrs Woolf" for *The Times Literary Supplement* (though in fact the reviews were anonymous) versus "Virginia" for the memoirs. The first, or "public" tone she attributes to her being brought up to play the "Victorian game of manners": "But the Victorian manner is perhaps – I am not sure – a disadvantage in writing. When I reread my old *Common Reader* articles I detect it there. I lay the blame for their suavity, their politeness, their side-long approach, to my tea-table training" (*MB* 151). The essays in *Moments of Being* are mostly occasional pieces for family and friends: "Reminiscences" is a 37-page letter to her nephew, Julian Bell, about the youth of his mother, Virginia's sister Vanessa; "22 Hyde Park Gate," "Old Bloomsbury," and "Am I a Snob?" are contributions read to the Memoir Club, which consisted essentially of the so-called Bloomsbury Group. Woolf had, as she was aware, a highly developed sense of audience, and her self-presentation to intimates is much freer and franker than to the hypothetical common reader sitting across the tea-table. These are all rich and fascinating essays, but her most intimate expression of her youthful experience is the 85-page "A Sketch of the Past," written near the end of her life as an intermittent respite from her taxing work on her life of Roger Fry. At times it approaches a dialogue between her past and present selves.

Despite its unpolished and probably unfinished state, "A Sketch of the Past" deserves to be acknowledged as a classic of Modernism, as well as of the autobiographical essay. In some respects it is comparable to Joyce's *Portrait of the Artist as a Young Man* (1916), in that the child's view is often imaginatively recreated through a childlike simplicity of language in the earlier parts, and develops in complexity with the child's growth. Another similarity is the presence of epiphanies (Joyce's term) and "moments of being" (Woolf's). Formally and historically, Woolf's sketch also makes an intriguing comparison with Thomas Mann's *Doktor Faustus* (1947). Both texts cut back and forward from the "present" in which the writing is taking place (the late 1930s and early 1940s), and the writer's remembered "past" (the late nineteenth and early twentieth centuries). Mann's novel is of course much more elaborate and layered, but the basic Modernist technique of interweaving widely separate time-sequences is the same, as well as the particular historical gap involved (1900 viewed from 1940).

But these fictional parallels do not lessen the quintessentially essayistic quality of Woolf's memoir. Here we can see the aesthetic and cognitive purposes interacting in the process of "forming" a view of the self. The essay is "informal" in tone, but also in the sense that it is "on the way" to a form which it never actually completes. Like the other autobiographical essays, it is "occasioned" by someone else's request. It begins: "Two days ago – Sunday 16th April 1939 to be precise – Nessa said that if I did not start writing my memoirs I should soon be too old" (*MB* 74). Twelve pages and two weeks later, Woolf chances on the formal principle latent in that opening sentence:

> 2nd May . . . I write the date, because I think that I have discovered a possible form for these notes. That is, to make them include the present – at least enough of the present to serve as a platform to stand upon. It would be interesting to make the two people, I now, I then, come out in contrast. And further, this past is much affected by the present moment. What I write today I should not write in a year's time. (*MB* 87)

Past and present are constantly shifting in relation to each other, and we remember that T. S. Eliot's *Four Quartets* is contemporary with Woolf's memoir, and in some ways can be seen as his poetic equivalent of it, like Mann's novel. Not only his reflections on time, but also those on the continuity and discontinuity of the self, besides the musings about the relation of the act of writing to both themes, can be paralleled in Woolf's text. Yet Woolf is writing an *essay* – not even a polished, urbane, finished one, like her literary pieces. The act of composition, of making an aesthetic whole, is explicitly deferred: "Perhaps one day, relieved from making works of art, I will try to compose this" (*MB* 87). Meanwhile the work goes on as an intermittent diary, through April, May, and June 1939, a break of almost a year, and a resumption from June to November 1940. The last "entry" is 17 November 1940. Woolf committed suicide by drowning on 28 March 1941.

This end was not precisely the one foreseen in the text. During the eighteen months of its writing, Britain declared war on Germany, evacuated its army from Dunkirk, and began fighting the Battle of Britain in the air over southern England.

> The battle is at its crisis; every night the Germans fly over England:
> it comes closer to this house daily. If we are beaten then – however

we solve that problem, and one solution is apparently suicide (so it was decided three nights ago in London among us) – book writing becomes doubtful. (*MB* 116)

The text itself nearly perished before the author; she almost discarded it when clearing away her papers after finishing the life of Fry. "June 8th 1940. I have just found this sheaf of notes thrown away into my waste paper basket" (*MB* 116). At any moment the writing could be abandoned under pressure from other tasks and outside circumstances: "19th July 1939. I was forced to break off again, and rather suspect that these breaks will be the end of this memoir" (*MB* 114). Thus the text contains references to its own possible destruction, abandonment, or incompletion through its author's suicide or death of old age. Both in mood and in form it remains "uncomposed," as the fears and weariness of 1940 make a highly precarious "plat-form" to view the 1880s and 1890s. Yet the inclusion of the present through the diary form was vitally necessary, since it provided the device for the "juxtaposition of viewpoints" characteristic of her most successful essays.

The death of the author is foreshadowed in the text through her own anticipation, and outside the text through the reader's knowledge of her imminent suicide. The essay is ended by death, not by an aesthetic completion. And just as death stands at the end of the time sequence of the writing (1939–40), so it stands within the narrated time sequence (1882–1904) as the structuring element. Those years are divided into three periods by deaths: of Julia Stephen, Virginia's mother, who died on 5 May 1895; of Stella Duckworth, Julia's daughter by her first marriage, who essentially took over her mother's role in the household, and who died on 27 July 1897; and of Virginia's father, Leslie Stephen, who died on 22 February 1904. This last death is not described but clearly forms the terminus of "the seven unhappy years" (*MB* 137) following Stella's death. The deaths of the two women are as precisely dated as the diary entries, and in the case of Julia, the date of writing almost coincides with the 44th anniversary of the death. The scenes of mourning and the domestic changes that resulted are described in detail, and each of the two deaths seems to create a chasm, inaugurate a new period in Virginia's life.

The constituents of the essay are those of a novel – character, setting, and consciousness (realized in "moments" or "impress-ions"). But the three elements are presented separately, intro-

129

duced or interrupted by reflections on the time of writing, on the act of writing, on the act of recalling the past. She begins with her earliest childhood "impressions" (she uses this word in the same way as Henry James, who, incidentally, is the distant object of one of them in the essay), which are spiritually closest to her consciousness as the 57-year-old writer. Then this combination of early impressions and late reflections gradually gives way to awareness of the physical world (setting) and the social world (character); the progression recapitulates the growing awareness of the growing child, which, as it develops, is less in need of being supplemented by mature explanation. Yet these earliest "moments of being" are the key to the "self," the link between "I then" and "I now," the experiencing girl and the writing woman. This sense of identity is what eludes so many memoir writers, she says: "They leave out the person to whom the events happened" (*MB* 75). By initially emphasizing her consciousness-as-writer and her consciousness-as-child as widely different *and* strongly linked, she avoids, or rather postpones until later, the usual level of autobiographical narrative, where the tone is conditioned by an imagined "social" relationship to the reader. Here the tone is far from the tea-table, and far from conversational; the writing is intensely private, as if to forge before her death a link between her earliest and latest selves.

Yet however strong the focus is on subjectivity, the physical and social worlds are for Virginia Woolf always present: consciousness is always consciousness *of* something. The basic concept of the essay as a form is that selfhood cannot be grasped independently; it can only be *configured* with an object. Virginia's key "moments of being" are thus all "impressions" of scenes and people. Her first memories are of seeing the flowers of her mother's dress as she sat in her lap, and of lying in bed at St Ives (in the summer house rented by the Stephen family until 1895) listening to the waves behind the yellow blind and hearing the acorn on the end of its cord being drawn across the floor by the wind. In these and other early "pictures" there is in fact very little *self*-consciousness, and the object has a much greater share: "I am hardly aware of myself, but only of the sensation" (*MB* 78). Self-consciousness seems to come with her habit of looking at herself in the mirror, and the accompanying feeling of shame, along with the horror she felt at imagining or dreaming once that a hideous animal face appeared in the mirror beside hers. And bodily shame entered with Gerald Duckworth's much analysed sexual molesting of her. But the three most vital moments (at least vital to her own self-understanding) come later: a moment of violence (her brother Thoby pummelling her), of rapture (a sense of the flowerbed as connected to the "whole" of nature), and horror (the news of an acquaintance's suicide). The last incident inaugurates the death theme, while the central one introduces her artistic vocation. For her, writing is healing, making whole. It expresses her deepest philosophy of existence, "that the whole world is a work of art; that we are parts of the work of art" (*MB* 84).

This rapture, this sense of oneness with the world, usually has to confront a sense of its otherness, in particular the sense that it is a world for others, structured and ruled by them. Just as subjective sympathy is countered by objective judgment in her literary essays, in her autobiographical essays the personal viewpoint is countered by the social one. She reflects:

> Consider what immense forces society brings to play upon each of us, how that society changes from decade to decade; and also from class to class; well, if we cannot analyse these invisible presences, we know very little of the subject of the memoir; and again how futile life-writing becomes. (*MB* 93)

The last phrase is a rich one; Woolf must have been thinking of her "life" of Roger Fry, as well as her own autobiographical text, but it also unites and sums up her own life-work and working life. Her point is that "life-writing" has to balance the expansion of sympathy and imagination into the world against the hard, objective limitations that society imposes on the individual consciousness: every individual has to be seen from outside as well as from within. As we have seen, her literary portraits take into account class, culture, and historical period as limiting and situating factors; the same is true of her characterizations here.

Yet the masterstroke is that all this only becomes clear to the reader gradually, in the same way as it becomes clear to the adolescent girl. The first character sketch is of her mother, who is too close, looms too large in her life, to be seen as an individual: "I suspect the word 'central' gets closest to the general feeling I had of living so completely in her atmosphere that one never got far enough away from her to see her as a person" (*MB* 96). This distancing was only accomplished by the mature artist, Woolf states, in her novel *To the Lighthouse* written over thirty years after her mother's death. The peripheral characters, on the other hand, have the crude visibility of caricatures. Her sketches of Mr Wolstenholme, C. B. Clark, and Mr Gibbs are Dickensian, partly because that is how she saw them as a child, and "partly because I am reading Nicholas Nickleby at the moment" (*MB* 85). Gradually, between the "too close" perspective and the "distant" caricatural vision, a middle range or social focus emerges; the portrayal of Stella has a near-adult understanding of the difficulties of her position. By the time Gerald Duckworth reappears, the viewpoint is completely social, even sociological. "For he accepted Victorian society so implicitly that an archaeologist would find him of the greatest interest. Like a fossil he had taken every crease and wrinkle of the conventions of 1890–1900" (*MB* 152). The art of characterization in the "Sketch" could be seen as developing from the Dickensian mode of the childhood scenes, via the late Victorian description of a typical "society" evening (starring Gerald) in 1900, to the Modernist or Woolfian vision it began with, somewhat like the parody of English literary development in Joyce's *Ulysses*.

Places are as important to the memoir as characters. The main ones are Kensington Gardens, St Ives, and 22 Hyde Park Gate. As with the characters, there is a progression of consciousness through the series, from the child's view of the Gardens to the adolescent's view of the little society of the family's London residence (the sequence continues in the Memoir Club papers on "22 Hyde Park Gate" and "Old Bloomsbury," the latter covering the years 1904–14). These places are not described in the Bennett mode that Woolf saw as putting the buildings first; rather, they are rendered as space-times, in the Proustian manner (many of her themes are also in Proust: the mother, the seaside resort, the city parks, sexual shame, snobbery, etc.). "I see myself as a child, roaming about, in that space of time which lasted from 1882 to 1895. A great hall I could liken it to; with windows letting in strange lights; and murmurs and spaces of deep silence" (*MB* 92). The specific settings change shape and size according to the time at which they are experienced. For example, Kensington Gardens is still a changing experience for the writer in the present:

I cannot see Kensington Gardens as I saw it as a child because I saw it only two days ago – on a chill afternoon, all the cherry trees lurid in the cold yellow light of a hailstorm. I know that it was very much larger in 1890 when I was seven than it is now. (*MB* 87)

But despite the disclaimer, she recreates effectively the child-hood version of the Gardens, in juxtaposition to the recent one. The summer house in Cornwall, however, ceased to be part of her experience: "Our lease was sold . . . and St Ives vanished for ever" (*MB* 136).

The house at Hyde Park Gate Woolf sees as containing quite distinct cultures: "Two different ages confronted each other in the drawing room at Hyde Park Gate: the Victorian age; and the Edwardian age" (*MB* 147). Vanessa and Virginia confront their father and the Duckworth brothers: "We were living in say 1910; they were living in 1860" (*MB* 148). This is like a rehearsal for the Edwardians vs. Georgians battle in "Mr Bennett and Mrs Brown." Here, the two cultures occupy different zones in space – "Downstairs there was pure convention; upstairs pure intellect" (*MB* 158) – and in time, since the sisters practice their respective arts (literature and painting) during the day, but starting with tea and intensifying with the evening's activities they are forced to participate unwillingly in "society," which they view at best satirically, and at worst as simple coercion. The sequel to this in their immense relief at the light, space, and freedom of 46 Gordon Square, where the four Stephen children set up house in 1904, is vividly expressed in "Old Bloomsbury." The whole sequence is an excellent example of Woolf's gift for showing how individuals experience, passively and actively, shifts of taste and culture in terms of their actual surroundings – rooms, furniture, decor, paintings and arrangement – a succession of space-times with quite distinct atmospheres.

Although the social world is of prime importance in the memoir, the deepest unity in the essay is the pattern of "moments of being" which connect the child and woman at the beginning and end of her life. These moments are also moments of vision, amidst what she calls the "cotton wool" of everyday consciousness. The contrast is between ordinary opacity and sudden, shocking clarity. To the sense of wholeness which motivated her to be a writer corresponds a sense of transparency in reading, where the linguistic medium becomes perfectly translucent. This moment comes when Virginia is reading a poem from *The Golden Treasury* in Kensington Gardens, and suddenly understands it: "I had a feeling of transparency in words when they cease to be words and become so intensified that one seems to experience them" (*MB* 108). Life and literature thus flow into and out of each other, as do the lived past of the memoir and the present of its writing. "The past only comes back when the present runs so smoothly that it is like the sliding surface of a deep river. Then one sees through the surface to the depths" (*MB* 114). This is not the conventional image of the river of time, for the present and past are related as surface and depth simultaneously present. And the image develops from vision to immersion: "Let me then, like a child advancing with bare feet into a cold river, descend again into that stream" (*MB* 115). We cannot avoid being chilled when we read this by our knowledge of her suicide by drowning: as in the whole of the essay, the stream of life is the same as the river of death. The essay is casual, spontaneous, open to life; but is in a sense completed by the image of a death it cannot include.

8

T.S. Eliot: the process of refinement

If we accept Adorno's dictum that "the law of the innermost form of the essay is heresy" (Adorno 171), we must see the position taken up in the essays of T. S. Eliot as paradoxical. It offers a rhetoric of order and orthodoxy to a reading public which, initially at least, found it extremely *un*orthodox. Eliot's rhetoric assumes that the established majority opinion in the early twentieth century is a continuation of nineteenth-century secular liberal individualism, just as established literary taste is governed by the Romanticism and Realism of the previous century. Among other things, this situation represents the triumph of the values which brought the essay into existence: free thought, concrete observation, and belief in the reality and worth of the individual personality. What might be called "essayistic culture," and its expression in a vast literature of personal opinion, had been growing throughout the nineteenth century, and in many ways was at its peak in 1920 at the time of Eliot's first prominence. Originality, personality, individuality had become a kind of orthodoxy. So that when Eliot enters proclaiming tradition, impersonality, and orthodoxy, the effect is, in the strict sense, *para*doxical: orthodoxy and unorthodoxy have changed places. Eliot is showing his independence by reasserting *in essayistic form* many of the medieval values in opposition to which the essay arose in the first place, as we saw in Chapter 1. The structure and rhetoric of Eliot's essays are conditioned by the paradox.

The usual approach to Eliot's prose is to treat it as *criticism* or more particularly as a body of critical thought whose actual shape, a large number of scattered essays, lectures, prefaces, etc., is accidental, and not of interest in itself. This approach tends to treat these forms almost as obstacles to grasping the system as a whole. Thus a number of commentators have tried schematizing Eliot's criteria for literary value-judgments, his theory of poetic creation or his view of literary history, or the meaning of certain key terms. In some ways these commentators are rewriting Eliot in terms of a real systematizer like Northrop Frye. They participate in the academic absorption of Eliot's criticism into the organized *discipline* of literary study, in which he acquired, and still to a great extent retains, the status of a canonical authority. The phrase "as Mr Eliot has said" became a standard validating phrase in criticism by the 1950s, and Eliot did nothing to discourage this beyond the occasional affectation of modesty and surprise at the weight given to his pronouncements. (The modesty may, of course, be the genuine diffidence of someone to whom quasi-doctrinal positions are attributed, but who lacks an official academic or ecclesiastical position.) The important point here is that Eliot's early and most influential criticism is in the essay form.

It is possible, though difficult, to put together a "theory" or system out of Eliot's critical work, but he himself did not do so. He *alluded* to theory without actually creating one. Like Roland Barthes, he wrote "essays" at system, fragments of one, gestures towards one. These pieces are often barely consistent internally, and certainly not with each other, yet they constantly indicate a "whole" beyond themselves. Like Eliot's poems, they are fragments "towards" a whole that is lost or absent, and cannot be realized as such. This "essaying" of completeness, while actually remaining incomplete, accounts for much of the essays' influence on criticism and for the abundance of "completing" commentary they have invited; fully articulated systems often have less influence simply because they leave less to do, less to debate. Eliot's essays seem to offer fragments of doctrine, hints of method, and glimpses of a perspective that has not been worked out, and thus incites the work of others. Yet, by a further paradox, this work of completing and applying Eliot's ideas in turn transforms the climate of opinion in which they were heterodox, so that from being a highly individual assertion of an unfamiliar "orthodoxy" the essays become an authority for a now familiar, accepted, and genuine orthodoxy, and are cited as such in academic discourse. Their quixotic assertion of orthodoxy turned out to be self-fulfilling.

In Chapter 1 I maintained that commentary was a characteristic form of medieval discourse, and that the essay decisively broke away from this collaborative accumulation of ideas, especially through the example of Montaigne. Yet with Eliot we face the paradox of the essay as the starting-point for just such a discursive accretion: "Tradition and the Individual Talent," in particular, must be easily the most commented-on essay in English in the twentieth century. Besides its paradoxical situation in regard to literary opinion (proclaiming a heretical orthodoxy which then ceases to be heresy), paradox is built into the fabric of the essay's thought about literary history. Although poetry is the focus, the title does not specify it, and some of the ideas could equally well be discussed in relation to prose. The two main sections attack the values of originality and personality as criteria of literary merit, values which are, as we have seen, fundamental to the essay: the fresh, unprejudiced, *unliterary* account of observed reality, which is at the same time an intensely personal expression. The triumph of the values Eliot recommends instead, tradition and impersonality, may have a lot to do with the low regard in which the essay genre has been held since the 1920s. In "Tradition" and elsewhere, Eliot champions the idea of the learned and *literary* poet, well versed in the poetry of the past and even citing it as a kind of poetic authority (as Eliot himself did Dante). This figure of the learned poet naturally succeeded in academia, and in particular with the new "discipline" of English: Eliot's studious, conservative kind of poet seemed to be much more like a critic than the popular Romantic image of the poet as rebellious, spontaneous, reckless, and youthfully dead; and the conservative poet's use of literary sources provided a task for commentary as well.

The two central paradoxes of "Tradition" are that the poet is most individual when he is most aware of his predecessors, and that the poet's emotional self-expression is most powerful when it is least apparent. In the first case Eliot is arguing against the (implied) proposition that the best poets are those who differ most from their predecessors, that is to say those who enact a historical discontinuity. He asserts that those who are most aware of the past make the strongest contribution to the present. He presents the poet's mind as a passive (though carefully prepared) area within which the *poetry* of the past can enter into contact with the *history* (or soon-to-be-history) of the present. Here a quasi-Hegelian fusion of poetry and history takes place, something far more important than mere self-expression. The poet's mind is for Eliot that through which the mind of Europe or the mind of one of its nations develops in the present, and the poet's duty is to be as good a vehicle as he can for this momentous process: i.e. both learned and self-effacing. The poet's work is created at least in part out of "existing" works (Eliot uses this word rather than "past" works to situate them in the present); then, if it is accepted into the canon ("order" is Eliot's term) it causes a reshuffling or readjustment of relationships throughout the canon. Thus it both *contains* and *causes* a recombination of the elements of the literary tradition.

But this is not all. The poet's mind is also to be as far as possible a passive receptacle for recombining his own experiences, impressions, and emotions with what he has read. The most concrete example of this process is given in "The Metaphysical Poets," where Eliot is arguing that after about 1650 (this is his equivalent of Woolf's 1910, though his date marks an ending, hers a beginning, of a great creative period) poets suffered from a "dissociation of sensibility" which adversely affected their work. Yet Eliot immediately goes on to present an ideal of poetic creativity which clearly applies after 1650 as well:

> When a poet's mind is perfectly equipped for its work, it is constantly amalgamating disparate experience; the ordinary man's experience is chaotic, irregular, fragmentary. The latter falls in love, or reads Spinoza, and these two experiences have nothing to do with each other, or with the noise of a typewriter or the smell of cooking; in the mind of the poet these experiences are always forming new wholes. (*SE* 287)

It is hard to believe that this passage is not comic in intention, and in general the levity in *Selected Essays*, the extent to which it can be read as "Old Possum's Book of Practical Criticism," has been underestimated. In the Preface to *For Lancelot Andrewes* (1929) he finds it necessary, just before announcing his famous classicist–royalist–anglo-catholic triple allegiance, "to refute any accusation of playing 'possum" (*FLA* vii). One suspects that Eliot sometimes "ventured" things like this to see whether the English literary world would "buy" them or not. In this case, everyone appears to have done so, though perhaps if they had tried to imagine the resulting poem they would have realized the absurdity of making a "whole" out of these items, other than through a parody of Eliot himself. It is obvious (at least to me) that "the poet" and "the ordinary man" are one and the same (not many ordinary men read Spinoza, nor do many poets), and further, that both are Eliot himself. It is another of Eliot's oblique self-revelations, like those in the poetry, as explicated in such books as *T. S. Eliot's Personal Waste Land*, by James Miller. Another prose example, potentially tragic rather than comic in tone, is the hint at personal suffering in "Tradition and the Individual Talent":

> Poetry is not a turning loose of emotion, but an escape from emotion; it is not the expression of personality, but an escape from personality. But, of course, only those who have personality and emotions know what it means to want to escape from these things. (*SE* 21)

Here the romantic figure of the suffering poet is rejected, but then reappears in the distance. His self-pity is not to be inflicted on his readers, but we are to sense its existence.

Both in the form and the content of the "Tradition" essay we confront the paradox of personal impersonality. Eliot's tone is one of aloof authority and doctrinal pronouncement. But what is he "authoritative" about? The process by which experiences become poems. How can anyone pronounce on this other than from personal experience? What grounds can he have for contradicting Wordsworth's formula for poetic creation, "emotion recollected in tranquillity," other than the fact that it does not correspond to his own experience of composition? The abstract figure he calls "the poet" is himself. The whole essay is a personal confession disguised as impersonal doctrine. It is a piece of ventriloquy: the suffering poet speaks through the mouth of the doctrinal critic, impersonating his impersonality. Despite this tone, the material of the essay is typical of the genre: personal observation and self-observation. It is also worth noting than when he turns to consider other poets, he does not stick to his precept that "Honest criticism and sensitive appreciation is directed not upon the poet but upon the poetry" (*SE* 17). Eliot's essays on Dante and Baudelaire use their quasi-autobiographical prose (the *Vita Nuova* and the *Journaux intimes*) as essential complements to the poetry, though especially in Dante's case this use is hedged around with fine distinctions. The "disguised confession" is a genre that clearly intrigued him, and which he practiced himself.

For Eliot, the creative faculty is passive, both on the historical level (tradition revitalizes and re-totalizes itself through the new poet) and on the individual level (disparate experiences combine into poetic wholes in the poet's mind). The active, conscious side is critical, and consists in selection and rejection, whether performed by the critic on the poetic tradition or by the poet on his own work. Passive recombination of (mostly) existing material is followed by active, critical judgment of it. In "The Function of Criticism" Eliot maintains that the important work is not so much "appreciation" as judgment, and he praises Middleton Murry for realizing that "now and then one must actually reject something and select something else" (*SE* 26). He also avers that the critical work of the poet, sifting through and revising his writing, has been much underestimated. Eliot minimizes the role of creative originality in art. For him, the poet moves directly from being a crucible to being a critic, from passive vehicle to active judge.

When certain forms of writing lose their authority in society, they are reassigned to the category of "literature"; no longer doctrine, they become "prose" or "prose style." We noted this phenomenon earlier, in discussing the seventeenth century. The same thing may be about to happen with Eliot's essays; if so, my analysis is a contribution to the process. Eliot's doctrinal status has until now occluded his prose artistry, his skill as an essayist, which includes playing with doctrinal tone and content. But if we view his essays as art, we see at once how well they exemplify his poetic. If we take "poetry" in the wide sense of the German *Dichtung* (the nearest equivalent in English would be the lame phrase "creative writing"), we could include his essays as well. In its language and rhetoric, the prose performs both functions Eliot assigns to Poetry and poems: *recombination* of existing materials until a "fusion" is produced, and *criticism*, the selection or rejection of the results. These operations form the basis of Eliot's "style."

Before demonstrating this in detail, we have to take into account another influence: the language of philosophy. In the Preface to his doctoral dissertation *Knowledge and Experience in the Philosophy of F. H. Bradley* Eliot wrote, "My own prose style was formed on that of Bradley" (quoted in Wollheim, *On Art and the Mind*, 220). The philosophical influence does not have to be confined to Bradley, however. A general feature of philosophical writing is the repeated use of certain words and phrases, only put into a slightly different form or relationship each time. Eliot's poetry also uses this effect in certain passages, but either abandons the train of thought in a suggestive way, or draws it into a religious style of repetition as incantation, where the echoing phrases produce a mystical resonance rather than a philosophical precision. The latter, the obtaining of a precise formulation of a proposition, is ostensibly the goal of the prose. But Eliot is writing essays, not philosophy. As we saw in Chapter 1, essays do not belong to disciplinary discourses, of which philosophy is one example. (Although there are some essayistic philosophers, like Nietzsche, and some philosophers who have switched to writing essays, like Heidegger, they are exceptions, and Bradley is not in exception.) So what happens when a disciplinary style (here philosophical) is used for essayistic (i.e. partly *aesthetic*) purposes? The result is very powerful, and in fact becomes the basis for a new *disciplinary* discourse: not "Philosophy," but "English." Not only did Eliot's essays become canonical sources for citation, they also provided much of the tone and many of the characteristic sentence structures of literary criticism for at least the half-century following "Tradition and the Individual Talent," just as *The Waste Land* pervaded the poetry of that period.

In the typical Eliot essay ("Tradition" is paradigmatic here) the two phases of poetic production, recombination and selection/rejection, operate together. There is a small number of conceptual counters (in "Tradition" they include "personality," "emotion," "the poet," "the present," the past," etc.) which are constantly being related to each other in different ways, from slightly different to completely opposite ways. The verb which most often relates them is the verb "to be": the thought proceeds by equations of the type "x is (not) y." This produces the same kind of reshuffling and reordering that Eliot attributes to the "tradition," except that there does appear to be a goal here, a progress towards precision. This progress is made by the discarding of erroneous or imprecise notions and formulations. The characteristic method for doing this is the distinction, the recurrent *not . . . but* structure which Eliot bequeathed to two generations of critics. This structure performs the same work of *rejection/selection* that Eliot assigns to the great "reordering" critic who appears in each century: Johnson, Arnold, Eliot (the critics themselves are selected very stringently). Combined with the equation, the distinction produces the typical sentence "It is not x, but y" (the "it is" pattern was another legacy to academic criticism). Here is a passage from "Dante":

> You are not called upon to believe what Dante believed, for your belief will not give you a groat's worth more of understanding and appreciation; but you are called upon more and more to understand it. If you can read poetry as poetry, you will 'believe' in Dante's theology exactly as you believe in the physical reality of his journey; that is, you suspend both belief and disbelief. I will not deny that it may be in practice easier for a Catholic to grasp the meaning, in many places, than for the ordinary agnostic; but that is not because the Catholic believes, but because he has been instructed. It is a matter of knowledge and ignorance, not of belief or scepticism. (*SE* 258)

The basic point is that Catholic belief isn't necessary to appreciate the *Divine Comedy*, but Catholic training might help to understand it. More or less the opposite thought is expressed in a parallel negative/positive hortation in *Four Quartets*: "You are not here to verify,/ Instruct yourself, or inform curiosity/ Or carry report. You are here to kneel/ Where prayer has been valid" ("Little Gidding," lines 43–6). In the prose, the belief/ understanding antithesis is developed through two not/but distinctions (in the first and third sentences), one conditional (in the second sentence – the "if/then" formation is another common academic-critical one), and a final distinction/ equation: it is x, not y (here the positive precedes the negative). A form of the word "belief" occurs eight times, even though the idea is finally discarded. A very precise rejection and a very precise selection have been achieved. Catholics have an advantage, but not the advantage you think (the context here is the whole 1930s debate about whether the reader needs to believe the author's creed to appreciate his work): Catholics have more *knowledge*.

Just as the religious *via negativa* figures prominently in Eliot's poetry, so in his essays negative propositions occupy as much space as positive ones. The negative is included to be discarded, so that the reader is shown first error, then the true way. The essayist is the author's guide, his Virgil helping the Dantean pilgrim not to stray from the true path. Eliot's reader follows a process of refinement or purgation, rejecting error and selecting truth. One sentence from Eliot's essay on Pascal sums up the paradox of the Christian essay (if such a thing can exist) as a personal search for truth rather than an official announcement of it: "The Christian thinker – and I mean the man who is trying consciously and conscientiously to explain to himself the sequence which culminates in faith, rather than the public apologist – proceeds by rejection and elimination" (*SE* 408). The sentence itself, with the parenthetic distinction which refines the notion of the "Christian thinker," perfectly enacts the essay-process, which is elsewhere expressed in the title of *Notes Towards the Definition of Culture*, giving a sense both of exploration and of a fixed goal. For Eliot, to define is to refine: one of his favourite lines from Dante follows Arnaut Daniel's speech in Provençal in *Purgatorio* XXVI: "Poi s'ascose nel foco che gli affina" ("then he withdrew into the flame that refines them [the sinners]"). Eliot quotes it in *The Waste Land* as well as in the "Dante" essay. The idea of refining precious metal out of dross is one of Eliot's key metaphors for poetic creation, and it applies equally to his prose as it rejects the inferior and even the approximate in favor of the true essence, the pure gold of the precisely formulated conclusion. The conceptual elements shift and recombine until the new compound is fused.

Eliot's own attempt at unifying his prose and creating a kind of canon from his own work is the volume of *Selected Essays*, which could in some ways be seen as a prose equivalent of *Four Quartets*. Both consist of fragments of an unrealized order, though the poem is of course far more unified on the level of theme and symbol. *Selected Essays* applied to Eliot's own prose the process he saw as the function of criticism in general, the selection of a canon by the rejection of anything inferior; we can imagine a sheaf of *Rejected Essays* as well. As with the general literary canon, the selection is subject to change: the 1932 edition was substantially expanded in 1951 to include most of the 1936 volume *Essays Ancient and Modern*, with the significant exception of "Catholicism and the International Order." This collection was in turn based on *For Lancelot Andrewes* (1929), "omitting two papers with which I was dissatisfied, on Machiavelli and on Crashaw" (*EAM* 5). Thus Eliot regularly reshuffled (or "reordered") his essays in a way strongly reminiscent of the "simultaneous order" of literary works in "Tradition and the Individual Talent," where the new work compels a repatterning of the existing canon. Even the grounds for selecting and recombining the essays seem to change: Eliot remarks in the Preface to *Essays Ancient and Modern* (1936), that, in contrast to the "unity" he had claimed for the collection *For*

Lancelot Andrewes, "I offer this book, as the title implies, only as a miscellaneous collection, having no greater unity than that of having been written by the same person" (*EAM* 7).

Selected Essays does, however, possess a clear architecture, and offers something more like an "impersonal order" than the personal miscellany of *Essays Ancient and Modern*. The 1932 edition's structure is preserved in the 1951 edition; the only difference is the addition of all the essays but one from *Essays Ancient and Modern*, demonstrating how the apparently miscellaneous pieces could be successfully ordered. The seven sections cover Eliot's areas of interest as follows: theory, poetic drama, Elizabethan drama, Dante, post-Elizabethan English poetry, religion, and a final "mixed prose" category containing essays on criticism, philosophy, fiction, and autobiography (the Baudelaire essay is a review of his *Journaux intimes*). This forms a kind of "ring" structure, from the peripheral topics of criticism and prose to the central topic of poetry. At the very centre, the only essay to have a whole section to itself, is the essay on Dante, which is itself divided into three parts, like the *Divine Comedy*. Only the parts don't correspond: Eliot's divisions are "The *Inferno*," "The *Purgatorio* and the *Paradiso*," and "The *Vita Nuova*." The centre of the essay and the almost exact centre of *Selected Essays* is Dante's vision of cosmic order in the *Paradiso*: "I saw ingathered, bound by love in one mass, the scattered leaves of the universe, substance and accidents and their relations, as though together fused, so that what I speak of is one simple flame" (quoted in *SE* 267). This moment of unity is clearly one source of inspiration for the end of *Four Quartets*, but it also "gathers in" some themes of Eliot's prose, such as refinement, fusion, and unity, and thus appropriately stands in the centre of the order of his prose. In a way this kind of ordering runs against the essayistic spirit: one can't imagine Montaigne imposing this kind of structure on his book, and in fact the *Essais* clearly reveal the organic, unplanned growth of the book. Another contrast is with Virginia Woolf's habit of arranging the pieces in chronological order of topic in her essay collections, reflecting her basically historicist perspective, just as Eliot's plan reflects his anti-historicist "simultaneous order" of literature.

We have seen various ways in which Eliot both uses and tries to escape the personal and provisional character of the essay through his gestures towards doctrine and system. This results in the paradoxical *essaying* of an authoritative, disciplinary discourse without actually delivering it. Now it is time to look at the content of some of the essays: how does the "impersonal" theory work confronted with the actual writer, whose distinct individuality was the goal of the literary essays of Hazlitt, James, and Woolf, and of essayistic criticism in general? It is worth noting that Eliot's studies are at least titularly focused on authors rather than works; "Hamlet" and "In Memoriam" are the only exceptions in *Selected Essays*. But even so, the sense of concrete individual character never really comes through; Virginia Woolf's approach through historical and personal empathy produces this effect much more. Eliot the strict judge is always present in the tone of his assessments, and the figures who come before him seem too inhibited by the courtroom atmosphere really to come to life. Somehow they resent being "simultaneously ordered." They are being judged as specimens of the abstract figure first introduced in "Tradition": the Poet. True to his theory there, Eliot does not single out the unique or *differentiating* features of each writer in the way Woolf does, and as a result most of them sound like variants of the same figure, like the composite poet of "Little Gidding," or like ghosts of Eliot himself.

What *is* different for Eliot is the Age from which each poet has to choose his material. But Eliot does not try to evoke, like Woolf, the lived reality of the period; he presents it as an intellectual and aesthetic problem which the poets have to solve. Eliot talks about them as if they were students facing examination questions, and finding themselves either lucky or unlucky with what is presented to them. Dante was luckier than Shakespeare, for example: "The difference between Shakespeare and Dante is that Dante had one coherent system of thought behind him; but that was just his luck" (*SE* 136). Massinger too was "as a comic writer, fortunate in the moment at which he wrote" (*SE* 216). Baudelaire had to confront "an age of bustle, programmes, platforms, scientific progress, humanitarianism and revolutions which improved nothing, an age of progressive degradation" (*SE* 427). Finally, Joyce (and by implication Eliot) has to deal with "the immense panorama of futility and anarchy which is contemporary history" ("*Ulysses*, Order, and Myth," 2626). The perspective is of increasing disorder in society, which sets more and more difficult problems of aesthetic ordering for the artist. Hence the importance of the solution Joyce come up with, what Eliot calls the "mythical method," and judges to be "a step towards making the modern world possible for art" (2626). Eliot's poets do not live as characters but have significance as "cases" of the problem of the poet's relation to history and philosophy, just as the "Ages" they have to deal with are described negatively in terms of their difficulties for the creative artist. They have to struggle, like the argument of an Eliot essay, slowly and painfully through a mire of negativity, or (to change the metaphor) suffer the refining fire which will make gold out of the dross of history. The struggle for artistic purity is quasi-religious, a struggle against the character of the age and of the poet, both of which are ideally overcome in the work. History and personality are never seen as vital or inspirational, but as things to be purged or transcended.

Eliot's reconstructions of the situations of his poets operate, like his typical sentence structures, through oppositions and paradoxes. His view of history is non-progresssive and non-dialectical. Each Poet confronts his Age as a fixed, static space within which he has to work, and though each Poet is set harder and harder problems to solve, we are given no clues as to why or how this happens. Each Age and Nation has a Mind, which together constitute the Mind of Europe, but its workings remain mysterious. We only know that it increasingly fails to do its job of providing the Poet with a coherent Order, forcing him to take on the task himself. In his later essays, Eliot saw Religion rather than Mind as the only possible way of ordering the chaos of modernity and preparing it for the artist. That religion was Catholicism specifically. Eliot's answer to the problems of the 1930s was the Dantesque political program of "the reunion of Christendom" (*EAM* 113), expounded in "Catholicism and International Order." Originally, this was an address to the Anglo-Catholic Summer School of Sociology at Oxford in 1933, and was the only paper in *Essays Ancient and Modern* not reprinted in the 1951 edition of *Selected Essays*. Here he dismisses the League of Nations as the product of the "exaggerated faith in human reason to which people of undisciplined emotions are prone" (*EAM* 120), brands as "heretics" a wide range of political positions (fascists and communists, rationalists and democrats), and recommends "the conversion of the whole world" to Catholicism (*EAM* 123). This essay is the key expression of Eliot's aesthetic politics, that is, the judgment of political systems and societal organizations by the art they produce or make possible. Since Dante's *Divine Comedy* is the most perfect work of art, the "order" which produced it must be preferable, Eliot implies. There is a further hint that Eliot the Poet could have approached Dante if his social and intellectual world had been as well ordered; Eliot approved the suggestion that Baudelaire was a "fragmentary Dante" (*SE* 420), and the same phrase could well apply to himself.

Chaos and order, fragment and whole: these opposites confront each other at every level of Eliot's essays. The chaos of individual consciousness (Spinoza, cooking-smells, typing noise, love) is ordered into a Poem. This is a passive, almost random occurrence, however; the poet can prepare himself for it by education and receptivity, but cannot make it happen. The reshaping of the literary Tradition to find a place for the new Individual Talent is also imaged as a recombination of chemical elements resulting from the addition of a new one. Other examples of Eliotean Order, however, are *willed*, and correspond in religion to the discipline of prayer rather than the unpredictable gift of grace. The poet's critical faculty has to go to work on the gratuitous recombination his sensibility has offered him. Similarly Eliot offers an active image, as well as the passive, chemical one, of the reformation of tradition as the task of a critic, judging, selecting, and rejecting. The active images of creation and criticism tend to predominate in the later essays: the chaos of modern society is willed into *aesthetic* order by the mythic imagination of the artist, which performs for the present what the critical judgment does for the creativity of the past. Society itself, now hopelessly fragmented, can only be reordered, according to Eliot's later prose, especially *Notes Towards the Definition of Culture*, through a reunited and reinstituted Christendom. The idea of order in Eliot is always under pressure from the sense of chaos, and the prose as much as the poetry gives the impression of emotional disintegration being fought by an intellectual will to control and composure and authority.

Eliot's ideal of order, as opposed to what he could actually accomplish, is static, inorganic, and hierarchic. This ideal is perfectly expressed in the *Divine Comedy*, where "every degree of the feeling of humanity, from lowest to highest, has, moreover, an intimate relation to the next above and below, and all fit together according to the logic of sensibility" (*SE* 269). Eliot stresses the completeness of the scale, the presence of every intermediate phase between absolute good and absolute evil. In the absence of this completeness (beginning with the "dissociation of sensibility" and ending with the "chaos" of modernity), the will to order has to find substitutes. But Eliot completely rejects modern forms of totalization; he rejects the Marxist and the Freudian forms of "totalization from below" for the Dantesque "totalization from above." Typically, he places them in absolute opposition: "Either everything in man can be traced as a development from below, or something must come from above" (*SE* 485), and rejects the Freudian *low* dream in favour of the Dantesque *high* dream (*SE* 262), and the Marxist base/superstructure model of society in favour of a hierarchic culture unified and *explained* by its religious faith.

What are the substitutes Eliot finds for the Dantesque order? They are, in poetry, as we have seen, the *juxtaposition* of fragments according to a mythic or symbolic "method," and the *fusion* of disparate experiences into new wholes. This can even happen on the level of personality, as in the case of Pascal (for Eliot a figure comparable to Donne and nearly as important for him): "Pascal is a man of the world among ascetics, and an ascetic among men of the world; he had the knowledge of worldliness and the passion of asceticism, and in him the two are fused into an individual whole" (*SE* 411). In prose and thought, the *opposition* is the key device. It is created by eliminating precisely the plenitude of intermediate categories Eliot valued in Dante, and by producing a direct confrontation between the extremes. Eliot's profoundly anti-dialectical way of thinking constantly eliminates transitions, gradations and middle terms. We saw how the essence of his style was to formulate and then reject *neighbouring* ideas to his own; approximations of it are more dangerous to him than direct opposition. In politics and religion it is easy to see how churches and parties worry more about positions that are *close* to theirs, and hence blur or dilute them, than about those which are overtly hostile: doctrinal purity is at stake, and must be defended with precision. As with Eliot's style, so with his content: once the approximations have been refined away, a stark opposition is left. This is not resolved by dialectical means, but by either a *choice* or a *paradox*. In the first case the alternatives are presented as *mutually exclusive*; in the second as *mutually enhancing.* Eliot's essays contain many examples of both, and both were duly bequeathed to later critical writing.

Let us take the *choice* first. On sex (from the "Dante" essay): "the love of man and woman (or for that matter man and man) is only explained and made reasonable by the higher love, or else is simply the coupling of animals" (*SE* 274). Eliot's attacks on Humanism largely characterize it as a temporary transitional phase between Christian faith and atheistic materialism, and hence as a confusing and blurring of the choice: "There is no avoiding the dilemma: you must either be a naturalist or a supernaturalist" (*SE* 485). Eliot even manages to imply that there is something unmanly about not facing up to these stark choices, something cowardly about taking mediating positions: "Baudelaire was man enough for damnation" (*SE* 429), as opposed to the ordinary modern man (a recurring stereotype in Eliot's essays as in his poems) who has no spiritual life at all. He writes: "it is better, in a paradoxical way, to do evil than to do nothing: at least, we exist" (*SE* 429).

Paradox, as we have seen in analyzing the "Tradition" essay, is the other basic way of resolving the oppositions, and Eliot's favourite form of it is where the opposites are mutually enhancing. In the essay on "Andrew Marvell," for example, we read of that poet's "alliance of levity and seriousness (by which the seriousness is intensified)" (*SE* 296). Similarly, in Chapman and Donne Eliot finds "a direct sensuous apprehension of thought, or a recreation of thought into feeling" (*SE* 286). Later in the same essay ("The Metaphysical Poets") he states that Tennyson and Browning "do not feel their thought as immediately as the odour of a rose" (*SE* 287), again bringing what are normally seen as opposites (thought and sensation) into direct contact by eliminating the usual mediating idea of emotion, though the ambiguous use of the word feeling (which could mean sensation or emotion) blurs the issue somewhat. For a final example, he sees Dante's local roots as *enhancing* his Europeanness, not detracting from it: "the localization ('Florentine' speech) seems if anything to emphasize the universality, because it cuts across the modern division of nationality" (*SE* 239). Once again the opposites are enhanced by the elimination of the middle term. Eliot seems to dislike mediations, transitions, and triads: his characteristic literary judgment is "Dante and Shakespeare divide the modern world between them; there is no third" (*SE* 265).

The individual paradoxes in the essays reinforce the paradoxical quality of Eliot's essay-writing as a whole. This quality has two main forms: the first is their status as fragments of an order that is never realized. In the "Dante" essay he writes "Let us entertain the theory that . . ." (*SE* 274), and this perfectly conveys the spirit of all his essays and their "towards" quality. What distinguishes them from the other essays we have considered is that they are "towards" doctrine, system, theory, authority: even though they are not themselves doctrinal pronouncements, a discipline grew up around the theories they "entertain." The second paradoxical aspect is that the "impersonal" and abstract quality of Eliot's case-studies of poets is partly due to their personal significance to him as versions of his own situation. Somehow he fails to seize the otherness of other writers' work through failing to present his own personality more openly; this would enable the *difference* to emerge. But true to his precept in "Tradition," he eschews the definition of a writer's distinctiveness as an essayistic goal. Instead, he uses them as articulations or allegories of himself, as "objective correlatives" (or "objectives correlative" – which is the noun?) for "Eliot and his Problems," to adapt the original title of his "Hamlet" essay.

The contrast with Virginia Woolf's essays makes much of this clear, particularly when the two authors discuss similar subjects, like the Elizabethans. Her approach draws attention to the concrete and cultural differences between her viewpoint and theirs, and uses this to enhance our sense of both. Fundamentally, she is a "both/and" thinker in the line of Montaigne, where Eliot is an "either/or" thinker in the tradition of Pascal, as is shown in their respective essays on their preferred writer. Woolf's "Montaigne" celebrates the acceptance of both sides of a contradiction, while Eliot's "The 'Pensées' of Pascal" emphasizes the need for choice and rejection. Eliot pays tribute here to Montaigne's skepticism, but joins Pascal in rejecting it. Contrasting Voltaire and Pascal, Eliot writes: "in the end we must all choose for ourselves between one point of view and another" (*SE* 409).

There could hardly be a stronger rejection of Montaigne's or Woolf's relativistic philosophy of the essay as the expression of double, multiple, or shifting viewpoints. Because she is more openly personal, Woolf is able to escape from her own viewpoint more effectively, while Eliot, trying to be more impersonal, lets his personal predicament show through every-thing he says about others. Her imagery of light and evanesc-ence, her visual strategies of blurring and focusing, convey her empathic approach to an author and his situation. Eliot's prose imagery draws typically on science and technology, and he deploys a rhetoric of dissociation and distinction, welding and fusion. The fact that his "hard" rhetoric of precise judgment and stern rejection prevailed in academic criticism over Woolf's "soft" rhetoric of empathy and changing viewpoint, her non-judgmental treatment of both major and minor writing as ways to imagine and recuperate the experience of other selves in other situations – this says as much about the nature of the academic discipline of "English" as it does about the respective merits of the two essayists.

9

George Orwell: myth and counter-myth

T. S. Eliot's great creative decade as an essayist (from "Tradition and the Individual Talent" in 1919 to "Dante" in 1929) roughly coincided with the 1920s. For George Orwell, the equivalent decade was the 1940s (Hazlitt's was the 1820s; perhaps essayists peak in the decade in which they turn forty). Apart from five brief "documentary" pieces from "The Spike" (1931) to "Marrakech" (1939), Orwell's major achievement in the essay runs from "Charles Dickens" in 1939 to "Writers and Leviathan" in 1948, including autobiographical and critical essays as well as pieces on literature, culture, and society and their interrelations. This period coincides with the hiatus in Orwell's career as a novelist between *Coming Up For Air* (1939) and *Nineteen Eighty-Four* (1949); during these ten years the only fiction he wrote was the fable *Animal Farm* (1945). The effect of the war years and their immediate aftermath was clearly to make the essay his main form of expression, and his production in it certainly bears the pressure of the time and its issues. However, Orwell did not write documentary prose about the war; his work in that genre (including *The Road to Wigan Pier*) belongs to the 1930s.

What occupied Orwell in the great essays of the 1940s was a retrospect on the recent past, going back about a century from 1940. That year's crisis in English, European, and world history provided a compelling occasion for inquiry into its cultural origins. Orwell's perspective on earlier periods tends to be polemically simplified and highly colored in comparison to the detailed attention and sympathy which, in their different ways, both Woolf and Eliot gave to them. Most of the individuals Orwell wrote about were still active and influential in his own lifetime: Wells, Kipling, Yeats, Dali, Wodehouse, Gandhi, and even Tolstoy (who died in 1910; Orwell was born in 1903). Swift was the only figure before Dickens to be the subject of a major essay.

The perspectives of Orwell and Eliot in their essays can be seen as almost diametrically opposed. Where Eliot's level of interest in, and approval of, literary and social developments declines after Dante and Shakespeare, Orwell's interest (though not always, or even usually, his approval) grows as they approach the present and his own experience. Both see deterioration in the modern period, but attribute it to different causes: Eliot to the decline of Christianity, Orwell to the rise of totalitarianism. Eliot in 1920 (a convenient point at which to date his basic outlook) saw liberal humanist individualism as a reigning orthodoxy to which his traditionalism was opposed, while in 1940 Orwell saw himself as conducting a last-ditch defense of humanist values against the coming of totalitarianism. Orwell vehemently distrusted both Catholicism and Communism, which Eliot saw as the only possible and logical ways of running a society (of course preferring the first). Where Eliot derogated the idea of national character in favor of Europeanism, or universalism as represented by those two world-wide organizations, Orwell strongly reasserted the importance of national character. The idea of Englishness, still dominant after the First World War and celebrated in Georgian poetry, had little to offer a Europeanized American like Eliot in 1920; but by the time Orwell championed it in 1940, the internationalist, ideological perspectives of the 1930s, especially Communism, had made it unfashionable again. Orwell was, of course, opposed to nationalism as an aggressive or anti-individualist force, as in Fascism; but he supported patriotism as the instinct to love and defend a shared way of life. He differs from Eliot (who was, after all, an expatriate) in seeing nationality as an important component of the individual's identity, something Eliot sought more in the universalism of Catholic faith. For Eliot national culture was necessary but limiting, something to be transcended in the direction of larger wholes, while Orwell's view of these supra-national entities is expressed in the three huge power blocs in *Nineteen Eighty-Four*. It is also worth noting that "national character" is a much more typical essay subject (in Latin America it is even the principal one) than international movements like Catholicism or Communism, which tend to be discussed doctrinally or ideologically.

In "England Your England" (first published as Part One of *The Lion and the Unicorn* but later issued as a separate piece), Orwell sees the English national character as both constant and endlessly transformed, "an everlasting animal stretching into the future and the past, and, like all living things, having the power to change out of recognition and yet remain the same" (165). This paradox is one reflection of Orwell's program of revolutionary patriotism, offered at a time when revolution was usually assumed to be anti-national and patriotism to be conservative. Progress towards socialism, he maintains, will not obliterate the distinctiveness of English life, but merely give it a new and better form. Orwell combines tradition and modernity in a social program, as Eliot had done in a literary one. He has the difficult task of praising the traditional English way of life without condoning the class structure, and of asserting English respect for liberty without appearing complacent.

Rather than beginning from a Marxist-style class analysis, Orwell starts from an appeal to intuition and experience: "When you come back to England from any foreign country, you have immediately the sensation of breathing a different air. . . . Yes, there *is* something distinctive and recognizable in English civilization" (145). Here Orwell, as he often did, inverts Marxist method by proceeding from individual experience to theory. Marxism generally treats nationalism as a mystique fostered by the ruling class to divide the different proletariats from each other, and individual nations are only treated as *cases*, that is advanced or retarded states of various historical forces that are essentially international in character. The particular, local conditions are primarily seen as obstacles to general processes. Orwell does not reject this perspective; his essays are full of international comparisons and class analyses, and he is constantly in dialogue with Marxism. Yet he does not adopt the *method* of Marxism, but rather the method (or non-method) of the essay. He appeals directly to his own and the reader's (he clearly has a purely English audience in mind) personal experience: doesn't England *feel* different? This is the level of experience that the essay characteristically describes and appeals to, and "national character" remains an essayistic subject simply because no sociology, whether Marxist or otherwise, has come up with a way of treating it scientifically –

somehow the subject of class division is much more tractable than that of national unity, often an emotional or symbolic matter.

After "England Your England" the argument of *The Lion and the Unicorn* does move on to sociological territory and eventually to a set of political proposals; but its origin in subjective impressions is not forgotten. The confidence of this essayistic invasion of sociology and politics stems from this beginning, so that the question of proof of the assertions never arises; conviction comes, if it does come, from the individual reader's agreement that the observations chime with his own. This is Orwell's manner of persuasion: "Here are a couple of generalizations about England that would be accepted by almost all observers. One is that the English are not gifted artistically. . . . Another is that, as Europeans go, the English are not intellectual" (146). As he continues with his list of characteristics – "the love of flowers" (146), "the English hatred of war and militarism" (148), and "the respect for constitutionalism and legality" (150) – he offers in support not so much "evidence" (statistics, for instance, would look completely out of place), as illustration by some kind of concrete image, often as vivid and simple as a caricature. Thus the anti-militaristic quality is supported by this, for example: "What English people of nearly all classes loathe from the bottom of their hearts is the swaggering officer type, the jingle of spurs and the crash of boots" (149). The aim here is to evoke a swift emotional response to a stereotype created by vivid yet conventional associations; this response is all the support that Orwell needs for his immediate purposes.

There are plenty of other stereotypes in the essay: the hanging judge (150), the lady in the Rolls-Royce car (176), and the old-style proletarian, "collarless, unshaven and with muscles warped by heavy labour" (164). In all of these cases, the figures are typified by physical attributes of the most conventional kind. And once Orwell plays one of his favourite tricks of pairing opposed groups in order to ridicule both. Here they are the imperialist Blimp and the left-wing intellectual:

These two seemingly hostile types, symbolic opposites – the half-pay colonel with his bull neck and diminutive brain, like a dinosaur, the highbrow with his domed forehead and stalk-like neck – are mentally linked together and constantly interact upon one another; in any case they are born to a considerable extent into the same families. (160)

These two caricatures are themselves part of the family group that makes up England, which for Orwell is "a family with the wrong members in control" (156). Class conflict becomes a domestic quarrel, and the family becomes the metaphor to hold together the hypotheses of the unity of national feeling with that of the diversity of classes, and support the contention that "Patriotism is usually stronger than class-hatred, and always stronger than any kind of internationalism" (152).

In some ways this technique of "sociology by stereotype" is akin to the modern politics of "image," and both are equivalent to the use of emblems, personifications, and icons in past historical periods. The popular images Orwell evokes give impact to his writing, but it is not a subtle technique. For one thing, they have to be established already in the popular imagination. Of the key points in his analysis of class changes between 1920 and 1940 – the decline in ability of the ruling class, the disaffection of the Blimps and intellectuals, and the emergence in large numbers of "people of indeterminate social class" (164) – the last crucial point is weakened because Orwell cannot produce an "image" for them. He can only give them a setting in the light-industry areas of southern England, "those vast new wildernesses of glass and brick" (164), and a set of attributes almost in the Homeric manner, a group of objects correlative to this new life-style: "It is a rather restless, cultureless life, centring around tinned food, *Picture Post*, the radio and the internal combustion engine" (164). This passage also undercuts Orwell's argument that "England will still be England" (165), since these features are clearly international and modern or Americanized rather than distinctively English. The picturesque vigor of the essay is devoted to the old class stereotypes, and the "new class" or "classless" class that Orwell the socialist wants to develop looks pallid and characterless in contrast.

"England Your England" provides a framework for Orwell's studies of the diverse class cultures of England in the period that especially preoccupied him, 1910 to 1940. Orwell was an individualist paradoxically attracted by mass culture, of which he was a pioneer student; conversely, he relished treating individualist "high" culture as if it were mass culture. He enjoyed disregarding its subtleties and complexities by reducing it to stereotypes, slogans, and stock attributes. This even-handedness – treating serious literature irreverently and popular culture seriously – implies a characteristically essayistic viewpoint: the detached outsider without allegiance to a particular class, even the amorphous "new" class. This "outsider" can see that what the different class cultures have in common is that they propagate myths, that is vivid images and compelling beliefs that are in some way *false*, or at best partial, accounts of reality.

Orwell's most provocative overview of the "high" literary culture of the 1910–40 period is found in the middle section of "Inside the Whale," where he gives a general context for the work of Henry Miller. Orwell's literary-historical sketch, which is worth comparing with Virginia Woolf's "Mr Bennett and Mrs Brown" and "The Leaning Tower" as a treatment of the same period, divides it up according to three sharply distinguished generations, each reacting strongly against the previous one. Each generation is dominated by a particular "group," which has a shared ideology, but despite the marked differences between them, these group tendencies are always *away* from contemporary reality, concealing, distorting, or ignoring it.

The first period Orwell deals with is the Georgian: "War poems apart, English verse of the 1910–25 period is mostly 'country'. The reason no doubt was that the *rentier*–professional class was ceasing once and for all to have any real relationship to the soil" (116). In other words, the poetry is a compensation fantasy for the urban middle class. The keynote of "the beauty of nature" gives way during the 1920s to "the tragic sense of life" (Orwell provides each generation with its own slogan) which typifies "the Joyce-Eliot group" now generally known as the Modernists. The new mood doesn't come any closer to reality, though. Orwell asks impatiently,

> Why always the sense of decadence, the skulls and cactuses, the yearning after lost faith and impossible civilizations? Was it not, after all, *because* these people were writing in an exceptionally comfortable epoch? It is in just such times that "cosmic despair" can flourish. (122)

For Orwell the two generations are simply choosing two different forms of evasion: the idyll of rural England gives way to myths of remoter times and places. Finally comes the "Auden–Spender group," and once again the tendency is "entirely different"; the new keynote is "serious purpose." Even so, the new ideology is as much at variance with reality as the previous ones. Like the rest of the comfortably off middle-class English left, this group "can swallow totalitarianism *because* they have no experience of anything except liberalism" (128). The repetition of the italicized *"because"* implies that literature is actually motivated by the desire to avoid facing reality. In presenting the "groups" as brought together by a common myth which they "propagate" for their generation, Orwell attacks or ignores the individualist assumptions of the culture; we hear nothing about personal vision or formal artistic qualities. Art is treated as "message," spelled out in the simplest terms, and treated as propaganda to be demystified.

But for the most part the individual writers Orwell treats in his essays do not belong to groups, and in various ways seem out of touch or out of sympathy with their times. Often he sees them as having outlived their formative generation, and as persisting in sounding the keynote of two or even three generations earlier. According to Orwell, "Kipling belongs very definitely to the period 1885–1902. The Great War and its aftermath embittered him, but he shows little sign of having learned anything from any event later than the Boer War" (211). The fascination of Kipling for Orwell was partly that he straddled the divide between high and low culture – Orwell points out the influence of *Stalky and Co.* on the boys' magazines. Wodehouse is another example of a borderline figure, and his work, too, is very dated; Orwell exculpates him for collaborating with the Nazis by saying, "It is nonsense to talk of 'Fascist tendencies' in his books. There are no post-1918 tendencies at all. . . . Success and expatriation had allowed him to remain mentally in the Edwardian age" (302). This datedness is a feature of nearly all the writers to whom Orwell devoted a separate essay: Swift he sees as estranged from the Enlightenment thinking of his age, Dickens is nostalgic for the Regency, Yeats cannot shake off the 1890s, Henry Miller is writing 1920s novels in the 1930s, while H. G. Wells's Edwardian belief in progress makes him incapable of understanding Nazism. Orwell seems to delight in reversing the popular idea of the artist being ahead of his time, and shows him lingering two or three generations in the rear.

Orwell shows a sneaking admiration for datedness, because it gives a limited autonomy from history in the form of the succession of fashionable "keynotes." Although they tend to misread contemporary reality, these anachronistic world views represent a challenge to the tyranny of the present ideology and values. Every writer, for Orwell, represents his formative generation, but in his own way. At least this is true of the writers he chose to devote separate essays to; the "grouped" writers (Joyce-Eliot and Auden-Spender, as he described them with derogatory hyphenation) he generally avoided lengthy commentary on. Orwell's literary essays are like a negative of Leavis's *The Great Tradition*, and include precisely the kind of minor writers Leavis was bound to omit: Orwell gathers up the neglected, the anomalous, and the scorned, who at the time he was writing included Kipling and even Dickens (the Leavisite exclusion of Dickens as a popular entertainer was fairly typical), as well as Wodehouse and Wells.

Besides his generation, the other main grouping a writer inevitably partakes of is his social class. Orwell was enough of a Marxist to include a class analysis of the writer under discussion, but he emphasizes that class society is experienced *personally*. Individuals respond very differently to their class position, often misreading it as well as trying to change it. "Snobbery" is a term Orwell often uses in these discussions, and it indicates the personal and moral level at which they take place. It is an untheoretical term rarely used by Marxists, and is keyed to the detail of individual response to class, rather than the broad categories of the class struggle between proletariat and bourgeoisie (terms he rarely used). Orwell had more to say about fractions and subdivisions of classes, like the upper working class he discusses in "The Art of Donald McGill" or the comical but precise "lower upper middle class" in which he placed himself in *The Road to Wigan Pier*.

Snobbery is something empirical for Orwell, regrettable but almost inevitable, the product of lived social experience, and as such more rewarding to study than large abstractions about class. Snobbery is also *ordinary*, a normal effect of living in a class society, and writers are not immune to it. In fact, they seem to be especially prone to it, to judge from the number of them he attributes it to. Shakespeare, he says, "liked to stand well with the rich and powerful, and was capable of flattering them in the most servile way" (419). Dickens was "not free from the special prejudices of the shabby-genteel" (59). Kipling, because of his "distorting class perspective" (214), cannot resist the temptation to mimic working-class accents in his ballads. Yeats is "not altogether free from ordinary snobbishness" (242), while Wodehouse's novels display "a harmless old-fashioned snobbery" (300), a phrase calculated to annoy both Wodehouses's devotees and his left-wing detractors. Orwell accepts neither the romantic idea that artists *transcend* the outlook of their class, nor the Marxist belief that they *reflect* it. Orwell's working assumption is that a writer's message is developed from his particular social situation, but is not conditioned by it. A writer's political views are for Orwell never a passive reproduction of a class ideology, but rather an individual, sometimes idiosyncratic, selection of sometimes contradictory tenets formed through personal responses to the surrounding society. Thus Kipling is seen as far from a simple spokesman for imperialism: Orwell stresses that Kipling's contemporaries in India were highly suspicious of him, and that many of his "Blimp" supporters could not have read his work very carefully if they had missed the subversive element in it. Similarly, Yeats's Fascist sympathies are bound up with the complexities of his own peculiar class position, and cannot be simply explained as a "typical" case of a right-wing bourgeois intellectual.

It must be acknowledged, Orwell seems to tell us, that a given writer has petty bourgeois prejudices or Fascist sympathies. But this is not the prelude to a contemptuous dismissal, but rather to an evaluation of what *else* the writer has to offer. There is often a kind of reversal in Orwell's literary essays, where after seeming to build a highly negative case, he states how admirable and enjoyable he finds the work he has seemed to condemn. In the Swift essay it comes near the end:

> From what I have written, it may have seemed that I am *against* Swift, and that my object is to refute him and even to belittle him. In a moral and political sense I am against him so far as I understand him. Yet curiously enough he is one of the writers I admire with least reserve. (389)

Similarly, he interjects half-way through the Dickens essay, "By this time anyone who is a lover of Dickens, and who has read as far as this will probably be angry with me" (73); yet he ends the essay with a strong endorsement of Dickens *as a personality*, despite all the limitations he has noted. Generation, class, political persuasion, or any other grouping, influence but do not determine the literary expression of a given personality. Orwell sets an individualist reading within and against a class reading. There is a double movement of a Marxist-influenced "placing" of the author (in categories of class, generation, etc.) and a differentiation of him; grouping and then individuating. Orwell celebrates in the latter phase of his essays what Eliot derogated in "Tradition and the Individual Talent": "our tendency to insist, when we praise a poet, upon those aspects of his work in which he least resembles anyone else" (*SE* 14). But much of the effect depends on the way the differentiation seems to reverse the earlier negative-sounding "placing."

These reversals mean that every author Orwell discusses comes out either as a bad good one or a good bad one. In "Lear, Tolstoy and the Fool" the pattern is doubled by the inclusion of two authors, both of whom are supposed to be "good" ("great," in fact). But one of them (Tolstoy) is appearing not as a creative writer but as a critic. Further, he is a critic who thinks that a writer (Shakespeare) universally acclaimed as "good" is actually "bad." This, of course, makes the critic in this case look like a "bad" critic, since he cannot see why the "good" is "good." Enter George Orwell, determined to exploit the situation to make both these "good" authors look "bad." First of all, he concedes an astonishing amount to Tolstoy's denigration of Shakespeare: "Tolstoy is right in saying that *Lear* is not a very good play, as a play" (412). Extending the criticism of his own account, Orwell shows disrespect for the playwright's intellectual capacities: "It is not because of the quality of his thought that Shakespeare has survived, and he might not even be remembered as a dramatist if he had not also been a poet. His main hold on us is through language" (419). Orwell even endorses the low self-estimate he attributes to Shakespeare, seeing most of his work as patched-together pot-boilers with no clear purpose. He implies that Shakespeare's disorganized creativity needed the discipline of a clear purpose in order to achieve greatness: "about a dozen of his plays, written for the most part later than 1600, do unquestionably have a meaning and even a moral" (415). One of these is *King Lear*; it has the kind of clear message Orwell is demanding: "The subject of *Lear* is renunciation, and it is only by being wilfully blind that one can fail to understand what Shakespeare is saying" (415). Nevertheless Tolstoy achieves this feat. So Orwell now turns from what he sees as Shakespeare's intellectual deficiencies to Tolstoy's.

As someone who had himself tried and failed to achieve

happiness through renunciation, Tolstoy could not afford emotionally to understand *Lear's* message. He protected himself by maintaining that there *was* no coherent message. This accounts for the misinterpretation; the failure of appreciation is partly due to cultural distance: "Tolstoy's native tongue was not English" (420), and thus he missed the main reason for Shakespeare's popularity in the English-speaking world, his gift of language. However, Tolstoy would have disapproved of the whole idea of enjoying poetry for its own sake anyway. For him, "literature must consist of parables stripped of detail and almost independent of language" (413). For Tolstoy, the medium is nothing and the message everything; since he refuses the message and cannot or will not enjoy the medium, he can find no value in the play whatever.

In the pattern of antitheses deployed in the essay, Shakespeare and Tolstoy represent the same contrasting principles as the Fool and Lear within the play. Orwell sees Shakespeare as endorsing the Fool's kind of wisdom, representing the values of ordinary life, while Lear is, like Tolstoy, identified with arrogance, poor judgment of people, and a revulsion from sexuality. In ideological terms, Shakespeare comes out as a humanist, Tolstoy as a religious propagandist. For Orwell, Tolstoy is a would-be saint, and the hostility to sainthood he shows here is as sharp as in the Gandhi essay. He sees Tolstoy as a spiritual bully, a self-righteous moralist whose pacifism actually enhances his authoritarianism, and whose renunciations rid him of none of his desire to coerce. In contrast Shakespeare's exuberance and curiosity make him a humanist, that is someone firmly committed to this world rather than the next, and someone who can accept and enjoy the physical reality of the world and the human body. In art, it means taking pleasure in the depicted objects and in the richness and texture of the medium of depiction. Orwell's definition of humanism is empiricist and aesthetic, and against it Tolstoy represents a puritanical religion, a rejection of the pleasures of life and art, and a propagandistic attempt to narrow the range of human consciousness. In the Shakespeare pamphlet this becomes an active endeavor to spoil other people's enjoyment. Orwell's essay seems to amount to a devastating indictment of religious puritanism and a stout defence of ordinary enjoyment.

But is the essay really as clear-cut and decisive as it seems? In the first place, why resurrect an attack on Shakespeare which

Orwell himself points out was completely ineffectual? What is there about the pamphlet which makes it worth a twenty-page essay? Does not Orwell find the pamphlet as worthless as Tolstoy finds the play? Finally: why is Orwell, the champion of the neglected and underestimated, *defending Shakespeare*? We have already seen how lukewarm that defence actually is, how much it concedes to the opposition, and perhaps this reflects Orwell's unease at finding himself defending an orthodoxy, a long-established reputation. Another interesting point is that Tolstoy's pamphlet adopts the same strategy as many of Orwell's own essays: attacking the conventional view by showing how it fails to accord with empirical experience. Tolstoy was taking on a massive consensus of educated opinion, backed by effusive praise of critics like Hazlitt and Brandes, all of whom Tolstoy claims to have read before turning back wearily to the text, still unable to appreciate it at all. This quixotic effort must have appealed to Orwell at some level. Again, Orwell disapproves of Tolstoy's disgust at physical life, comparing it to Swift's. But in the Swift essay he also says that Swiftian disgust forms at least a part of most people's response to the body and the world. Certainly it appears often enough in Orwell's own novels and essays, more often, perhaps, than a mood of simple physical enjoyment.

In the last sentence of the essay Orwell says that the Shakespeare pamphlet would have been forgotten altogether if "Tolstoy had not also been the author of *War and Peace* and *Anna Karenina*" (420). This is one of the reversals typical of Orwell's essays, but here the reprieve comes at the last possible moment. Tolstoy as an epic novelist had once been a kind of Shakespeare himself, a lord of life and language. Orwell invites parting consideration of this dramatic reversal in Tolstoy, through which he denounced the very thing he had so well exemplified. The essay seems to offer us a clear-cut choice, or rather set of choices: Shakespeare or Tolstoy? The Fool or Lear? Ordinary humanity or sainthood? This world or the next? Art or propaganda? Orwell's answers at first sight seem equally clear: in each case he chooses the first option. But there is also a sneaking sympathy for the second. His own literary career started out with the record of a kind of renunciation and a kind of disgust: his first essay, "The Spike" ends with the essayist-tramp being offered four soggy cigarette ends as a gift. Orwell himself on his tramping expeditions had been a renouncer of the comforts of existence, and it was only by a second renunciation, the renunciation of the temptation of asceticism, self-mortification, and even sainthood, that he came to be the champion of ordinary enjoyment. In repudiating Tolstoy, he is repudiating an earlier self, just as Tolstoy is doing in repudiating Shakespeare. But the strongest images left by the essay are of Tolstoy and Lear, while Shakespeare and the Fool remain relatively vague. Orwell's own experience of inner division is what articulates and energizes the essay, producing a characteristic pattern of reversal of sympathy.

At any rate, both Tolstoy and Shakespeare are brought down to size as (at least sometimes) "bad good" authors. Their treatment is balanced by that of the "good bad" authors who are the subjects of Orwell's essays on mass culture. Frank Richards was the main author discussed in "Boys' Weeklies" and although Orwell discussed his work with affection and respect (certainly compared with the way he wrote about Shakespeare and Tolstoy) Richards was angered and wrote a stinging reply to the "charges" he thought Orwell had brought against him. This is in itself a minor gem of prose, and expresses something of what we might imagine the victim of an Orwell essay to feel. His unexpected and spirited reply in the next issue of *Horizon* (unfortunately it is not reprinted in the *Penguin Essays of George Orwell*, but is available in vol. I, pp. 531–40 of the Penguin *Collected Essays, Journalism and Letters*) makes one wish for replies from Kipling, Yeats, and Dickens, not to speak of Shakespeare and Tolstoy. The editors were as amazed at getting this response as Richards was to see his work discussed in a highbrow magazine like *Horizon*. "Boys' Weeklies" are, like most of the "keynotes" of "high" culture Orwell discusses, unrealistic fantasies: "Needless to say, these stories are fantastically unlike life at a real public school" (88). They are caught in a time-warp: "the boys are now using slang which is at least thirty years out of date" (87); in 1940 the language, atmosphere, and behavior are those of 1910. Like the "dirty joke" postcards Orwell discusses in "The Art of Donald McGill" (the title itself is a joke against "high" culture), the magazines present an unchanging world, where the cataclysms of the 1930s find not even the faintest echo. They are simply another way of getting "inside the whale," i.e. hiding from the real world. They also satisfy social fantasies, since their readership is at least one class below the class that is supposedly represented, as well as being at least two generations later. They include the crudest kind of stereotypes: "The assumption all along is not only that foreigners are comics who are put there for us to laugh at, but that they can be classified in much the same way as insects" (94). (Orwell, of course, used the caricature technique himself often enough, as we saw in "The Lion" essay.)

Youth culture creates an overlap between mass and élite culture, in Orwell's view. The "keynote" tendencies in "high" culture are set by younger people: "When one says that a writer is fashionable one practically always means that he is admired by people under thirty" (115). Accordingly, he treats Housman (his own adolescent favorite) and Rupert Brooke as constituting a mass culture for middle-class youth. He defends Housman, but not Brooke: "Considered as a poem 'Grantchester' is something worse than worthless but as an illustration of what the thinking middle class young of that period *felt* it is a valuable document" (117). Like Virginia Woolf, Orwell valued minor literature and art because of the light it sheds on ordinary life in the past, not through accurate depiction of reality but by expressing the emotional make-up of its period. Orwell showed little interest in the "major" or "great" authors stressed by Eliot and Leavis, except to mock them or catch them at moments when they were not being great, as in the Tolstoy and Shakespeare essay. His review of *The Great Tradition* (*Observer*, 6 February 1949) caricatures Leavis as a schoolmaster who would give six of the best to anyone caught reading a "minor" author like George Moore. Orwell invented the category of "Good Bad Books" in his essay of that title, where he maintained that works like *Uncle Tom's Cabin*, *Dracula*, or *Sherlock Holmes* [sic] will outlast the work of people like Virginia Woolf. He believed that childhood and adolescent reading, whatever its quality, could have a profound influence on one's sensibility for the rest of one's life. This influence may even be in inverse proportion to literary quality: "the worst books are often the most important, because they are usually the ones that are read earliest in life. It is probable that many people who could consider themselves extremely sophisticated and 'advanced' are actually carrying through life an imaginative background which they acquired in childhood from (for instance) Sapper and Ian Hay" (104). Hence the importance of the "Boys' Weeklies" Orwell is discussing; they leave a substratum in the English male psyche of incredibly dated and dangerously irrelevant emotional assumptions like the absurdity of foreigners, the permanence and rightness of the British Empire, and the non-existence of poverty, unemployment, or other social problems. Even the minority who go on to acquire "high" culture may unconsciously retain this deposit at a deep level of their sensibility.

All the cultures or subcultures Orwell examines have one thing in common: they propagate myths which conceal or distort reality. They actively hamper perception, even at the basic level of seeing what is in front of your nose. Impercipience and stupidity are Orwell's incessant themes; examples could be taken from almost any page of his essays. The cause is always the same: the belief in cultural myths, from the tragic sense of life in Modernism to the gutter patriotism of the boys' magazines. Orwell is consistently incredulous as he describes the credulity of others (this, of course, is reproduced in *Nineteen Eighty-Four* through Winston's amazement at the way most of his fellow citizens swallow the ever-changing government propaganda). But Orwell's own childhood experience provided him with a theory of how this credulity originates. In "Such, Such Were the Joys," his account of his years at preparatory school, he writes: "my own main trouble was an utter lack of any sense of proportion or probability. This led me to accept outrages and believe absurdities" (457). This is common to other children: "The weakness of the child is that it starts with a blank sheet. It neither understands nor questions the society in which it lives, and because of its credulity other people can work upon it" (457). This accounts for the "incredibly distorted" (457) view children have of the world, which is either carried through life or simply replaced by a different myth, in the same way as the Auden group, in Orwell's view, simply switched from the Boy Scout mentality to the Communist (123), without ever escaping from indoctrination to think for themselves.

If all cultures and ideologies propagate myths, how is anyone ever to grasp the truth? In fact Orwell sees this as a rare event, as exceptional in the world of his essays as it is in the novels. In Orwell's view, most people stumble blindly and stupidly through their lives, oblivious even to simple facts, ignoring even the evidence of their own senses. The individual awakens to truth only at the price of isolation and alienation from culture and class. When culture is equated with myth, to demystify is an act of treachery. To Orwell, the essay is such an act. In a sense all his essays are Dostoyevskian "notes from underground," and have the Underground Man's determination to reject all alliances and explode all theories. The essays could also be seen as passages, though much better written, from Winston Smith's diary. Orwell seeks to cancel the stereotypes created by cultures and groups (though ironically he often does so by stereotyping *them* in revenge).

Truth, for Orwell, is only available to the isolated individual adult. Hence the air of desperation which the essay form has in his hands; since the whole culture of individualism with which it originated and on which it depends is felt as collapsing, no emotional or intellectual support is assumed or expected. The tone of leisured, friendly conversation which is traditional in the essay often gives way in Orwell to a high-pitched harangue, as if he feels the reader is not going to be convinced by anything less. A conventional essay-device like the "defense" of something deemed to be unpopular, like idleness, becomes in Orwell's "In Defence of P. G. Wodehouse" something closer to a legal defense of a hounded and misunderstood individual, though his "In Defence of English Cooking" has a more traditional tone and content. But mostly his essays are full of the apprehension that the essay world is vanishing, that the world of doctrine has almost reconquered it.

Orwell's 1946 essay "The Prevention of Literature" is an elegy for the kind of referential prose of which the essay is a leading form: "in any totalitarian society that survives for more than a couple of generations, it is possible that prose literature, of the kind that has existed during the past four hundred years, must actually come to an end" (340). This is because "to write in plain, vigorous language one has to think fearlessly, and if one thinks fearlessly one cannot be politically orthodox" (341). Orwell's sees this kind of thinking more as reporting than as theorizing: "Freedom of the intellect means freedom to report what one has seen, heard, and felt, and not be obliged to fabricate imaginary facts and feelings" (337). Orwell equates the age of "free" prose with the "Protestant centuries" (335). In opposition are Catholicism and Communism: "Each of them tacitly claims that 'the truth' has already been revealed, and that the heretic, if he is not simply a fool, is secretly aware of 'the truth' and merely resists it out of selfish motives" (337). Thus each of these organizations would, for Orwell, deny the grounds of the essay: the individual *discovery* and recording of truth, or rather of *a* truth. Orwell was working in a form which he himself saw as probably doomed. This is why the tone of his essays is so different from the leisured, confident one of the Victorian essay, which assumed a basic liberal consensus even while exploring the peripheries of its society's value structures. To adapt his original title for *Nineteen Eighty-Four*, "The Last Man in Europe," we could say he wrote as if he was "the last essayist in England."

As such, he is in some ways curiously reminiscent of the first. Bacon's emphasis on sorting out true from false propositions, his empiricism, his anti-dogmatism, and his love of aphorisms and "arresting" openings can all be paralleled in Orwell. The suspicion of "idols" and culture myths is also common, and one might be tempted to add the plain style, if Orwell's style were in fact plain (and it is even questionable whether Bacon's prose can be called plain). We have seen that Orwell was an individualist fascinated by mass culture; yet he was also *part* of that culture, and it plays a part in his work, on the level of style as well as content. This tension is manifested at every level of his work from individual sentences to the authorial "image" he cultivated. The populist element is as strong in his work as the individualism. The world-famous slogans he coined in *Nineteen Eighty-Four* can be paralleled on almost any page of his writing. Along with the "image," the memorable catch-phrase or provocative dictum are key features of his work. The two key operations in his prose, typification (producing an "image" or stereotype) and generalization (producing a slogan or dictum) are common to advertising and propaganda.

Yet Orwell was so successful (though largely posthumously) at projecting his own "image" as the courageous individualist that little note has been taken of how much he borrowed from the enemy. The ambiguity of the word "Orwellian" captures this ambiguity perfectly: it can mean either the values he fought *for* or those he fought *against*. Both are woven into his prose; it includes its own opposition. Orwell's prose is *supposed* to be scrupulously honest, accurate, supple, spare, plain, concise, and concrete, and indeed it often is so; but it is equally often abstract, generalized, and wildly exaggerated. "All" and "always" occur frequently in his essays: "All art is propaganda" (73); "All sensitive people are revolted by industrialism" (462–3); "All writers are vain, selfish, and lazy" (12). The power of these statements is in being provocative, conspicuous, and memorable (this last was a key test of literature for Orwell), rather than scrupulously accurate, detailed, and specific, as Orwellian prose is reputed to be. Too minute a fidelity to particular facts would leave too much power to the big simplifications he wanted to oppose. When Orwell does go into concrete detail, it is usually as illustration or support for a generalization, not for its own sake. Rather than inhabiting a middle range of qualified generalizations, his writing moves abruptly from extreme generality to extreme specificity, both extremes gaining in impact from the difference. He seeks both kinds of convincingness: the provocative generalization, and the appeal to sensory evidence and concrete instances.

This move between general and specific is often articulated by two of Orwell's favorite introductory adverbs, "obviously" and "curiously" (his use of "probably" is worth a separate study). His essays on individual writers often follow a pattern of alternation between spelling out the general tendency or "message" of a writer in the simplest possible terms, almost in slogan form, and noting small, seemingly irrelevant details. Rapid changes of focus can bring a statement like "Yeats' tendency is Fascist" (242) into relation with an observation of an unnecessary word in one of his poems. With Dickens he moves from spelling out the "change of heart" platitude he sees as the basic message, to noting the irrelevant details which fill his novels. Orwell's "documentary" essays of personal testimony are also governed by broad generalizations about something like colonialism ("Shooting an Elephant") or poverty ("How the Poor Die" – the title itself makes a large claim from a limited specific experience).

Even in these largely descriptive pieces Orwell is far from maintaining a sober and restrained accuracy. They often rely on amplifying and exaggerating the impact of events and objects with words like "immense," "enormous," "huge," or "endless" (these words are taken almost at random from "Shooting an Elephant"). Abrupt switches and crude contrasts are frequent. Both in abstract debate and concrete description, Orwell's style strains for vivid effect, and it is more often combative than patient in its tone, as if this pitch was needed to get people to sit up and take notice. His writing is pugnacious and vehemently polemical (a simple indication of this is the freqency of words italicized for emphasis), seeking to score clear points against

competing accounts. Unlike the other essayists we have
discussed, Orwell enters the field of discourse to attack an
enemy already in possession and fortified in place with lies and
evasions. In many respects his style is shaped by his opponents, i.e. it is in part *determined by other discourses* rather than
by a calm look at the facts. His writing is forced to match the
"enormity" of what he sees. All of his essays implicitly begin
with the opening words of "My Country Right or Left":
"Contrary to popular belief . . ." (139).

This dialectic of orthodoxy and dissent produces the typical
form of Orwellian essay. Many of his essays follow this pattern:
(1) exposition of an orthodox belief or assumption; (2) disproof
of this from a specific incident or personal experience; (3) new
generalization. Or in another form: (1) personal experience; (2)
common belief; (3) disproof of common belief. We might take
the short essay "Some Thoughts on the Common Toad" as an
example of the second structure. Orwell begins with the
concrete description of toads spawning to show one of his own
"unorthodox" pleasures in the coming of spring. He mentions
the toad because "unlike the skylark and the primrose, [it] has
never had much of a boost from the poets" (367). Already the
desire to rebel against conventional discourses is evident.

Having separated his own pleasure in spring from the usual
ones, he moves on to defend all pleasure in Nature, whether
conventional (crocus and cuckoo) or unconventional (toads),
against the main orthodoxy, which now emerges: the supposedly Marxist assertion (contained in a letter to Orwell) that
joy in Nature is sentimental and reactionary, and is in any case
a luxury of comfortable city dwellers. Orwell rounds on these
arguments, claiming that "this last idea is demonstrably false"
(368). This is a characteristically "forthright" short sentence,
Baconian in spirit, moving from abstract to concrete with a
promise of empirical demonstration. But the proof is too brief to
be very convincing, and Orwell himself had maintained
something like the contrary in discussing the Georgian "country" poets, as we saw. The other idea (love of Nature is
reactionary) is rebutted with an appeal to the human need to
enjoy Nature regardless of the state of social progress. Finally,
the group of "opponents" of Spring is widened from "Marxists"
(actually just one correspondent) to include "all the important
persons who would stop me enjoying this if they could" (369).
This typically Orwellian exaggeration is extended to sheer

hyperbole in the last sentence, where he maintains that "the dictators and the bureaucrats" actually disapprove of the fact that the earth goes round the sun (thus implicitly aligning them with the persecutors of Galileo).

Orwell's dictum "Good prose is like a window pane" (13) hardly applies to his own work, which is a highly-colored medium, not a transparent one. Its concreteness is usually polemicized, its perceptions sharpened by the desire to refute some orthodoxy or convention, to take on some doctrine that he exaggerates to the point of caricature. "Shooting an Elephant" takes the stereotyped image of the white man's dominance in the East, which he memorably pictures in his essay on Kipling as a "pukha sahib in a pith helmet kicking a coolie" (210), confronts it with the shooting incident, and then inverts the original generalization by asserting that in order to live up to the natives' expectations the white man becomes "a sort of hollow, posing dummy" living in constant fear of ridicule. The new sense of the powerlessness of the supposedly powerful is reinforced by the great difficulty and slowness of actually killing the elephant. Even the smallest details of the story are chosen to confound expectations, and sometimes an imaginary interlocutor is actually addressed: "Never tell me, by the way, that the dead look peaceful. Most of the corpses I have seen look devilish" (27). Orwell's style is highly "dialogical" in Bakhtin's sense, and is often reminiscent of one of Bakhtin's most effective examples, the Underground Man.

The characteristic movement of Orwell's essays comes from this alternation of myth and counter-myth, false image and true. He presents his stance as demystifying, but he also gives powerful presentations to the myths he attacks. The false images are often replaced by true images that are presented by the same means: the vivid image and the provocative phrase. However, the "true" image has a different source: it results from shutting your eyes and thinking of the object; in his advice to writers in "Politics and the English Language" the stress is on *first* forming a clear mental image and *second* putting it into words. Visualization should precede verbalization: "When you think of a concrete object, you think wordlessly, and then, if you want to describe the thing you have been visualizing, you probably hunt about till you find the exact words that seem to fit it" (364).

This passage, with its assumptions that (1) mental images can be exactly matched to real objects, and (2) words can be found to match the mental images, has annoyed some recent theorists who are committed to the notion that words create reality rather than describe it. They accuse Orwell of epistemological naïveté; but Orwell's own work also undercuts his thesis by showing repeatedly that *false* or imaginary mental pictures are usually more powerful than the true ones. Vividness does not depend on accuracy, in other words. Nor, despite Orwell's reiterated claims, does it depend on individual perception. The two kinds of images, the realistic ones produced by the individual and the imaginary ones created for popular consumption, cannot finally be separated. Let us take an example from Orwell's essay on Tolstoy and Shakespeare:

> Shut your eyes and think of *King Lear,* if possible without calling to mind any of the dialogue. What do you see? Here at any rate is what I see: a majestic old man with flowing white hair and beard . . . wandering through a storm and cursing the heavens. (412)

Orwell seems completely unaware that what he has called up by this method is probably a Victorian illustration of a children's Shakespeare. His personal experiment produces *the* popular image of the old king, not at all an original insight.

But this does not detract from its power, or the pleasure it can give. "True" and false" images can be equally pleasurable, and in practice Orwell relishes and produces wild inaccuracy as much as strict accuracy. He loves stereotypes for their comic vitality, as we saw in "England Your England," and even when he is demystifying them, he manifestly also enjoys them. For example, "Chesterton had not lived long in France, and his picture of it as a land of Catholic peasants incessantly singing the *Marseillaise* over glasses of red wine – had about as much relation to reality as *Chu Chin Chow* has to everyday life in Baghdad" (310). In "Such, Such Were the Joys" he describes another false image of a national culture, the image of Scotland presented to the boys of St Cyprian's: "Our picture of Scotland was made up of burns, braes, kilts, sporrans, claymores, bagpipes and the like, and somehow mixed up with the invigorating effects of porridge, Protestantism and a cold climate" (448). In this case the demystification follows immediately: the image is produced by snobbery (only the rich spent the summers there) and bad conscience (of the "occupying" English). But there is no mistaking the iconic power of the false image, which shows us *in practice* how these crude stereotypes and stock associations can overpower the truth.

Orwell's proclaimed *objectivity* is actually more a stance of *objection* to prevalent suppositions. Orwell is an objector; his concreteness is not impartial, but results from a desire to point out things that everyone else seems to be ignoring. Then, he usually prefers the drama of *reversing* the orthodoxy to merely qualifying it or making it more precise. His appeals to "truth," "fact," and "reality" show little awareness of the problematic nature of these concepts, or the unavailability of a version of a reality that is not already partly formed by the perceiver's purposes and prejudices, although in "The Prevention of Literature" he rightly rejects the argument "that since absolute truth is not attainable, a big lie is no worse than a little lie" (339). He also rejects the "totalitarian" view (also the Nietzschean view, recently popularized in the work of Foucault) that "history is something to be created rather than learned" (338). But Orwell's own "production" of reality is itself partly rhetorical, relying on abrupt, dramatic contrasts between what others *say* and what he *sees*. The switch from *their* statement to his is presented as a switch from purely verbal assertion to verifiable fact. Orwell's characteristic "reality effect" (Roland Barthes's phrase) is achieved by exaggerating the lies he is attacking: the more blatant they are, the more dramatic and convincing the truths will appear by contrast. In this sense they are simply reversed lies, or counter-myths. If they are also a shift from a comfortable illusion to an uncomfortable shock, their power is all the greater. Orwell's essay on his schooldays gives a recurring incident which perfectly symbolizes this effect: "That bump on the hard mattress, on the first night of term, used to give me a feeling of abrupt awakening, a feeling of: 'This is reality, this is what you are up against'" (439). He describes an unpleasant feeling of waking up just when you should be going to sleep, an effect such as he sought in all his essays: waking up an audience narcotized by myths.

Perhaps the incident could also symbolize what Orwell did to the essay. Even in the 1930s writers like Robert Lynd were producing cosy, whimsical pieces on traditional Edwardian themes, as if bourgeois England had not changed since 1900, and in some quarters this is still the dominant image of the essay as an outdated, belletristic genre. Orwell brought the essay into the age of the mass media and mass politics, but at the price of adopting some of their devices. Perhaps to him the only way of gettting attention amidst the vast outpouring of opinion was to fix provocative slogans and bright images in people's minds. This changed the essay completely; no longer would the old gentlemanly (or ladylike, as Virginia Woolf saw her own early work) tone be available. Orwell made the essay possible for the post-war period, just as his brand of realism dominated the post-war English novel. With him, the essay moved out of the backwater of rural sentimentality, antiquarian preciousness, and social complacency, and underwent the pressures of the age, the mainstream of political and social conflict. For him the essayistic attitude, the offering of independent views based on individual thought and experience, came to have an immense *political* significance. If it continued to linger in the byways of the culture, it would end up incarcerated, like P. G. Wodehouse caught by surprise by the Nazi invaders of France (293).

There are elements of tradition and continuity in Orwell's essays, however. He can be seen as reviving the tradition of the political essay (as distinct from the party pamphlet, broadsheet, or policy paper) which runs from Swift through Hazlitt. In fact Swift's essay on politics and language is an interesting precursor of "Politics and the English Language." Many of its ideas about style are also found in Sir Arthur Quiller-Couch's *The Art of Writing*, which is based on his lectures as the Professor of English Literature at Cambridge, so that Orwell's essay can be seen as, in part, reasserting an Edwardian orthodoxy about plain writing, brevity, and unpretentiousness. The subject matter of Orwell's essays on mass culture is not new either: the predecessors of "Boys' Weeklies" include Stevenson's "'A Penny Plain and Twopence Coloured'" and Chesterton's "A Defence of Penny Dreadfuls." What is different is the seriousness, intensified by the levity (to adapt Eliot's phrase), with which he treats these magazines. For Orwell mass culture is fascinating but also politically sinister. In "Boys' Weeklies" he traces the ownership of many of them back to a certain Lord Camrose, to whom he attributes the intention of ideological conditioning (104). Orwell's belief that "all art is propaganda" (73) holds true for popular culture in so far as it is controlled and manipulated from above.

The idea of culture as *politically* important energizes all of Orwell's essays on literature and art. The consequent sense of urgency distinguishes his work from the tone of calm, detached contemplation which is traditional in the essay from Montaigne onwards. With Orwell the essay emerges from retirement; observation is no longer detached, but caught up in polemic. Orwell said his aim was to "make political writing into an art" (11); he also succeeded in making the art of the essay political. He politicized the critical essay, and to a great degree also the travel essay and the autobiographical essay. He saw politics and culture as a totality, where the individualism which is essential to the essay is constantly at risk, and where the truths which can only be vouched for by individuals are in constant danger of being suppressed or ignored or co-opted by the cultures of groups, classes, and organizations. With him the essay acquires an edge of anger, a quicker temper, needed to fight for its existence and its values in the era of homogenized discourse, high-impact slogans, and images. As we have seen, the cost of fighting back is to adopt some of the enemy's techniques. But the only alternative he saw for independent prose was irrelevance, obscurity, and extinction.

10

The essay and criticism

In the 1950s – "The Essay as Form" was composed between 1954 and 1958 – Adorno's view of the west's cultural future was as bleak as Orwell's in the 1940s (it is curious how little the end of the war seems to have lightened the pessimism of either). Adorno looks back on the essay as representing the best in bourgeois individualism, just as Orwell's idea of "good prose" sums up the best features of the culture of "the Protestant centuries." For Adorno the triumphant enemy is the pseudo-culture of modern mass society, in east and west alike, where for Orwell the enemy is political totalitarianism and its planned manipulation of culture. For both writers, the culture which produced the essay is dying or dead, and both are unmistakably nostalgic. How valid is this gloomy outlook?

Adorno, in Orwellian fashion, makes a distinction between the good essay and the bad essay. He describes the "capitulation" (154) of the essay as beginning with Sainte-Beuve and continuing with Stephan Zweig's romanticized studies of artists. The bad essay, Adorno tells us, vulgarizes high culture for mass consumption, providing a "washed-out pseudo-culture" (155) which is complicit with "the reification of consciousness" (155). In other words, it lacks the quality of independent probing thought, and instead produces easy, superficial images. It offers no advantages over the official discourse of academia, of which Adorno was now himself a part as a professor at the University of Frankfurt: "bad essays are as conformist as bad dissertations" (154). This flood of inferior "popularizing" commentary over the domain of art is partly a result, he maintains, of the reduction of art to aesthetic technique and the monopoly of science over cognition. Modern culture is split, he claims (in a way reminiscent of the "two cultures" debate of the 1950s in Britain), into "a sealed and flawlessly organized science, and . . . a conceptless intuitive art" (156). This division, reminiscent also of Eliot's "dissociation of sensibility," is potentially, or partially, overcome by the essay's attempt at aesthetic cognition, although "a consciousness in which perception and concept, image and sign would be one is not, if it ever existed, to be recreated with a wave of the wand" (154).

Adorno attributes to the essay the same possibility of "unified sensibility" Eliot finds in the poem. For Adorno, Proust's essayistic fiction was a final attempt to "save or reproduce a form of knowledge that was still considered valid in the days of bourgeois individualism when the individual consciousness still trusted itself and was not yet worried about organizational censure: the knowledge of an experienced man" (156). It is worth noting that Adorno sees unified sensibility as a product and expression of bourgeois individualism, not, like Eliot, as being destroyed by it. Adorno strongly preferred individualism to modern mass culture, and made a sharp distinction between them, where Eliot saw the extension of liberal-humanist individualism as *producing* the atomized, alienated mass that constitutes modern society.

For Adorno, then, the essay is one of the high forms of bourgeois culture now being degraded. "The relevance of the essay is that of an anachronism. The hour is more unfavourable to it than ever" (170). He equates the essay with intellectual freedom, as Orwell does "good prose," and sees both as lacking in his own national culture: "In Germany the essay provokes resistance because it is reminiscent of the intellectual freedom that, from the time of an unsuccessful and lukewarm Enlightenment, since Leibniz's day, all the way to the present has never really emerged" (152). Adorno takes up the Orwellian stance of a proudly independent intellectual, alienated from all the available ideologies and institutions, even from his period and his society, and the essay becomes the form and vehicle of his defiance – another last man in Europe, in fact. But how real is this isolation? How appropriate is this valediction to the essay? How true is his premise that the essay has disappeared between the disciplinary structures of university learning and the tide of popularized culture, between academia and the media?

I discussed in Chapter 1 the way in which the essay is a

much-used form in the lower levels of the educational system, gradually replaced by the less personal "research paper" (both these remain below the level of publication) and finally by the impersonal "scholarly article" complete with a double set of quotations, one set to "prove" or illustrate the points, the other to substantiate the ideas or theories used from the appropriate, validating authorities. But by a curious phenomenon, essayistic form tends to re-emerge at the very top of the academic hierarchy, where there is less need for validating authority and a greater indulgence of personal opinion (and also a greater number of invitations to give the lectures which often reappear as essays). As we saw with Eliot, an essay can become authoritative in academia partly because it does not cite authorities and speaks on its own authority. But in general the academic system does not use the essay as a form of writing any more than it attends to the essay as an object of study (though there are signs, like this book, that this may be changing). We need to look in a little more detail at the different phases of institutionalized literary study to understand the relative neglect of the essay.

The study of modern literature (i.e. post-classical vernacular literature) was first organized along national-historical lines, and was seen as representing the spirit of the nation through the different stages of its evolution. This idea dominated the nineteenth century, from Hazlitt's lecture series down to the early twentieth century. The assumptions were historicist and the structure was sequential narrative; the objects so ordered were seen as "works" or "products" of the author's personality, his society, and his age. The essay fared reasonably well in this period, since it could be "personally" expressive as well as "historically" revealing. At the end of the period in England it received its own history, Hugh Walker's *The English Essay* (1915), which gives the names, dates, and circumstances of the essayists, along with accounts of the kinds of essays they wrote. Several other studies of the essay appeared around the same time, but although, as I have maintained earlier, the essay was a key expression of the Modernist movement, it was not, apart from Virginia Woolf's studies of Montaigne, Addison, Hazlitt, and "The Modern Essay," the object of much critical attention in itself. Although it is certainly true that the Modernists wanted to displace the Victorian idea of "character and environment," this was not with a view to depersonalizing art, but rather to providing a new and in many ways freer concept of personality as consciousness. Despite the "impersonal" theory of poetry, the key Modernists made highly successful use of the "personal" essay. However, this was not acknowledged as Modernism gained acceptance in academia through professorial critics like Leavis, Trilling, and Levin, perhaps because *at the same time* the essay was being replaced by the professional article as the form of literary criticism. The essay disappeared from view simultaneously as an object of study and as a vehicle of that study.

As Modernism and the Modernist poetics of Eliot and Pound became established after about 1920 (though changes of this kind spread very slowly) the object of literary study was reconceived, not as the historically produced work, but as the autonomous Poem, relatively independent of its author and age, and not yet dependent on its reader. The other genres were valued by the degree to which they approached the condition of poetry, and this obviously did not encourage close attention to the essay. The assumptions were organicist, stressing the wholeness, unity, and self-sufficiency of the verbal artifact, and the method was explication – *ex*plication of the *com*plications in the poem. The more dense and complex the internal relationships were, the greater the poem was felt to be. The prevalent tone was reverential before poetic works that were agreed to be truly great, and little attention was spent on minor talents and minor forms like the essay, though particularly post-Orwell there was talk of prose style – "firm" and "supple" were the approved qualities. An interregnum followed in the 1960s, when systems of "poetics" like Frye's or the various derivatives of Saussure's were dominant, and the privileged object was Fiction, finally rescued from the shadow of the Poem, but still the object of analytic techniques largely derived from poetry criticism.

In the late 1960s the present phase began. Now, in contrast to the Work as Product, the object of study became the Text as Process. Instead of autonomy and wholeness and solidity, the text displayed a highly provisional and precarious set of significances, hardly waiting to be unraveled. Tensions and paradoxes became fissures, ruptures, and contradictions; the tone of reverence gave way to one of suspicion or even resentment. Where organicism had seen the Poem (or at least the "great" poem) as a timeless refuge from the horrors of modern mass society, "literature" (in protective quotation marks, which are another sign of the times) is now seen as just another instance of the textual processes which construct the culture, and which are all more or less suspect as ideological fictions on the same basis as advertisements and propaganda.

In this phase, close reading is seen as a "construction" of the text (as in "reader-response" criticism) which immediately invites "deconstruction." The object is not even so definite as a text; rather it is an instance of textuality. This word was formed on the analogy of "sexuality" (itself modeled on "sensibility") as the condition, or set of conditions, under which a text comes into existence. The author is ruled out of account or out of existence, and the "reader" becomes not an individual person responding, but a neutral subject position or text-activator, through which the text is constructed and/or deconstructed. In a curious way, in textualism (in its radical form epitomized by Derrida's "il n'y a pas d'hors-texte") the text is as autonomous as in organicism, but as a process, not a finished product. Curiously, too, the sources of this *post*-modernist criticism are *pre*-modernist – the three "masters of suspicion," the "authorities" for textualism, are Marx, Nietzsche, and Freud, whose birthdates are 1812, 1844, and 1856.

At first sight, this third phase of literary study might seem conducive to the development of criticism of the essay. The hierarchy of genres, which usually ranks the essay low, is attacked or disregarded, the canonization of "great" works is in disfavor, and even the distinction between kinds of discourses (literature and philosophy, for example) is ignored: textuality is a universal condition. All this would seem to favor the essay. But there are more powerful countervailing factors. In current terms the essay would be dismissed as a combination of the bourgeois liberal-humanist subject and a naïve-realist epistemology believing in accurate linguistic construction of "real" objects. The essay's assumptions are both more subjective and more objective than textualism's; but both aspects are particular and individual. The essay claims to articulate *this* self and *that* object, but not as instances of general laws. Textualism, operating at the level of general laws (or anti-laws), would dismiss the essay's self and object as illusory textual "constructs." As we have seen, the essay is skeptical in its traditional attitude; but it is skeptical precisely about general laws, even general laws of skepticism. Textualism, at least in its deconstructive form, is a universal, even dogmatic skepticism. The essay is skeptical about *other* accounts of reality, but not its own, which stem from personal experience. That is the essay's ultimate "ground"; but that, or any other ground for discourse, would be rejected by deconstruction. The essay takes a "demystifying" approach to reality precisely because, within the limits of an individual's "situation," it claims to produce an unmystified account of it. We can make a similar contrast with the idea of "indeterminacy," which is common to the essay and deconstruction, Montaigne and Derrida. For Montaigne, the self and the object are both indeterminate, but the language in which he records the temporary determinations of himself or the world around him is not. Textualist approaches to Montaigne have only succeeded in turning him into "Montaigne," a textual construct apart from the "real" person. But Montaigne was already aware of this possibility; however, he did not go on to commit the textualist fallacy of assuming that a construct is *completely* fictitious. He accepted that a construct (admittedly inexact, temporary, possibly prejudiced) is *of* something actual – something of which different constructs can be made at other times by other people, and then compared and selected or rejected. Deconstructive skepticism, on the other hand, carried to its extreme, turns into a form of credulity, a naïve *un*realism believing that we can perceive *nothing but* our own constructs, which we can only endlessly deconstruct and reconstruct. Effective perception and communication need a judicious mixture of suspicion and trust: universal skepticism and universal credulity are equally disabling.

The analogue of textualism Montaigne had to deal with was medieval scholasticism; for Orwell it was the propaganda of the 1940s, fictionally reflected in the endlessly indeterminate textuality of *The Times*, which never had reflected reality or even tried to. O'Brien in *Nineteen Eighty-Four* is the ultimate Nietzschean "fictionalist," holding that history is only the myth enforced by the victor. The modern concern in government and the media for projecting favorable "images" regardless of their accuracy can also be seen as a form of Nietzschean "fictionalism." Textualists, of course, are not friends of totalitarianism, and in fact generally see their activities as radically subversive; however, even on the textual level their epistemology leaves them ill-equipped to contest the "constructs" of those actually in power. American deconstructionists, for example, should

181

logically abandon the political field to "the Great Communicator" since they have disallowed the "grounds" for believing that one account of what is happening can be more accurate than another. Many or most deconstructionists are left-wing, but they have to practice a kind of doublethink about language, where textualism is suspended when some effective practical discourse is needed, but reinstated in literary contexts. From a textualist position, they cannot say "This is untrue." Orwell's essays could, because his aim "to make political writing into an art" enabled him to maintain a unified view of language, where aesthetic quality was identical with effective referentiality. Montaigne and Bacon would also undoubtedly have rejected Derrida's textualism as scholastic, as privileging the order of words over the order of things. It was exactly against that mentality that the essay originally reacted. But academia, with its concern to organize discourse into disciplines, will always tend to give priority to "theory," to the structures of learning; the unstructured, or rather, personally and provisionally structured, world of the essay is all the more necessary as a counterweight.

There is a strong case for increasing the role of the essay in academia, both as an object to study and as a form of writing *for* that study. This does not imply a return to an élitist, belletristic cult of sensibility as a form of personal superiority – this "gentlemanly amateur" image of the essayist belongs mainly to the Edwardian period and is by no means typical of that anyway. Anyone who can look attentively, think freely, and write clearly can be an essayist; no other qualifications are needed. Potentially, as Addison and Steele showed, the essay is one of the most popular forms of expression, the most available to writers and readers. It is a direct individual-to-individual communication. As such it is likely to offer divergent views rather than express a consensus. It is not free from ideology, because no individual consciousness is free of it, though the essay encourages a critical attitude. A positive description might call the essay an anti-ideological expression of the free individual reporting and reflecting on his experience in defiance or disregard of authority; a negative account might see it as embodying bourgeois ideology, the world view based on the isolated self, separated from community, and forced to construct its own precarious significance in an alien world. But regardless of whether the essay is seen as a happy form or a sad one (like the epic and novel respectively in Lukács's theory of the novel), it provides an opening to individual experience of the past. Theory and system are powerful and necessary organizers of human knowledge, and they usually hold pride of place in academic institutions; but the lived individual experience which eludes system, and which the essay expresses and symbolizes, has an important place as well.

What of the essay outside academia? This, of course, has always been its situation as an unofficial vernacular discourse, first in non-academic books in the seventeenth century, and then in the periodical press from the eighteenth century onwards. At present all branches of the essay are flourishing, except perhaps the moral essay, which seems to have fallen into the gap between academic philosophy and journalism, neither of which provides much of a market for it. But there are gifted writers practicing most other forms of the essay, usually outside academia: Susan Sontag, Joan Didion, Clive James, Jan Morris, Conor Cruise O'Brien, Richard Cobb, Dan Jacobson are variously practicing the travel essay, the autobiographical essay and the critical essay, and dozens of other names could be added to this list. The non-academic critical essay is a particularly important survival, though it needs an interested non-professional audience, and also usually the context of a large metropolis. Clive James's concept of "the metropolitan critic" (Edmund Wilson is a key example), which is sketched in the Preface to his essay-collection of that title, is a vital alternative to the academic critic. The metropolitan critic does not have an identifiable "approach" or theory of art, but offers a personal response of intellect and sensibility to the individual work, for which the natural form is the essay.

Thus the pessimism of Orwell and Adorno about the death of the essay looks unjustified at present. Part of what this means is that the idea of individual personality is still flourishing outside academia *in practice*, though it has generally been ignored or attacked by academic disciplines *in theory* in the twentieth century. Where the disciplines have developed the determinisms of the nineteenth century from an historical to a structural framework, the essay has held on to the other legacy passed on by that century, the belief in individual autonomy. The impersonal and anti-referential tendency of twentieth-century literary theory has kept poetics in harmony with other disciplines in this regard, and has also kept the essay, with its assumptions of personality and referentiality, out of favor. Its belief that individual viewpoints differ but can be shared through language, that an objective reality can be provisionally constructed through these viewpoints and can be described in language, that degrees of truth and falsity in accounts of reality can be distinguished – these beliefs are politically and aesthetically salutary. These beliefs, and the essay form based on them, have remained strong outside academia because individual opinion and observation are still valued in the general culture more than scholastic ideas and styles.

In academia literary criticism is governed by the idea of method: although there is disagreement about *which* method or methods are appropriate, there is agreement that *some* method is desirable. This produces the "approaches" model of literary study, where the text is made the object of various predefined procedures based on intellectual systems like Marxism, Freudianism, or semiotics. Here the text is viewed as an instance of general laws of ideology, psychology, society, textuality, etc. Or we could discern an "application" model for the relationship between literature and ideas, whereby ideas are taken from a system and methodically "applied" to a text. All of these models are indifferent to the essay either as an object or a form of criticism.

But this double neglect will leave the essay well placed in both capacities when the inevitable reaction against deconstruction has dissolved the whole "theory" phase of criticism. This reaction should not consist of a return to a Leavisite or New-Critical combination of vitalist moralism and organicist formalism, but could produce a move forward to an *essayistic* relationship between literature and ideas. That is, instead of the ideas being applied to the text, they would be evoked by it in a non-systematic way. These ideas could be those of the text, or of its contemporary intellectual context; ideas taken from philosophers like Nietzsche, Marx, or Freud, or simply the critic's own ideas. The point is to characterize the object in terms of the ideas its different aspects evoke in the mind of the individual observer. The results of this spontaneous and non-methodical free play between subject and object are then arranged aesthetically, not as a formal or logical argument governed by established rules, but as a unique configuration, a constellation of ideas around an object or experience. Thus a revival of the essay tradition could rejuvenate academic literary criticism.

The final image I would give to this process is one which has unexpectedly become a theme in this book: the portrait, explicitly discussed in connection with Lukács, Hazlitt, James, Woolf, and Montaigne, but implicitly present in the other writers as well. The portrait is an image of one individual by another, and that definition can be extended to places (in travel essays, such as those of James) or works of art and literature (most critical essayists agree with Orwell in discerning a "face behind the page") or experiences (as in the autobiographical essay, which is a self-portrait in a past situation). Although the "type" (or stereotype or caricature) also has a long tradition, the modern essay tends to be critical of it, though Orwell was ambivalent on this. We can also see the essayistic literary history practiced by Hazlitt, Woolf, Eliot, and Orwell as a kind of group portraiture (for example, Woolf's "The Russian Point of View" contains sketches of Dostoyevsky, Tolstoy, and Turgenev) or a portrait of two or more groups (like Orwell's depiction of Henry Miller against a background of groups representing three generations). In all these cases the portrait is built up by observing and recording the "traits" of the object until some kind of vital configuration of aspects makes the separate objective features come to life as a likeness, that is, as another "subject" or quasi-subject; an image which is "like" the sitter but also "like" the artist; an image which is a convergence of individual identities. There can be no definitive portrait, in that each artist will have and express a different view of a given individual; nevertheless that individual will be recognizably the same person in the different views. A portrait is like an essay: the objectification by a subject of another subject; the permanent record of a temporary impression; an image which is a brief determination, momentarily fixed in a configuration, of an open and shifting and indeterminate relationship.

The essay offers aesthetic knowledge, despite an intellectual milieu which has come to see the two dimensions as mutually exclusive, and despite the threat from another direction by the "methodical" manipulation of mass politics and the "formula" products of the mass media. Despite the pessimism of Orwell and Adorno, the essay remains a focus of individual resistance to "systems" of various kinds, political, intellectual, and cultural. This form of individualism lies between the élite and scholastic "high" styles of academia and the manipulated and sensationalized "low" styles of the media, both of which tend to

185

approach their content through "systems" of analysis and "models" of presentation which determine its construction in advance. The essay is neither an élite form nor a mass form, and when it treats those forms it is generally critical of both. It is a democratic form, open to anyone who can see clearly and think independently. As such it is vital to our educational, cultural, and political health.

Reference list

The following lists works cited, other than the principal works by Montaigne, Bacon, Johnson, Hazlitt, Henry James, Virginia Woolf, T. S. Eliot, and George Orwell discussed in Chapters 2–9. These sources are given at the beginning of the Bibliographical Notes for each chapter, and are followed by notes on the secondary literature for each essayist. The notes for Chapter 1 include a survey of general discussions of the essay form in various languages.

Adolph, Robert, *The Rise of Modern Prose Style*, Cambridge, Mass.: MIT Press, 1968.

Adorno, Theodor, "The Essay as Form," tr. Bob Hullott-Kentor, *New German Critique*, 32 (Spring-Summer 1984): 151–71.

Auerbach, Erich, *Mimesis: The Representation of Reality in Western Literature*, tr. Willard R. Trask, Princeton: Princeton University Press, 1953.

— "Figura," tr. Ralph Manheim, in *Scenes from the Drama of European Literature: Six Essays*, New York: Meridian, 1959.

Benjamin, Walter, *The Origin of German Tragic Drama*, tr. John Osborne, London: New Left Books, 1977.

Bense, Max, "Uber den Essay und seine Prosa," *Merkur* 1:3 (1947), 414–24.

Buck-Morss, Susan, *The Origin of Negative Dialectics: Theodor W. Adorno, Walter Benjamin, and the Frankfurt Institute*, Brighton, Sussex: Harvester, 1977.

Colie, Rosalie, *The Resources of Kind: Genre-theory in the Renaissance*, Berkeley: University of California Press, 1973.

Crane, R.S. "The Relation of Bacon's *Essays* to his Program for the Advancement of Learning, "in *Schelling Anniversary Papers*, New York: 1923, 87–105.

Curtius, Ernst, *European Literature and the Latin Middle Ages*, tr. Willard R. Trask, Bollingen Series 36, Princeton: Princeton University Press, 1973.

Descartes, René, *Discourse on Method and Other Writings*, tr. F. E. Sutcliffe, London: Penguin, 1968.

Eliot, George, *Adam Bede*, Everyman edn, London: Dent, 1906.

Foucault, Michel, *The Order of Things: An Archeology of the Human Sciences*, New York: Pantheon, 1970.

Guillén, Claudio, *Literature as System*, Princeton: Princeton University Press, 1971.

Holquist, Michael, and Clark, Katerina, *Mikhail Bakhtin*, Cambridge, Mass.: Harvard University Press, 1984.

James, Henry, "The Figure in the Carpet," in *Henry James' Shorter Masterpieces*, ed. Peter Rawlings, vol. 1, Brighton, Sussex: Harvester, 1984.

Johnson, Samuel, *Lives of the English Poets*, Everyman edn, London: Dent, 1925.

Lukács, Georg, "Solzhenitsyn: *One Day in the Life of Ivan Denisovich*," tr. William David Graf, in *Solzhenitsyn*, Cambridge, Mass.: MIT Press, 1971.

— "On the Nature and Form of the Essay," in *Soul and Form*, tr. Anna Bostock, Cambridge, Mass.: MIT Press, 1974.

Mazzeo, Joseph Anthony, *Renaissance and Revolution: The Remaking of European Thought*, London: Secker & Warburg, 1965.

Pater, Walter, *The Renaissance*, intro. Kenneth Clark, London: Collins, 1961.

Watt, Ian, *The Rise of the Novel*, Berkeley: University of California Press, 1967.

White, Hayden, *Metahistory: The Historical Imagination in Nineteenth-Century Europe*, Baltimore: John Hopkins University Press, 1975.

Williams, Raymond, *Marxism and Literature*, Oxford: Oxford University Press, 1977.

Wollheim, Richard, *On Art and the Mind: Essays and Lectures*, London: Allen Lane, 1973.

Bibliographical notes

Chapter 1: The essay as genre

The best recent comparative overview of the genre is Richard M. Chadbourne, "A Puzzling Literary Genre: Comparative Views of the Essay," *Comparative Literature Studies* 20:2 (Summer 1983), 133–53. This discusses the various national traditions and cites many of the major practitioners and theorists. A useful early attempt at a genre definition is Charles Whitmore, "The Field of the Essay," *PMLA* 36 (1921), 551–64. On the English essay, Hugh Walker, *The English Essay and Essayists* (London: Dent, 1915), gives a thorough history including minor writers. Bonamy Dobrée, *English Essayists* (London: Collins, 1946), gives a much more selective but stimulating treatment. Ted-Larry Pebworth has an interesting group of articles on the early English essay: "Not Being, but Passing: Defining the Early English Essay," in *Studies in the Literary Imagination* 10:2 (1977), 17–27; "'Real English Evidence': Stoicism and the English Essay Tradition," *PMLA* 87 (1972), 101–2; "Wandering in the America of Truth: *Pseudodoxia Epidemica* and the Essay Tradition," in C. A. Patrides (ed.), *Approaches to Sir Thomas Browne* (Columbia: University of Missouri Press, 1982); and "Jonson's *Timber* and the Essay Tradition," in Thomas A. Kirby and William J. Olive (eds), *Essays in Honor of Esmond Linworth Marilla* (Baton Rouge: Louisiana State University Press, 1970), 115–26. Chapters on Donne, Browne, Felltham, Hazlitt, De Quincey, Hazlitt, Emerson, Thoreau, and T. S. Eliot are contained in Laurence Stapleton's *The Elected Circle: Studies in the Art of Prose* (Princeton: Princeton University Press, 1973). A good scholarly monograph on the early English essay, including a chapter on Bacon, is Elbert N. S. Thompson, *The Seventeenth-century English Essay* (University of Iowa Humanistic Studies, 1926).

On the essay in France, the best starting-point is the collection *The French Essay* (University of South Carolina French literature Series, vol. 9, 1982), which includes discussions of essayists over the range of French literature from Montaigne to the twentieth century. H. V. Routh, "The Origins of the Essay Compared in English and French

Literature," *Modern Language Review* 15 (1920), 28–40, 143–51, offers an interesting discussion of the question of why, given the example of Montaigne, France did not develop as strong an essay tradition as England. Two other useful general sources in French are Robert Champigny, *Pour une esthétique de l'essai* (Paris: Lettres Modernes-Minard, 1967) and Jean Terasse, *Rhétorique de l'essai littéraire* (Montréal: Les Presses de l'Université du Québec, 1977). *Etudes littéraires* 5:1 (April 1972) is a special issue on the essay; it includes a French translation of Lukács's "Nature et forme de l'essai."

In German, the most comprehensive source is Ludwig Rohner, *Der deutsche Essay: Materialen zur Geschichte und Asthetik einer literarische Gattung* (Neuwied: Luchterhand, 1966), which includes good general and theoretical material as well as discussion of the German essay specifically, as does the shorter introduction by Gerhard Haas, *Essay* (Stuttgart: Metzler, 1969). On theory purely, the three most important texts are Georg Lukács, "Über Wesen und Form des Essays," in *Die Seele und die Formen* (Berlin: Fleischel, 1911); tr. Anna Bostock, *Soul and Form* (Cambridge, Mass.: MIT Press, 1974); Max Bense, "Über den Essay und seine Prosa," *Merkur* 1:3 (1947), 414–24; and Theodor Adorno, "Der Essay als Form," in *Noten zur Literatur* (Frankfurt: Suhrkamp, 1974); tr. Bob Hulott-Kentor, "The Essay as Form," *New German Critique* 32 (Spring-Summer 1984), 151–71. The main collection of Adorno essays in English is *Prisms*, tr. Samuel and Shierry Weber (London: Spearman, 1967). Walter Benjamin collections in English include *Illuminations*, ed. and intro. Hannah Arendt, tr. Harry Zohn (London: Cape, 1970) and *One-way Street and Other Writings*, tr. Edmund Jephcott and Kingsley Shorter (London: New Left Books, 1979).

On the Spanish essay the broadest treatment is Donald Bleznick, *El ensayo español del siglo XVI al XX* (Mexico City: Ediciones De Andrea, 1964). Shorter considerations of the particular significance of the essay in Spain are Alfredo Carballo Picazo, "El ensayo como genero literario. Notas para su estudio en Espano," *Revista de literatura*, 5 (1954), 93–156, and Jean-Marcel Paquette, "Forme et fonction de l'essai dans la littérature espagnole," *Etudes littéraires*, 5 (1972), 75–90. An excellent introduction in English to the peculiar importance of the essay in Latin America is Martin S. Stabb, *In Quest of Identity: Patterns in the Spanish-American Essay of Ideas, 1890–1960* (Chapel Hill: University of North Carolina Press, 1967). A useful collection on another aspect of this topic is Kurt Levy and Keith Ellis (eds), *El ensayo y la crítica literaria en Iberoamerica* (Toronto: University of Toronto Press, 1970). A wide-ranging comparative work in Spanish is Marcos Victoria, *Teoría del ensayo* (Buenos Aires: Emece, 1975), which includes Emerson, Carlyle, Barrès, Valéry, and Kenneth Clark as well as Spanish-language writers. An excellent recent study with implications for study of the genre as a whole is Antonio Urello, *Verosimilitud y estrategia textual en el ensayo hispanoamericano* (Mexico: Premia editora, 1986), which deals with textual strategies for establishing verisimilitude within the essay.

Chapter 2: Montaigne

The most used modern French editions of the *Essais* are those edited by Maurice Rat (Paris: Garnier, 1962) – this is the text I have cited as G – and Albert Thibaudet (Paris: Editions de la Pléiade, 1950). The standard modern English translation (cited as F) is Donald Frame, *The Complete Essays of Montaigne* (Stanford: Stanford University Press, 1958), but I have sometimes preferred to cite (as C) the versions of J. M. Cohen, *Montaigne: Essays* (Harmondsworth: Penguin, 1958).

There is an abundance of good studies on Montaigne's *Essais*. The classic scholarly treatment is Pierre Villey, *Les Sources et l'évolution des Essais de Montaigne* (Paris: Hachette, 1908; rev. edn 1933). A broader study, though still focused on the *Essais* and with a good general chapter on the essay as genre, is Hugo Friedrich, *Montaigne* (Bern: Franke, 1949; Fr. trans. R. Rovini, Paris: Gallimard, 1968). The best general introduction in English is R. A. Sayce, *The Essays of Montaigne: A Critical Exploration* (London: Weidenfeld & Nicolson, 1972). The best biography in English is Donald Frame, *Montaigne: A Biography* (New York: Harcourt, Brace & World, 1965). Sayce and Frame, the doyens respectively of British and American Montaigne studies, were each honored with an admirable collection of essays by others: I. D. McFarlane and Ian Maclean (eds), *Montaigne: Essays in Memory of Richard Sayce* (Oxford: Clarendon Press, 1982); and Raymond C. La Charité (ed.), *O un amy! Essays on Montaigne in Honor of Donald M. Frame* (Lexington: Kentucky University Press, 1977). A good recent thematic study is M. A. Screech, *Montaigne and Melancholy: The Wisdom of the Essays* (London: Duckworth, 1983). *Yale French Studies* 64 (1983) is devoted to Montaigne, and provides a good sampling of recent approaches, including Jean Starobinski, "The Body's Moment," a study focused on Montaigne's "De l'experience."

Three essayists who have devoted pieces to the founder of their genre are: Ralph Waldo Emerson, "Montaigne; or, the Skeptic," in *Representative Men* (1850); John Middleton Murry, "Montaigne: the Birth of the Individual" in *Heroes of Thought* (1938); and Virginia Woolf, "Montaigne," in *The Common Reader: First Series* (1925). Outstanding among academic studies are: Erich Auerbach, "L'Humaine Condition," Chapter 12 of *Mimesis: The Representation of Reality in Western Literature*, tr. Willard Trask (Princeton: Princeton University Press, 1953); Georges Poulet, "Montaigne," in *Studies in Human Time*, tr. Elliott Coleman (Baltimore: Johns Hopkins University Press, 1956); W. G. Moore, "Montaigne's Notion of Experience," in Will Moore, Rhoda Sutherland, and Enid Starkie (eds), *The French Mind: Studies in Honour of Gustave Rudler* (Oxford: Clarendon Press, 1952); Anthony

191

Wilden, "Par divers moyens on arrive à pareille fin: A Reading of Montaigne," *Modern Language Notes* 83 (1968), 577-97; and the chapter on Montaigne in Terence Cave, *The Cornucopian Text: Problems of Writing in the French Renaissance* (Oxford: Clarendon Press, 1979). See also Cathleen M. Bauschatz, "Montaigne's Conception of Reading in the Context of Renaissance Poetics and Modern Criticism," in Susan R. Suleiman and Inge Crossman (eds), *The Reader in the Text: Essays on Audience and Interpretation* (Princeton: Princeton University Press, 1980); and Jules Brody, "From Teeth to Text in 'De l'experience,'" *L'Esprit créateur* 20:1 (Spring 1980), 7–22.

Chapter 3: Bacon

Quotations from Bacon's essays are taken from Francis Bacon, *The Essays*, ed. and intro. John Pitcher (Harmondsworth: Penguin, 1985). Quotations from Bacon's other works, and from the two discarded Prefaces to the essays, are from vol. 1 of *The Works of Francis Bacon*, 5 vols (London: A. Millar, 1765), cited as W.

The topic of seventeenth-century English prose has attracted a number of good general studies. The scholarly originators of the twentieth-century debate on it are Morris W. Croll, whose major papers are collected in *Style, Rhetoric, and Rhythm*, ed. J. Max Patrick *et al.* (Princeton: Princeton University Press, 1966); and R. F. Jones, *The Seventeenth Century: Studies in the History of English Thought and Literature from Bacon to Pope* (Stanford: Stanford University Press, 1969). Their controversy is summarized in Chapter 1 of Robert Adolph, *The Rise of Modern Prose Style* (Cambridge, Mass.: MIT Press, 1968); Chapter 2 is on Bacon. Joan Webber, *The Eloquent "I": Style and Self in Seventeenth-century Prose* (Madison, Milwaukee and London: University of Wisconsin Press, 1968) is a good general study, but does not include Bacon. George Williamson, *The Senecan Amble* (London: Faber, 1951), has Chapter 6 on "Bacon and Stoic Rhetoric." Stanley Fish has a long chapter called "Georgics of the Mind: The Experience of Bacon's *Essays*" in *Self-Consuming Artifacts* (Berkeley: University of California Press, 1972). Bacon is the subject of Chapter 4 in Joseph Mazzeo, *Renaissance and Revolution: The Remaking of European Thought* (London: Secker & Warburg, 1965).

Articles on Bacon's literary and intellectual context include: R. S. Crane, "The Relation of Bacon's *Essays* to his Program for the Advancement of Learning," in *Schelling Anniversary Papers* (New York, 1923); Jacob Zeitlin, "The Development of Bacon's *Essays*," *Journal of English and Germanic Philology*, 27 (1928), 496–519; and L. C. Knights, "Bacon and the Seventeenth-Century Dissociation of Sensibility," *Scrutiny* 11 (1943), 268–85; reprinted in *Explorations* (Harmondsworth: Penguin, 1948).

Chapter 4: Johnson

The standard edition of Johnson's essays is in *The Yale Edition of the Works of Samuel Johnson* (New Haven and London: Yale University Press) as follows: vol. 2: *The Idler* and *The Adventurer*, ed. W. J. Bate, John M. Bullitt, and L. F. Powell (1963); vols 2, 3, and 4: *The Rambler*, ed. W. J. Bate and Albrecht B. Strauss (1969). Quotations from this edition are followed in parenthesis by the volume and page number, and then the series title (*R = Rambler; A = Adventurer; I = Idler*) and essay number.

There are many general treatments of Johnson's prose style. Modern discussion starts with W. K. Wimsatt, Jr, *The Prose Style of Samuel Johnson* (New Haven and London: Yale University Press, 1941). A good recent contribution is Brian McCrea, "Style or Styles: The Problem of Johnson's Prose," *Style* 14:3 (Summer 1980), 201–15. There are also many studies of Johnson's criticism. A major modern treatment is Jean H. Hagstrum, *Samuel Johnson's Literary Criticism* (Minneapolis: University of Minnesota Press, 1952). Two key articles are by W. R. Keast, "The Theoretical Foundations of Johnson's Criticism," in R. S. Crane (ed.), *Critics and Criticism: Essays in Method* (Chicago: University of Chicago Press, 1952; abridged edn 1957), 169–87, and "Johnson's Criticism of the Metaphysical Poets," *English Literary History* 17 (1950), 59–70.

On Johnson's essays specifically, O. F. Christie, *Johnson the Essayist: His Opinions on Men, Morals and Manners* (London: Grant Richards, 1924) offers a survey, arranged by topic, of the essays' content. All students of the essays have cause to be grateful for Robert C. Olson, *Motto, Context, Essay: The Classical Background of Samuel Johnson's* Rambler *and* Adventurer *Essays* (Lanham, Md: University Press of America, 1984), which provides the original context for Johnson's classical epigraphs and elaborates on their relevance to the particular essay. Two good discussions of *The Idler* are Patrick O'Flaherty, "Johnson's *Idler*: The Equipment of a Satirist," *English Literary History* 37 (1970), 211–25, and James F. Woodruff, "Johnson's *Idler* and the Anatomy of Idleness," *English Studies in Canada* 6:1 (Spring 1980), 22–38. On *The Rambler*, see Patrick O'Flaherty, "Towards an Understanding of Johnson's *Rambler*," *Studies in English Literature* 18:3 (Summer 1978), 523–36; James F. Woodruff, "Johnson's *Rambler* and Its Contemporary Context," *Bulletin of Research in the Humanities* 85:1 (Spring 1985), 27–64, a historical study of topical references in the essays; Leopold Damrosch, Jr, "Johnson's Manner of Proceeding in the *Rambler*," *English Literary History* 40 (1973), 70–89; Peter T. Koper, "Samuel Johnson's Rhetorical Stance in *The Rambler*," *Style* 12:1 (Winter 1978), 23–34; and Alan T. Mackenzie, "Logic and Lexicography: The Concern With Distribution and Extent in Johnson's *Rambler*," *The Eighteenth Century* 23:1 (Winter 1982), 49–63.

Quotations from *The Spectator* are taken from the Everyman edition, ed. E. Rhys, 4 vols (London: Dent, 1906) and identified by issue number.

Chapter 5: Hazlitt

The standard edition of Hazlitt, which I have cited in parenthesis by volume number and page number, is *The Complete Works of William Hazlitt*, Centenary Edition, ed. P. P. Howe, 21 vols (London and Toronto: Dent, 1931). Useful selections are *Selected Essays of William Hazlitt*, ed. Geoffrey Keynes (London: Nonesuch Press, 1948) and *Selected Writings: William Hazlitt*, ed. Ronald Blythe (Harmondsworth: Penguin, 1970).

Good background on the journalistic scene in Hazlitt's day is contained in John O. Hayden, *The Romantic Reviewers, 1802–1824* (London: Routledge & Kegan Paul, 1969). Melvin R. Watson, *Magazine Serials and the Essay Tradition, 1746–1820* (Baton Rouge: Louisiana State University Press, 1956) sees Hazlitt, along with Lamb and Hunt, as re-establishing the "familiar" essay tradition of Montaigne after the interregnum of the Addison–Steele form. The standard recent life, thorough and readable, is Herschel Baker, *William Hazlitt* (Cambridge, Mass.: Harvard University Press, 1962). There are two recent critical books: John Kinnaird, *William Hazlitt: Critic of Power* (New York: Columbia University Press, 1978); and David Bromwich, *Hazlitt: The Mind of a Critic* (New York and Oxford: Oxford University Press, 1983). A good short study of *Table Talk* is Robert Ready, *Hazlitt at Table* (East Brunswick, NJ: Associated University Presses, 1981); it includes Charles Lamb's previously unpublished review of *Table Talk*. Other studies relevant to specific themes are Elizabeth Schneider, *The Aesthetics of William Hazlitt: A Study of the Philosophical Basis of his Criticism* (Philadelphia: University of Pennsylvania Press, 1933); and Roy Park, *Hazlitt and the Spirit of the Age: Abstraction and Critical Theory* (Oxford: Clarendon Press, 1971).

Among essay-length studies, Virginia Woolf's is, as always, outstanding; her "William Hazlitt" is in *The Common Reader: Second Series* (London: Hogarth Press, 1932). Ronald Blythe's essay "My First Acquaintance with William Hazlitt" is collected in *From the Headlands* (London: Chatto & Windus, 1982), as well as serving as the introduction to his Penguin selection of Hazlitt. Also noteworthy is Terry Eagleton, "William Hazlitt: An Empiricist Radical," *New Blackfriars*, 54 (1973), 108–17. Hazlitt's essays are the subject of Chapter 4 of Laurence Stapledon, *The Elected Circle: Studies in the Art of Prose* (Princeton: Princeton University Press, 1973). More recent articles include: W. P. Albrecht, "Structure in Two of Hazlitt's Essays," *Studies in Romanticism*, 21 (1982), 181–90; by the same author, "Hazlitt's 'On the Fear of Death': Reason versus Imagination," *The Wordsworth Circle*, 15 (1984), 3–7; and

Stanley Jones, "First Flight: Image and Theme in a Hazlitt Essay," *Prose Studies* 8:1 (May 1985), 35–47, an exemplary study of "On My First Acquaintance with Poets."

Chapter 6: Henry James

For the travel essay section of this chapter I have cited *Portraits of Places* (1883; repr. Freeport, NY: Books for Libraries Press, 1972) and *The American Scene*, ed. and intro. Leon Edel (Bloomington: Indiana University Press, 1968). James's other collections of his own travel essays are *Transatlantic Sketches* (1875); *A Little Tour in France* (1884; repr. with intro. by Leon Edel, New York: Farrar, Straus & Giroux, 1983); *English Hours* (1905; repr. with intro. by Alama Louise Lowe, London: Heinemann, 1960); and *Italian Hours* (1909; repr. New York: Grove Press, 1979). An excellent general selection of the travel essays is in *The Art of Travel: Scenes and Journeys in America, England, France and Italy from the Travel Writings of Henry James*, ed. and intro. Morton Dauwen Zabel (New York: Doubleday Anchor, 1962). Aside from these introductions, there is little extended comment on James's travel writings.

I have cited James's critical essays from Morris Shapira (ed.), *Henry James: Selected Literary Criticism* (New York: McGraw-Hill, 1964), which also contains as its introduction the essay "James as Critic" by F. R. Leavis. James's own collections are four in number: *French Poets and Novelists* (1878; repr. with intro. by Leon Edel, New York: Grosset & Dunlap, 1964); *Partial Portraits* (1888); *Essays in London and Elsewhere* (1893); and *Notes on Novelists* (1914). A useful trio of selected reviews and essays organized by the art referred to is: Henry James, *The House of Fiction: Essays on the Novel*, ed. and intro. Leon Edel (London: Rupert Hart-Davis, 1957); Henry James, *The Painter's Eye: Notes and Essays on the Pictorial Arts*, ed. and intro. John L. Sweeney (London: Rupert Hart-Davis, 1956); and Henry James, *The Scenic Art: Notes on Acting and the Drama*, 1872–1901, ed. and intro. Allan Wade (New Brunswick: Rutgers University Press, 1948).

A thorough survey of the criticism is Sarah B. Daugherty, *The Literary Criticism of Henry James* (Athens: Ohio University Press, 1981); unfortunately it lacks a bibliography. An early book-length study is Morris Roberts's *Henry James' Criticism* (Cambridge, Mass.: Harvard University Press, 1929). The James–Flaubert relation has attracted some comment: David Cook, "James and Flaubert: the Evolution of Perception," *Comparative Literature* 25 (1973), 298–307. Broader studies are by Philip Grover, *Henry James and the French Novel: A Study in Inspiration* (New York: Barnes & Noble, 1973); and Lyall Powers, *Henry James and the Naturalist Movement* (East Lansing: Michigan State University Press, 1971).

Chapter 7: Virginia Woolf

My quotations from Woolf's essays (except for the autobiographical pieces cited from *Moments of Being*, which is abbreviated as *MB*) are followed by reference to volume and page of Virginia Woolf, *Collected Essays*, ed. Leonard Woolf, 4 vols (London: Hogarth Press, 1966). Virginia Woolf herself published two collections during her lifetime (both Hogarth Press): *The Common Reader* (1925), and *The Common Reader: Second Series* (1932). After her death Leonard Woolf published four more collections of her essays (all Hogarth Press): *The Death of the Moth* (1942); *The Moment* (1947); *The Captain's Death Bed* (1950); and *Granite and Rainbow* (1958). All of the material in the six volumes is included in the four-volume *Collected Essays*, but there remains a substantial number of essays which have not yet been reprinted in book form. Since Leonard's death, two further volumes have appeared: *Moments of Being: Unpublished Autobiographical Writings*, ed. Jeanne Schulkind (London: Chatto & Windus, 1976; repr. Triad/Granada, 1978); and *Books and Portraits: Some Further Selections from the Literary and Biographical Writings*, ed. Mary Lyon (New York: Harcourt Brace Jovanovich, 1977). The first volume (of a projected six) of a complete scholarly edition of the essays was published recently: *The Essays of Virginia Woolf, Vol. I: 1904–12*, ed. Andrew McNeillie (London: Hogarth Press, 1986).

Most critical books on Virginia Woolf refer to her essays in passing, but few offer a separate consideration of them. The major exception is Dorothy Brewster, *Virginia Woolf* (New York: New York University Press, 1962), which contains a long second chapter called "Criticism: The Uncommon Reader as Critic." There is one book exclusively on Woolf's criticism: Vijay L. Sharma, *Virginia Woolf as Literary Critic: A Revaluation* (New Delhi: Arnold-Heinemann, 1977); this work contains a useful bibliography. There are several articles on Woolf's criticism: Mark Goldman, "Virginia Woolf and the Critic as Reader," *PMLA* 80 (June 1965), 275–84, reprinted in Claire Sprague (ed.), *Virginia Woolf: A Collection of Critical Essays* (Englewood Cliffs, NJ: Prentice-Hall, 1971); Desmond Pacey, "Virginia Woolf as a Literary Critic," *University of Toronto Quarterly*, 18 (April 1948), 234–44; Louis Kronenberger, "Virginia Woolf as Critic," in *The Republic of Letters: Essays on Various Writers* (New York: Knopf, 1955); and Denys Thompson, "The Common Reader II," *Scrutiny* I (December 1932). An interesting article partly on the autobiographical essays is Harvena Richter, "Hunting the Moth: Virginia Woolf and the Creative Imagination" in Ralph Freedman (ed.), *Virginia Woolf: Revaluation and Continuity* (Berkeley: University of California Press, 1980).

Chapter 8: T. S. Eliot

SE stands for *Selected Essays* in the 1951 edition: *EAM* for *Essays Ancient and Modern*; and *FLA* for *For Lancelot Andrewes*. Eliot's first collection of criticism was *The Sacred Wood: Essays in Poetry and Criticism* (London: Methuen, 1920; 2nd edn 1928). It was followed by *For Lancelot Andrewes: Essays on Style and Order* (Garden City, NY: Doubleday, Doran, 1929), which formed the basis for *Essays Ancient and Modern* (London: Faber, 1936). The first edition of *Selected Essays* (London: Faber, 1932) was expanded in the second edition (London: Faber, 1951) by selections from *Essays Ancient and Modern*. Also worth noting are Eliot's Harvard lecture series, *The Use of Poetry and the Use of Criticism* (London: Faber, 1933); *After Strange Gods* (London: Faber, 1934); *Notes Towards the Definition of Culture* (London: Faber, 1948); *On Poetry and Poets* (London: Faber, 1957); Eliot's doctoral dissertation, *Knowledge and Experience in the Philosophy of F. H. Bradley* (London: Faber, 1964); and *To Criticize the Critic* (London: Faber, 1965). Eliot frequently wrote a "Commentary" as editor of *Criterion*, but these pieces have not been collected – some have not worn well. The uncollected piece "*Ulysses*, Order and Myth" is quoted from *The Norton Anthology of English Literature, Major Authors Edition* (New York: Norton, 1968), 2623–6.

In contrast to most of the essayists treated in this book, there is an abundance of commentary of Eliot's criticism. Here I will list only those which discuss the form of the essays or are relevant to the specific issues I deal with. Vincent Buckley, *Poetry and Morality: Studies on the Criticism of Matthew Arnold, T. S. Eliot, and F. R. Leavis* (London: Chatto & Windus, 1959) is an excellent and still not outmoded account of the basic themes and contexts of Eliot's criticism. Useful collections of essays include Graham Martin (ed.), *Eliot in Perspective* (London: Macmillan, 1970), which includes Richard Wollheim, "Eliot and F. H. Bradley," revised and enlarged in Wollheim, *On Art and The Mind: Essays and Lectures* (London: Allen Lane, 1973); and David Newton-De Molina (ed.), *The Literary Criticism of T. S. Eliot: New Essays* (London: Athlone Press, 1977), which contains Roger Sharrock on "Eliot's 'Tone.'" Among recent relevant books are: Brian Lee, *Theory and Personality: the Significance of T. S. Eliot's Criticism* (London: Athlone Press, 1979), which contains an excellent close analysis of "Tradition and the Individual Talent"; Edward Lobb, *T. S. Eliot and the Romantic Critical Tradition* (London: Routledge & Kegan Paul, 1981), especially ch. 3, "Eliot as Rhetorician"; and Gregory S. Jay, *T. S. Eliot and the Poetics of Literary History* (Baton Rouge: Louisiana State University Press, 1983), especially ch. 8 on "Critical Figurae: Shakespeare, Dante, and Vergil." After my chapter was completed I was alerted to J. P. Riquelme, "The Modernist Essay: The Case of T. S. Eliot – Poet and Critic," *Southern Review* 21:4 (October 1985), 1024–32; and Sanford

Schwartz, *The Matrix of Modernism: Pound, Eliot, and Early Twentieth-century Thought* (Princeton: Princeton University Press, 1985), esp. ch. 4, "Incarnate Words: Eliot's Early Career."

Chapter 9: George Orwell

The edition I have cited is *The Penguin Essays of George Orwell* (Harmondsworth: Penguin, 1984). A fuller collection of his prose, including reviews and columns, is George Orwell, *The Collected Essays, Journalism and Letters*, ed. Sonia Orwell and Ian Angus, 4 vols (Harmondsworth: Penguin, 1970). Orwell himself published four volumes of essays: *Inside the Whale and Other Essays* (1940), containing "Charles Dickens," "Boys' Weeklies," and "Inside the Whale"; *The Lion and the Unicorn: Socialism and the English Genius* (1941), consisting of "England Your England," "Shopkeepers at War," and "The English Revolution," a linked separate piece; *Critical Essays* (1946), published in the USA as *Dickens, Dali and Others*, included "Charles Dickens" and "Boys' Weeklies" (but not "Inside the Whale") in addition to eight further wartime essays on Wells, Kipling, Yeats, Koestler, Wodehouse, Salvador Dali, James Hadley Chase, and Donald McGill; and *The English People* (1947), a more extended treatment of the "national character" theme of *The Lion and the Unicorn*. After Orwell's death came three further collections: *Shooting an Elephant* (1950), which includes "Politics and the English Language" and the early autobiographical pieces, along with various shorter essays: *England Your England* (1953), which took Part One of *The Lion and the Unicorn* as its title piece; and *Such, Such were the Joys* (1953), the equivalent American edition; the title piece was omitted from the English collection for legal reasons.

In this chapter I have used material from two of my own articles: "Ideology and Personality in Orwell's Criticism," *College Literature* 11 (1984), 78–93; and "Language, Truth and Power in Orwell," *Prose Studies* 7:1 (May 1984), 55-69.

Commentary on Orwell's essays is often mixed in with commentary on his other work, fictional and non-fictional. But the following chapters from books contain relevant separate discussions of the essays: Keith Alldritt, *The Making of George Orwell* (London: Edward Arnold, 1969), ch. 4 – a full and valuable treatment; J. R. Hammond, *A George Orwell Companion* (London: Macmillan, 1982), Part 3; Jeffrey Meyers, *A Reader's Guide to George Orwell* (London: Thames & Hudson, 1975), ch. 2; and Raymond Williams, *Orwell* (London: Fontana, 1971), chs 2–4. See also John Wain, "George Orwell as a Writer of Polemic," *Essays on Literature and Ideas* (London: Macmillan, 1963); reprinted in Raymond Williams (ed.), *George Orwell: A Collection of Critical Essays* (Englewood Cliffs, NJ: Prentice-Hall, 1974)); and Alaric Jacob, "Sharing Orwell's 'Joys' – But Not His Fears," in Christopher Norris (ed.),

Inside the Myth: Orwell: Views From the Left (London: Lawrence & Wishart, 1984).

Chapter 10: The essay and criticism

It would be impossible to list those who have practiced the essay successfully since 1950. Here I will only cite a representative volume by each of the writers I mention in this chapter: Susan Sontag, *Under the Sign of Saturn* (New York: Farrar, Straus & Giroux, 1980); Joan Didion, *The White Album* (New York: Simon & Schuster, 1979); Clive James, *The Metropolitan Critic* (London: Faber, 1974); Jan Morris, *Among the Cities* (London: Viking, 1985); Conor Cruise O'Brien, *Writers and Politics* (New York: Pantheon, 1965); Shiva Naipaul, *Beyond the Dragon's Mouth* (London: Hamish Hamilton, 1984); and Richard Cobb, *Still Life: Sketches from a Tunbridge Wells Childhood* (London: Chatto & Windus, 1983).

Index

All works are entered under the name of the author

view of order 146, 148
datedness in writers 158–9
de Man, Paul 116
death: Montaigne on 31–2; Woolf on
129, 131, 134
"deconstruction" of text 180–2
Derrida, Jacques 180, 181, 182
Descartes, René 4; *Discourse on
Method* 37–8; philosophy 37–8, 39
detective stories, James's essays as
101, 105–10
"dialogical" style (Bakhtin) 171
diaries, use of 125
Dickens, Charles 158, 159, 160, 164,
169; *Nicholas Nickleby* 132;
snobbery 159
Didion, Joan 183
disinterest, in essayist 11–12
"dissociation of sensibility" (Eliot)
138–9, 148, 177
doctrine; and essay 5; withdrawal
from 31–2
Donne, John 86
Dostoyevsky, Feodor 117, 167; use of
"Underground Man" 85–6
Doyle, Sir Arthur Conan, *The
Casebook of Sherlock Holmes*
101–2, 165
drama, Johnson on 68–9
dream-visions, in eighteenth-century
essay 57
Dryden, John 84
Duckworth, Gerald 131, 132
Duckworth, Stella 129, 132
dynamic process, essay as 17, 18

Edinburgh Review, The 72
Edwardian literature 119, 173
Eliot, George (Mary Ann Evans) 90,
97, 98; *Adam Bede* 14
Eliot, T. S. 20, 24, 119, 135–51, 159, 174;
aesthetic politics 145–9, 153; and
Modernism 157, 179; and
tradition 125, 135–40, 165, 185;
influence on criticism 111, 135–6,
140, 151; literature and order
143–4, 147–8; on impersonality
21, 139, 150; on originality 140;
philosophy applied to essay
140–3; poet's relationship with
society 145, 146–7; revival of
medieval commentary 135; style
140–3, 146, 149, 150; Woolf and
144, 150–1; "Andrew Marvell"
149; "Catholicism and the
International Order" 143, 146–7;

"Dante" 139, 142, 143, 144, 145,
149, 150, 152; *Essays Ancient and
Modern* 143–4, 146; *Four Quartets*
19, 128, 142, 143, 144; "The
Function of Criticism" 140;
"Hamlet" 145; "In Memoriam"
145; *Knowledge and Experience in
the Philosophy of F. H. Bradley*
140; *For Lancelot Andrewes* 138,
143–4; "The Metaphysical Poets"
138, 149; *Notes Towards the
Definition of Culture* 143, 147;
"The 'Pensées' of Pascal" 150;
Selected Essays 125, 138, 143,
144–5, 146; "Tradition and the
Individual Talent" 137, 139, 141,
143, 145, 149, 150, 152; "Ulysses,
Order, and Myth" 145–6; *The
Waste Land* 141, 143
Emerson, Ralph Waldo 71
"English", study of 141, 178–9
environment, and James's placing of
moral ideas 91
epiphanies ("moments of being") 76,
127
Erasmus, *Adagia* 1
error, treatment of 65–6
essay 58, 99; and academic system
4–6, 71, 141, 178–81; as aesthetic
knowledge 14–25; as art 9–14;
and demystification 166–7;
development of 2, 24; Eliot and
136, 140; future of 167–8, 182–6;
as genre 1–2, 9–10, 12, 90;
Hazlitt's theories of 73–4, 85; and
individualism 62–6, 113, 135, 153,
177, 183–4; and intellectual
freedom 177; as knowledge 1–9;
and Modernism 178–9; and
musical structure 19, 20, 25; and
novel 9–13; Orwell and 167–8,
173–4; resistance to systems 4,
185–6; *see also* critical essay;
moral essay; travel essay
essay v. treatise 23–4
essayist: historical development 10;
nature of 9, 11
essayist as "errant" 12
"essayistic culture", growth of in
nineteenth century 135
Euripides 116
Examiner, The 73, 74
existentialism 23; and nature of essay
12; and physical experience 39
experience 1, 42; Bacon's use of 47–8;
as basis of essay 7–8; Johnson